# The Lord of the Sabbath Opens His Book of Revelation

# The Lord of the Sabbath Opens His Book of Revelation

CHRISTOPHER FUNG

RESOURCE *Publications* • Eugene, Oregon

THE LORD OF THE SABBATH OPENS HIS BOOK OF REVELATION

Copyright © 2017 Christopher Fung. All rights reserved. Except for brief quotations in critical publications or reviews, no part of this book may be reproduced in any manner without prior written permission from the publisher. Write: Permissions, Wipf and Stock Publishers, 199 W. 8th Ave., Suite 3, Eugene, OR 97401.

Resource Publications
An Imprint of Wipf and Stock Publishers
199 W. 8th Ave., Suite 3
Eugene, OR 97401

www.wipfandstock.com

PAPERBACK ISBN: 978-1-5326-1857-4
HARDCOVER ISBN: 978-1-4982-4426-8
EBOOK ISBN: 978-1-4982-4425-1

Manufactured in the U.S.A.                    AUGUST 29, 2017

Unless indicated otherwise, all biblical quotations are taken from the New American Standard Bible.

Permissions have been received from the respective sources to use the three images (first and second from the left and the lower right) in Figure 5 of this book. These are respectively from:

http://www.andrewgrahamdixon.com/archive/temptation-in-eden-lucas-cranachs-adam-and-eve-at-the-courtauld-institute-of-art-gallery.html

http://learn-biblical-hebrew.com/hebrew-scripture/story-cain-abel/

https://commons.wikimedia.org/w/index.php?search=picasso+Guernica&title=Special:Search&go=Go&uselang=en&searchToken=1y9dpnagimg4cennlptsmycrs#/media/File:Mural_del_Gernika.jpg

# Contents

*List of Figures* | ix
*List of Tables* | x
*Preface* | xi

1    First Reading—Diagnosing the Hurdles of Time, Style, and Tumors | 1

      1. Revelation's Promise and Our Expectations

      2. Step by Step through Revelation

      3. Starting Point in Receiving Revelation

      4. Some Suggestions and Two Observations

          4.1 First General Observation: One Chapter is Glaringly Different

          4.2 Second General Observation: The Essence of Revealed Time

      5. Some Basic Interpretative Approaches and Pitfalls

2    Second Reading—Gathering the Gems of Revelation | 22

      1. Jesus' Self Introduction (chapter 1)

      2. Seven Churches in Anticipation (chapters 2–3)

      3. The Heavenly Worship

          3.1 First Heavenly Worship (chapter 4): The Eternal God and His Creation in Praises

          3.2 Second Heavenly Worship (chapter 5): The Redeeming Lamb and Creation's Forward Movement

4. Seven Seals: Starting with the Custodians (6:1—8:1)

   4.1 The First Four Seals

   4.2 The Fifth Seal

   4.3 The Sixth Seal

   4.4 The Final and Most Uncharacteristic Seal—An Incomplete One

   4.5 Testimony of the Scroll—Seven Seals Together

5. Seven Trumpets: How God Works in All Creation (8:2—11:19)

   5.1 Lead up to the Trumpets

   5.2 The First Four Trumpets

   5.3 The Fifth Trumpet

   5.4 The Sixth Trumpet—Turning Point of Creation and of History

      5.4.1 First Episode of the Sixth Trumpet (9:13–21)

      5.4.2 Second Episode of the Sixth Trumpet (chapter 10)

      5.4.3 Third Episode of the Sixth Trumpet (11:1–13)

   5.5 The Seventh and Last Trumpet (11:15–19)

6. The Shape of an Intensified and Focused War (chapter 12)

7. Two Opposing Camps

   7.1 Anatomy of Satan's Camp (chapter 13)

   7.2 Anatomy of God's Camp (chapter 14)

8. Seven Bowls of Wrath—The End Game (chapters 15–16)

9. Physiology of the Beast and the Mortal Internal Struggle (chapter 17)

10. Three-Way Split of Babylon Explained

    10.1 Downfall of Babylon (chapter 18)

    10.2 Celebration and Judgment of the Beasts (chapter 19)

    10.3 A Précis of God's History and Satan's Downfall (chapter 20)

11. Advent of New Heaven and Earth (21:1—22:5)

12. Call to Action (22:6–21)

## 3 Third Reading—Stringing together the Gems of Revelation | 103

1. A Synoptic Outline of Revelation
2. Who are the Two Witnesses? A Key to Unlock Revelation
3. Revisiting some Key Passages to Grasp the Real Struggle

    3.1 The Enigma of the Saints' Prayers from Under the Altar (5:8, 8:3–4)

    3.2 Why are the 144,000 Sealed? (6:12—8:1)

    3.3 Seven Forbidden Thunders . . . Jesus . . . Seven Outpoured Bowls of Wrath

    3.4 From Ark to Ark

4. The Three Series of Sevens

    4.1 Why are there Three Series of Sevens?

    4.2 Some Peculiarities of the Three Series of Sevens: An Interlude and others

    4.3 What do the Seals, Trumpets, and Bowls Symbolize?

5. The Morphing Symbols of the Beasts, Women, Woes and Holy City

    5.1 Beasts

    5.2 Two Women, Two Cities; Is there a Role for Israel?

    5.3 The Enigma of "Threes"—Woes, Split in the Great City

    5.4 The Destiny of the Holy City—from Temple to No Temple, from "Seven" to "Twelve"

6. It is a Matter of Time
7. Symbols and How do the Players Fit in to the Overall Game?

    7.1 The Major Players

    7.2 The Ultimate Prize—God's Creation in Revelation

    7.3 The Grand Game

## 4 Fourth Reading—Hear God Speak Plainly through Revelation | 171

1. Interpreting Revelation through its Position in the Bible
2. What Lessons can the Seven Churches Draw from Revelation?

    2.1 A Meta-Narrative

    2.2 Four Encounters that Register

- 2.3 The Leader—Lord of the Sabbath
- 2.4 Focus of Revelation—The Key that No One should Miss
- 2.5 How are the Saints to Conduct Themselves by the Light of Revelation?
- 2.6 The Advent

3. Why is My Take so Irreconcilably Different?

4. An Epilogue

*Bibliography* | *219*

    *Commentaries/books consulted as basic references*

    *Other commentaries*

*Subject Index* | *223*

*Scripture Index* | *233*

# List of Figures and Tables

Figure 1.   The Beast(s) in Biblical Perspective | 79
Figure 2.   Structure of Revelation | 111
Figure 3.   Who are the two witnesses? | 114
Figure 4.   Schematization of the two major timescales used in Revelation | 159
Figure 5.   The Cosmic Struggle | 170

# List of Tables

Table 1. Features in Revelation that are absent from chapter 20 | 7

Table 2. Units of time in Revelation | 16

Table 3. A summary of the opening of the first four seals | 31

Table 4. Aspects of the first four trumpets | 40

Table 5. Major issues raised and addressed in Revelation | 106

Table 6. Structural comparison between the three series of "Sevens" | 131

Table 7. General comparison of the three series of "Sevens" in Revelation | 134

Table 8. Contrasting the two women in Revelation | 142

# Preface

TWO BROAD APPROACHES HAVE usually been taken to make sense of the book of Revelation. The popular approach pays scant attention to the Old Testament roots of many of the symbolisms in Revelation and reads Revelation as a book of foretelling major, and exact, events that are destined to come upon this hapless world. These purported events lead up to the grand finale of world's history as we know it. Individuals are largely bystanders or movie-watchers beholding the giant divine theatrics playing out before their eyes. The fitting response is to escape from this unstoppable onslaught, hence the fanciful notion of "rapture" coming out of the blue. Believers in God are transported out of this material world and spared the disasters and sufferings that will inevitably come upon the non-believers being left behind.

The more scholarly approach places strong emphasis on how Revelation gathers Old Testament symbols and reinterprets them in light of Jesus' accomplishments. Indeed, John has drawn heavily from the Old Testament, as only appropriate for the God who is the Alpha and Omega, and applied these to Jesus who, because of his death and resurrection, has put his ineradicable stamp on history, and as such would bring history to a fitting finale. Beauty is revealed in the consistent themes that run through the Bible. Profound teachings that impel actions would follow from this earnest and time-honored approach. However, even this has its limitations since some of Revelation's key symbols, especially those concerning numbers and times, *do not seem* to have apparent roots in either the Old or New Testaments. It is precisely here that the popular sentiment runs amok with unanchored speculation, eventually succumbing to theories that blatantly negate clear biblical teachings.

Much of the confusion that feeds the popular fancy surrounds *a few symbols which have not been properly deciphered*: 3.5 days, 1,260 days, 42 months, "time, times and half a time," the two witnesses, the number of the beast of 666, and a thousand years . . . etc. However, *it is clear that if Jesus is taken to be the Lord of the Sabbath, as he himself insists, the first six symbols above would make complete and consistent sense biblically and the rest of the more enigmatic passages would yield a clear meaning accordingly*. Contextual analyzes of how time is used would also reveal the meaning of the last symbol mentioned here. Following this direction, some other enigmatic symbols, e.g., the seven-headed beast . . . etc. would yield their secrets one after another like falling dominoes. This then is the contribution of my book.

Ever wonder whether all the fanciful popular beliefs said to be from Revelation—bodily transport of believers out of this earth (rapture), seven years of universal suffering (great tribulation), coming of two witnesses tormenting unbelievers, the rise of a universal demonic power under an anti-Christ figure, a millennium of godly administration by Christ and his resurrected saints, a final military showdown at a place in the Middle East called Armageddon . . . etc.—are actually taught in the Bible? Based on the above key to unlocking Revelation, the answer is a resounding "No" to all.

Where then does this book fit between the popular and scholarly? On the one hand, it unlocks the "secrets" of Revelation using nothing more than major themes consistently taught in the Bible—a key to avoiding unwarranted fancy. On the other hand, the popular yearning for meaning of the many esoteric symbols in Revelation is fully satisfied. The two poles in dissecting Revelation are brought together to bring out a clear and final message from Revelation. An important gap has been filled and Revelation is *understood realistically theologically*.

One of the possible titles for this book I toyed with was: "The Book of Revelation—If i Can Make Sense of It, So Can You." But this would turn off potential readers even before I have a chance to explain the uniqueness of the Sabbath as key to the interpretation. Now the explanation is done, let me say what that title conveys.

What is Revelation? Some believers have told me that they are not too concerned about the message of Revelation since they have already secured their personal passage to "heaven" and are living according to biblical teachings. These believers have assumed that Revelation, by and large, has nothing to tell them about Christian living. Such is a very counter common sense position as they cannot dispute that Revelation, being the last book, somehow concludes the Bible.

Yet the above unexamined sentiment is spurred on by the seeming difficulty in grasping Revelation's message: If most people, myself included, cannot make sense of Revelation, then we cannot all be missing a lot, so why bother? Herd mentality sets in.

But more fundamentally is the unspoken assumption in all these: Revelation is a timetable of things to come. As long as I remain faithful to God, how and when the "foretold events" come upon the world does not matter to me. I would rather not know as knowing causes fear and panic!

Is the "Revelation is timetable" impression correct? And does Revelation have no further teaching to crystallize for us, something that we can easily miss by reading the individual books making up the Bible?

Given the enormity of the above popular misunderstanding, I just cannot resist to jump ahead to state here that *Revelation is not a time-table*. It is not even a sequence of events that will happen in the future. It uses time to express some very profound truths which crystallize the most important messages that one indeed can miss if one is not careful. Through this very powerful conclusion in Revelation, the rest of the Bible and its teachings are now put into perspective. Under the guidance of the Holy Spirit, the early Christians placed Revelation at the end of the Bible for a reason. One must not judge the relevance of Revelation through other books in the Bible. The reverse must be true: *All Christian teachings must be read in the light of the Bible's conclusion—Revelation*. Is this not sensible?

Then who am i? My formal education does not extend to theology or biblical hermeneutics (just a PhD in physics). Neither does my professional work (numerical modeling of air pollution). But going for me are just a belief and a desire to investigate what puzzles me. My belief is simple: The Bible is God's words to his followers (both potential and extant). As such, it is open to all and sundry, even to those who are not academically trained in the Bible. Like the early Christians (e.g., church fathers) who have no "principles of biblical interpretation" to guide them on how they should read the writings of the Apostles and other Bible writers, but only armed themselves with common sense or simply logical reasoning, I have similarly equipped myself when approaching the Bible. I then approach the Bible with the seriousness it demands—being the inspired word of God (2 Tim 3:16).

This attitude has given me some success—publishing in scholarly theological journals. Further, one reader of my "Sabbath" paper in a theological journal suggested me to write a book on the same topic. I did, but that led me further to investigate the message of Revelation after previous attempts have failed. For this suggestion of Dr. Paul Bendor-Samuel, I am very grateful.

At one point in this investigation, I clearly told myself and God: "Though I have been able to make sense of one rather 'difficult' book (Ecclesiastes) and some important but often neglected teachings of the Bible (the

Sabbath), *I will never be able to make sense of Revelation* given its many knotty symbols and timescales . . . etc. I just have to content myself with what I have been able to understand so far."

But not long after I said the above, God shattered my confidence in my life-long ignorance. Starting with what I consider obvious in 20-20 hindsight, the dominoes started to fall one after another until *my confidence is re-established, not in my own ignorance, but in the wisdom of God and the intelligibility of his communication to us mortals*. I have learnt never to say "never" to God.

Because I have published in theological journals, a disclaimer is necessary. I have no strong interests in theology per se. I always learn theology from the Bible rather than read summarized truth (theology) back into the Bible. This counter-mainstream approach has won me praise from some, but also a near miss with a theological journal which, before coming to the end of my submission, got the impression that I was doing biblical studies which were not their specialty. To me, theology must start from the Bible and every complete biblical study should end in sound and practical theology.

As such, i am just one of the uncountable believers desiring to know what God is speaking to us through Revelation. What sets me apart from many is perhaps my persistence in trying to get to the bottom of some puzzles.

Now who am i writing this book for, or who are you? Basically everyone (lay or professional people) who wants to understand Revelation, but so far has been frustrated by its narration. Included among "you" are those who are confused by the many books and Internet material and want a clearer "fresh-eye" look at Revelation. Of course, i am writing for those who share my belief in the Bible being inspired by God and its intelligibility to the earnest.

But what is to make sense? Does my sense jibe with your sense? If not, "making sense" is solely personal. Such a concern is legitimate. Yet there are things that are indeed common and must be held fast—e.g., contextual reading, natural and logical flow of the narrative, responsive to the introduction and content of the whole Bible (since Revelation concludes the Bible) . . . etc. All these and some others are what one would expect to be true of any reading. Apart from these basics, i ask no more and indeed *need no more for making sense of Revelation*. Since i believe there is almost universal acceptance of these principles, my reasoning in applying these basics would also resonate with you and you would likewise see the beauty of Revelation as i have seen it. It is often said that "beauty is in the eyes of the beholder," but i always add a corollary: "yet all eyes are created equal to see beauty, hence the truth."

Of all the criteria, the beauty that leaps out of Revelation must be the clincher in our interpretation. "Eureka" strikes when all the pieces resonate together to reinforce the self-claimed central message—Revelation is of Jesus Christ. This Jesus brooks no rival.

In the end, it is my wish that this book would not only provide a realistic and solid framework for understanding Revelation, but also inspires its readers on a life-long journey to understand the word of God and to live out daily the very down-to-earth teachings therein.

# 1

# First Reading— Diagnosing the Hurdles of Time, Style, and Tumors

## 1. REVELATION'S PROMISE AND OUR EXPECTATIONS

Revelation is:
One biblically coherent and complete narration
That uses only natural and biblical symbols
To retell God's consistent work from beginning to end
That reveals Jesus and his resurrection as the focus
To call for decisive response from every person
For the creation which God loves and will glorify
To close God's written oracle to humankind.

Yet most readers would protest at these shockingly sweeping statements: How is this possible? Many of these seem to go against everything we have known and been taught about Revelation.

In the following pages, I will show that each of the above seven expectations is indeed true and most sensible. Even the most enigmatic symbols would reveal their meanings, as promised by Revelation. If I succeed, you will gain a better understanding of one of the most important books in the whole Bible. Not only so, the frequent sense of despair (both at grasping its meaning as well as the purported future Revelation points to) will be dispelled. It is my hope that you can approach other "difficult" books in the Bible, books that might have put you off, with renewed enthusiasm and confidence. Joy and excitement in studying the Bible will be restored.

One very common complaint about the purported teachings of Revelation is that no sooner after hearing or reading about them, one forgets. This is probably no fault of the reader's aging (even old people remember things that excite them!), but rather that the storyline (the logical sequence gluing the "events" together) seems to be missing. My very first statement above—*Revelation is one biblically coherent and complete narration*—sets my interpretation apart from the rest. The result? When one sees the bones, flesh, organs . . . etc. functioning elegantly in their assigned places, one can name the resulting animal properly. This was what Adam did and the animal became his friend. One usually has no trouble remembering good friends.

Yet based on what can I make such an outstanding claim?

Different approaches have been used to "unlock the secrets" of Revelation. Many of these attempts revolve around one belief: after Jesus' resurrection, God has given humans a roadmap or a timetable to a divinely pre-determined future through Revelation. Variations around the same theme have led to different schools of highly entrenched interpretation. It is common to find works on Revelation being classified into one of the God-knows-how-many schools.

If grasping the true message of Revelation is our goal, it is always detrimental to commit oneself to any school of thinking before diligently investigating the book's content. Instead, one should start with the book and try to make sense of it before deciding which school, *if any*, makes the most sense. Familiarity with the subject must be the first and irreplaceable condition of any study; interpretations by third parties should always be the last resort. But here I seem to be contradicting myself by expecting my readers to accept my analyses while I discourage pre-mature commitment to any school of thinking! Yet being a layman equipped only with common sense and common knowledge of the Bible, and not having delved into any school of interpretation in any depth, I am not starting a rival school. Given my interesting journey to discover the message of Revelation, I offer my findings to those who have a lingering interest in Revelation, but have decided that further self-reading is not going to take them further in their struggle with Revelation. Then perhaps my discovery would help. I only ask you to judge for yourself if my observations (inexplicably frequently overlooked), logic and reasoning make sense.

## 2. STEP BY STEP THROUGH REVELATION

A common practice in commenting on a biblical book is to present its overall structure as best one understands it, then delve into each part identified in the structure to put flesh on this skeleton. Such an approach works well for most books and it may also work for some readers of Revelation. Yet this approach would deprive the reader of the privilege of discovering the exciting building blocks that make up Revelation. Because of the seemingly complicated structure of Revelation, it does not do the reader much good without going through the reasoning in arriving at the structure in the first place. Needless to say, familiarity with Revelation's contents is a prerequisite. Hence I have chosen to leave the presentation of the structure after the passages making up Revelation are studied.

Instead, I have taken a more heuristic route to guide my presentation here in a four-reading approach. In the first reading which is this chapter, I will highlight some of the salient features that observant readers may notice. This will not be a synopsis, but it raises questions to be answered. Some basic principles from these observations will be pointed out.

In the second reading, we will go through all the passages one by one to understand their meanings. A natural-structure division will be used as appropriate. For example, chapters 4 and 5 both describe heavenly worship, but from two different angles. As such, the two chapters will form one unit, but the emphasis of each chapter will be highlighted. On the other hand, Revelation describes seven seals, seven trumpets . . . etc. These series cover more than one chapter and they will be taken up as a natural unit without regards to the chapter division. In doing so, we will focus on the immediate context of the passage and only draw from knowledge in the rest of the Bible if necessary.

The third reading will try to connect the different passages together through comparing the major series of sevens—the seals, trumpets, and bowls, and tracing the developing and morphing of the symbols used for the same entity (e.g., Jesus is the son of man, Lamb, rider on a white horse . . . etc.). This will place the passages explained in the second reading into proper context. The last run through Revelation—fourth reading—will determine what lessons one can learn from Revelation.

This four-reading approach can be likened to seeing some salient features, the interesting façade of a building that catches our attention (first reading); then trying to understand how this edifice is put together through its different bricks and components (second reading), which is obviously insufficient because the mortar to set the bricks in place has not been studied; so we try to understand how the bricks are being held together by the

## 3. STARTING POINT IN RECEIVING REVELATION

mortar and other reinforcement . . . etc. (third reading). Having now understood how the building is constructed, we want to see whether we can likewise construct a building suitable for our situation and these lessons are brought out in the fourth reading.

When reading the Bible, we have often been told to research and respect the historical and cultural setting within which the biblical book was written. The author is supposed to be addressing an audience facing certain issues in their situation. In other words, the author wants to convey a message that his target audience needs. Sensible and robust this approach may be, it has its limitations. An obvious example is the Old Testament book of Ecclesiastes in which the author—Qoholeth—claims that he has seen everything under the sun and that his writing is applicable to all humans (Eccl 1:13, 14, 12:13). If so, what is his target audience but all humankind? And what is the historical setting but all of human existence from time immemorial to time indefinite? The obvious inference is that the book is not tackling the issues particular to a certain time and culture and it would be futile to search in this direction to determine *what particular* situation or audience the book is speaking to.

Revelation goes much further than Ecclesiastes which concentrates only on humans. Its avowed scope is nothing less than cosmic, encompassing all of creation from beginning to end (1:17, 22:13). If so, like Ecclesiastes, it cannot only be addressing one or a few historical problems within a cultural setting. Whatever real history is mentioned therein (e.g., the seven churches) takes on far greater representation than particular historical snapshots can supply. With the scope of Revelation being so clear, it would be unnecessarily constraining the message if one uses the particular setting of its writing as a lens for its interpretation as if it were addressing only a local situation. No doubt, its writing may be prompted by specific situations, e.g., the frustrated expectation of Jesus' return and the sporadic persecutions Christians faced, but to say that the symbols and narration therein specifically address those first century happenings is barking up the wrong tree once the cosmic dimension of Revelation becomes clear.

As in approaching Ecclesiastes, here we have a crucial choice to make about the grandiose claim of the author: Either he has succeeded in his claim to writing something cosmically valid, which means that historical and geographical target audience and happenings, being extraneous particulars, are only relevant insofar as it has prompted the writing, but would serve no further purpose, or that he has failed and his work is not worth our effort to unravel since falling back on particular history to interpret the book blatantly betrays all the overt claims of Revelation.

Taking the second position a priori, i.e., being dismissive of the wisdom or ability of the author to address a cosmic problem, is unworthy of truth seekers. So in face of such a choice, only the first position is tenable. We then have to conclude that the usual extraneous cultural and historical analyzes would be largely futile for shedding light on Revelation's content because the piece of writing we are dealing with has mercilessly transcended the time, locale, socio-political, and cultural setting within which it was penned.

But is this not tantamount to having a book dropping down from heaven with no human imprints? Is this at all possible given that humans are authors, and despite divine inspiration, the human trait can really not be eliminated? No, I am not advocating such a view at all. If I am, then this world would not be a fitting abode for me! Revelation, though being divinely inspired like all other books of the Bible, is penned by a mortal called John who shares his humanity with you and me. Let me further elaborate.

While we gain very little by researching the historical setting (late first century Jewish and Hellenistic culture and events under Roman rule, specific target readers . . . etc.), the symbols used in Revelation are mostly based on history, very specifically biblical history. As such, *one has to draw heavily from the rest of the Bible, but not from the history and culture specific to the time and place of Revelation's formation.* Since the Bible is shot through with the gory little details of what happened on the human plane, the human imprints in Revelation come in through the rest of the Bible.

This expectation is nothing but common sense since if we believe that the divine hand is behind the arrangement of the books in the Bible, with Revelation concluding what have been said before, then knowing all that lead up to the last book, particularly the introduction (Genesis), would naturally put the reader in a good position to understand the conclusion. Reading the conclusion without the benefit of the previous developments and arguments could easily lead the readers away from the true message with potentially disastrous consequence. Though this "out of context" approach gives us a lot of leeway to interpret, it is fundamentally wrong.

Is there any other guide that can help us with making sense of Revelation? God is revealing his work to the churches, i.e., to the entire body of believers who live in this world. With this target audience, esoteric knowledge outside the Bible can be ruled out because the Bible is the only common inheritance the community of believers has received from the Holy Spirit. If so, apart from biblical knowledge, the only "interpretative" tool left would be common sense, or simple common reasoning using observations of Revelation as building blocks.

Of course, one can debate what is common reasoning endlessly without coming to any useful convergence. To avoid such unproductive detour, I have chosen to go directly to interpreting Revelation and let the process and findings naturally spell out more clearly what I mean. You can then decide whether what emerges from this journey justifies my above contention.

After reading Revelation a few times without the benefits of outside explanatory notes, most readers would come away baffled and confused. In fact, in exasperation, some have claimed that John has written Revelation in a drunken state! But alcohol and incomprehension aside, the other feeling that one comes away with is an awe-filled sense of its magnificent scope. The subject matters range from mundane communities called churches, to lofty and unreachable heavenly worship, to the final judgment that incites fear or longing, to a surreal future totally unimaginable from our present standpoint. Our finite human senses are taxed beyond their limits.

Yet, we are not hopeless since we know that *Revelation, as its name implies, is meant to be understood*—to reveal to those who earnestly want to appreciate its message the way Jesus sees it. So where do we start?

## 4. SOME SUGGESTIONS AND TWO OBSERVATIONS

The writings making up the Bible were initially written without chapter division. Such divisions were inserted by Archbishop Stephen Langton of Canterbury in the twelfth to thirteenth century based on his understanding of the sense of each section while keeping the length manageable. Modern Bible scholars usually ignore those chapter divisions for fear of being misled into missing the meaning of the original work. But I have found the chapter division quite helpful as a start to decipher some books. Thank you, Stephen. Judge then for yourself whether the current chapter divisions in Revelation by and large make sense through a cursory reading.

Being prompted by statements like "things which must soon take place" in Revelation, one constantly faces the temptation to correlate its content with historical or current events, global or local, to see what has or will soon come to pass. But unless the author explicitly refers to the purported events, such reading is to be strongly discouraged before one gets the sense of what the Apostle John is trying to convey from his standpoint. As far as I can tell, John has not referred to any specific event that human history has recorded that was future to his writing then. So my suggestion is for you to suspend your curiosity, no matter how natural it may seem, about how Revelation relates to current happenings, but to turn your attention first to how the passages making up Revelation are related to each other. Such relationship can take many forms, sometimes through continuity of one theme, similarity or contrast between passages or entities . . . etc. Needless to say, such endeavor takes determination and discipline, yet it is richly rewarding. Giving up too early is an iron-clad guarantee of failure. So let us now start with some interesting observations.

## 4.1 First General Observation: One Chapter is Glaringly Different

In going through all the twenty two chapters of Revelation, the careful reader would notice that one chapter stands out as completely different in the style it narrates as compared with all the other chapters. Revelation is replete with fanciful symbols that are described in colorful and lively terms with active participation of many parties. That makes Revelation vivid and exciting to read, yet difficult to grasp. But when it comes to chapter 20, the vividness, life, and exotic symbolism that infuse all the other chapters seem to have been drained from it. Let us take a cursory look in table 1 below.

Table 1. Features in Revelation that are absent from chapter 20

| ch. | Sample features that lift the chapters from being a dry nonchalant description |
|---|---|
| 1 | Personal encounter with Jesus; Jesus appears in exotic and colorful forms and attire; air of completeness and finality; the number seven repeated; a personal commission to John . . . |
| 2–3 | Very personal messages—admonition, encouragement, warning; individual circumstances of each recipient church in history; Jesus individualizing his exotic appearance for each church . . . |
| 4 | Rainbow-ringed throne; enigmatic and exotic living creatures; twenty four gold-crowned elders; wild and emotional acclamation by all life forms; profound sense of eternity . . . |
| 5 | Very personal interaction with the author with strong emotion; Lamb with seven horns and seven eyes; symphony of praise from every creature in creation . . . |
| 6 | Series of enigmatic sevens—seals opened, reappearance of the four living creatures, colored horses, enigmatic actions of riders; supplication of saints; cosmic disturbance; great apprehension towards the future . . . |
| 7 | Repetition of twelve thousand for each tribe; each tribe named; loud acclamation from a great multitude; a great tribulation to come out of; a poignant promise of bliss everlasting . . . |

| ch. | Sample features that lift the chapters from being a dry nonchalant description |
|---|---|
| 8 | Silence in heaven; starting another series of sevens—trumpets; disasters striking nature; an enigmatic destructive quota of one third; announcement of three woes ... |
| 9 | Bottomless pit opened with smoke coming out; mutated locust; an enigmatic five months of non-fatal torment; second release—from Euphrates; $2 \times 10^8$ horsemen; one third mankind killed; room for the survivors to repent, but they did not ... |
| 10 | Mighty rainbow-capped angel; a little scroll in the angel's hand; anti-revelation with thunders not allowed to be recorded; angel swearing to God; God's mystery is finished; John eating the little scroll; John commissioned to prophesy again ... |
| 11 | John measures the temple; two enigmatic witnesses; beast kills the witnesses; people gloating with celebration; specific timescales—42 months, 1,260, and 3.5 days; two witnesses resurrecting and taken to heaven; proclamation of God's eternal reign and final recompense ... |
| 12 | Nature-adorned woman; giving birth; a cosmically destructive red dragon; vulnerable male child chased by dragon; cryptic "time, times and half a time"; war in heaven; proclamation of salvation from heaven; formula for victory revealed; earth helping the woman; dragon is angry; struggle between Satan and offspring of the woman ... |
| 13 | An exotic beast with seven heads and ten horns; a powerful beast being worshipped; blasphemy from beast; another beast trying to deceive; saints are vulnerable; endurance of saints called for; buying and selling controlled; cryptic number—666 ... |
| 14 | One hundred and forty four thousand with names on their forehead; an exclusive new song; blameless firstfruits; an eternal gospel; Babylon destruction announced; personal warning; endurance of saints called for again; son of man reaping the earth; the earth reaped twice; wine press pouring out blood for 1,600 stadia ... |
| 15 | Seven plagues being the last; song of Moses merged with song of the Lamb; angels to deliver plagues garbed in pure bright linen with golden sashes; temple barred entry temporarily ... |
| 16 | Seven plagues in bowls; emotional responses to God's righteous judgment from both the saints and their opponents throughout; air of finality—people blaspheme God in response to his wrath; the throne proclaiming: "It is done"; unprecedented earthquake, the great city split into three; huge hailstones ... |
| 17 | Explanation volunteered by angel; litany of the great whore's poison; two-color woman riding on a beast; mystery of seven heads and ten horns revealed; hidden relationship between the beast and the whore revealed ... |
| 18 | Righteous indignation, rejoicing, astonishment, mourning coming from different sides; call to come out of Babylon; "merchants" form a distinct group; everyday activities of Babylon catalogued; very swift ending; millstone thrown into the sea symbolizing Babylon's eternal destruction ... |
| 19 | Multi-party, multi-faceted rejoicing at Babylon's fall; John's very human blunder; profligate portrait of the rider on a white horse; a gruesome banquet; wrathful punishment of the two beasts ... |

| ch. | Sample features that lift the chapters from being a dry nonchalant description |
|---|---|
| 20 | ~~~~~~~~~~~~~~~ NONE ~~~~~~~~~~~~~~~ |
| 21 | Proclamation from the throne; air of finality—Alpha and Omega; end to previously unavoidable miseries; God presence assured; colorful foundation stones and pearly gates of the city; specific number of twelve; John measuring the city; glory and honor of nations brought into the city . . . |
| 22 | Surreal portrait of river, tree, and street; personal encounter with Jesus; dialogue between John and an angel; another John's human blunder; direct instructions from Jesus, the Spirit, and the angel; promises and warnings given . . . |

All the characters we encounter in chapter 20 have made their debut in previous chapters, but now they are cast in a different light. Looking outward from chapter 20, we see these contrasts:

**Major Players**

1. A lone (not one of four or seven), non-descript (not mighty . . . ), unadorned (no rainbow on his head) angel coming down out of heaven with the sole task of locking up Satan.
2. Even the dragon has lost its color—scarlet; God's throne is now plain white without the emerald (white is not a color, just the lack thereof).
3. The many epithets attached to Jesus before are now absent, he is plainly Christ.
4. The multitude is not counted (e.g., 1000×1000, or 2×myriads of myriads before), but just as numerous as "the sand of the seashore."
5. Those who resurrected are neither stamped nor given names. The same is true for those opposing God.
6. The ubiquitous throne attendants—twenty four elders and four living creatures—seem to have deserted their usual place before God!

**Earthliness**

7. No physical measurements (e.g., stadia, cubits, denarius, talents) come into the picture; neither do objects like precious stones, scale, swords . . . etc.
8. No earthly creatures (horses, lion, leopard, eagle, fish, locusts, scorpions, green plants . . . etc.) or celestial objects (sun, moon, stars . . . etc.) are found.

9. In place of the familiar biblical geography (Zion, Jerusalem, Egypt, Sodom, Euphrates) and personage (David, Moses, twelve tribes of Israel) is now found the utmost obscured conflation of personnel and geography (Gog and Magog).

**Time and Number**

10. Timescales are given to only one significant digit (1,000 years) or as the indefinite "a little while" rather than the more precise "durations" before (1,260 and 3.5 days . . . etc.).

11. No reference to other specific numbers, e.g., 144,000 which was repeated twice before for the chosen of God. The only number is the non-specific 1,000.

12. Things or events do not come in series of sevens or fours or threes. Every event seems to be one-off and final.

**Struggle and Participation**

13. There is no meaningful contest between the parties. Whereas the dragon was angrily chasing after the woman in chapter 12, it has not put up any resistance to its binding and imprisonment here. Heaven's fire to destroy the opposition just goes unopposed.

14. All events seem effortless and proceed as if by auto-pilot without further divine instructions, e.g., no seal needs to be broken to open the book of life, the destruction of Satan is not illustrated like the mighty angel throwing down a great millstone into the sea as for Babylon . . . etc.

15. The actions of the players are minimally described: the resurrected simply reign, the deceived nations simply surround the saints' camp.

16. John's multiple first-hand participations in the process of revelation—weeping bitterly, asking, being answered, being instructed, measuring, swallowing, mistaking . . . etc.—are all absent. Here, he seems to be an outsider.

**Mood**

17. Joy and pain, rejoicing and cursing which are so prevalent before are all absent. Emotionally loaded words of all kinds are mostly kept out. The most loaded words—blessed and holy; tormented day and night forever and ever—are mild factual descriptions rather than emotive.

18. Judgment goes by the books (scrolls) rather than from God in person. The saints are no longer given names directly by God, but are just

registered as a name in the book. Personal details—who these people are and their deeds—are not mentioned.

19. There are no mysteries and enigmas to explain (e.g., 666, the woman on the beast . . . etc.). Everything seems plain and simple with no new encryption! It is assumed that the reader needs no assistance in grasping the meaning of the symbols.

**Outcome**

20. No promise of an alternative; no call to repentance is given. Indeed repentance, which is called for even in chapter 18 with the destruction of Babylon, is not expected here. The opposition is straightforwardly eliminated with fire from heaven.

21. Those reigning with Christ do not sing praises to the creator or to the Lamb. The frequent and unreserved accolades that resound throughout creation before have conspicuously fallen silent.

22. Satan's destruction is not described by a plague or as resulting from the wrath of God, but he is nonchalantly thrown into the lake of fire.

23. Despite the seeming finality in vanquishing God's final enemy, there is no fanfare, no banquet, no voice or proclamation from heaven befitting such a victory that caps all victory. Neither is there any specific mention of reward.

Gone are all the emotive and vivid elements that are in abundance in other chapters. The whole chapter seems to have been deliberately written from a detached perspective and made to stand out among other chapters. This total drabness is even more remarkable when one considers the subject matter of the chapter which seems like the final consummating battle, the negative grand finale. In going over the previous chapters, one encounters many conflicts between two camps, with God, the Lamb, his angels, and his followers on one side and Satan with his beast(s), false prophet, and followers as opposition. If we follow the order in chapters 18–20, though not as chronological, then all except Satan have already been defeated before chapter 20. What seems to remain now is Satan with some followers of *unexplained origin* (see section 10.3 of the second reading) facing God in a final showdown. And even in this ultimate retribution, the contrast is unmistakable: "these two (beast and false prophet) were thrown *alive* into the lake of fire which *burns* with brimstone" (19:20) versus "And the devil (Satan) who deceived them was thrown into the lake of fire and brimstone, where the beast and the false prophet are also" (20:10). In this description of the war to end all wars, one would only expect the most colorful, lively, and fanciful display followed by unprecedented celebration of vanquishing the final foe, to be capped by a happily-ever-after ending as in chapters 21–22. *But as opposed to a most grandiose and exciting climax, the Apostle John brought it to a complete black and white detached anti-climax.* Hollywood would frown on such a plot!

As if this is not enough, the contrast between the Greek words used for "time" is absolutely striking. The Greek word *kairos* is used for significant moments and appears five times in Revelation. They are at the beginning and end (1:3, 22:10) saying with all urgency that the time is near. Three more times *kairos* is used, right in the center of Revelation to designate very significant happenings. The first (11:18) talks of the time to judge the dead and to reward God's servants, an event which corresponds to the judgment before the great white throne in chapter 20. The second (12:12) says that the devil only has a short time on earth. The third ("time, times and half a time," 12:14) is enigmatic which we will unravel in our second reading through Revelation. On the other hand, the Greek word *chronos* describes linear time without significance, a word which gives rise to the English word "chronology." *This is used only three times in Revelation.* In talking to the churches in 2:21, a sinning woman is given *chronos* to repent. In 10:6, a strong angel promises God that there will be no more delay (*chronos*). But significantly, the only other usage is in 20:3 in asserting that Satan will be released for a short *chronos*, which recalls the short time the devil has on earth in 12:12. But as we have just seen, *kairos* and not *chronos* is used in 12:12. This glaring contrast between the epochal significance of the first "short time" and the nonchalant flatness of the second in referring to what seems to be the same thing further reinforces the distinctiveness of chapter 20 we have already noticed.

All these cry out for an explanation.

It may seem that since all the characters in chapter 20 have been encountered in preceding chapters, there is no need to repeat such extravagant description, hence the drabness. Yet such explanation does not hold water since many of the features have been repeated throughout the book (e.g., sword in Jesus' mouth (in three events), twenty four elders or simply elders (in 6), four living creatures (in 6), Euphrates (in 3), hundred and forty four (in 2), singing (in 2), worshipping God (in 5), ten horns and seven heads (in 3) . . . etc., just to name a few). It would come naturally to the person who has penned the first nineteen chapters in exotic details to continue with the same style in chapter 20, unless he has a specific message to get across.

Are we then to take chapter 20 to be written by a different author? Of course not! The flow of the message rules that out. Rather, we should seek an explanation from the author's intention which I will set forth in our next reading of Revelation.

Let us turn now to another aspect of Revelation which has caused much confusion: the symbols of time and their associated numbers.

## 4.2 Second General Observation: The Essence of Revealed Time

If Revelation is about the future—what must surely take place, then a proper understanding of how time units are used would be crucial to unlocking its messages. Even before getting into the details, one gets a sense that these time units cannot be taken as we moderns understand them, e.g., an hour for 60 minutes, a day for twenty four hours . . . etc. So what do the time units convey? I have catalogued all the time references in Revelation in table 2 to provide a bird-eye's view to help discussions.

Time is punctuated by units marking out durations. Only four proper time units are found in Revelation—hour, day, month, and year. An enigmatic reference to "time" is given as if time is itself a measure of time: "time, times and half a time" (12:14). As such, "time" (*kairos* and *chronos*) is also included in table 2. The time units give us the impression that those four units in Revelation refer to fixed durations because we have other terms, e.g., eons, era, ages, a split second . . . etc. to specify indefinite duration. Yet whether John has intended these to be interpreted as fixed durations can only be determined by examining the context. The first entry in the table is a case in point. There all four time units used in Revelation appear together, suggesting that any one of these four units—hour, day, month or year—can convey a decisive or appointed moment. Thus contextual understanding is paramount.

Time units in Revelation can either be used with a number or in the general sense without being counted. In the table, I have ascribed to all non-numeric used of time unit a meaning which would adequately give the sense of how these time units are to be taken. For example, the non-numeric use of the word "hour" always signifies the arrival of a decisive moment, e.g., "because the hour of His judgment has come" (14:7) . . . etc. That being clear, our attention should be focused more on how the "counted" time units are used.

Among the counted time units, I would discuss the extremes (longest and shortest) here and leave the other to the next reading when we go through Revelation section by section.

Hour is the shortest time unit in Revelation. When it is counted, it is associated with only two numbers, one (four times), and half (once). We will discuss the half hour in the next reading, but we note here that three of the four "one hour" usages are found in chapter 18 when describing the destruction of Babylon and they reinforce the same theme—the ignominious fate of Babylon will come very soon, sooner than expected. The remaining "one hour" also carries that sense (compare 17:10 and 12).

The longest time unit, year, in Revelation, when it is counted, is *without exception* associated with one number—one thousand, and this combination is *all found (6 times) in one chapter* (and *one in each of six successive verses* (20:2–7)): the most monotonic chapter that we have just encountered, namely 20!

In invariably associating a fixed but large number—1000—to the longest time unit used in Revelation and the smallest whole number (or half thereof) to the shortest time unit used, what could the Holy Spirit be conveying through John? To me, the answer is unequivocal: "hour" is to convey briefness and imminence while "year" a very long duration. For the thousand years, the contrast in 20:3 makes it clear: "and he threw him into the abyss, and shut it and sealed it over him, so that he would not deceive the nations any longer, until the *thousand years* were completed; after these things he must be released for *a short time*." But one could ask: If John has intended a thousand years to mean a very long time, why does he not say so directly, as with the "short time"? An explanation is that "a long time" can connote neither beginning nor end while "a thousand years" does. Not specifying the duration runs the risk of portraying history as an endless stretch with no beginning and no end, hence also no creation and no New Jerusalem. What is conveyed through a thousand years is a very long duration, but capped at both ends. On the contrary, a short time does not run the risk of being similarly misinterpreted, hence the asymmetry in the juxtaposition.

Only if our common sense is cruelly suspended when we encounter the "one hour" in chapter 18 can we come off with anything but a sense that Babylon's destruction is expected any time. And not surprisingly, the same sense of imminence is conveyed through a very similar verse (18:10) when hour is replaced by day: "For this reason in *one day* her plagues will come, pestilence and mourning and famine, and she will be burned up with fire; for the Lord God who judges her is strong." If one day and one hour are used somewhat interchangeably, then neither of them can be humanly literal nor arithmetical to indicate a preset duration.

Both the longest and shortest timescales in Revelation—year and hour—can then be called "indefinite" based on the generic nature of how they are counted (1 or 1,000) in contrast with the more particular, specific numbers used elsewhere with timescales (1,260, 3.5, 42). I will refer to the latter timescales as "definite" or "specific" since by using very exact (with two significant digits or more) numbers, the author is probably trying to convey a particular message. Unlike the definite timescales, the meanings of the indefinite timescales probably does not go beyond very long or very short, though they can be nuanced for the context. What all the definite timescales (and another timescale of "five months" in chapter 9) convey will be discussed in our next reading through Revelation.

In discussing timescales in Revelation, what is not explicitly mentioned can be just as puzzling (and revealing) as what is mentioned. *Conspicuously absent is the week.* Why is this absence so startling? Because John is a Jew well versed in the Old Testament. For the Jewish faith, the week is more fundamental than any other time units mentioned since unlike other time units, the week is explicitly commanded for observance by God. Six days the Jews should work, but on the seventh, a Sabbath is to be observed. John was fully immersed in the Sabbath practice. Not coincidentally, a week is not only marked by seven days, but by the Sabbath, hence the Greek word for week is *Sabbaton*, same as Sabbath. It recalls the work of God, and humans are to do what God did through observing the weekly cycle of work and rest. While hours, days, months and years follow the rhythm of nature, the Sabbath imposes God's rhythm on his creation through humans and is thus the *festival of all festivals in the Bible* (Exod 31:13). Our curiosity is further piqued by the profuse use of "seven" in Revelation which even the most casual reader cannot miss. But John never uses the term "week" though it was in common use then (e.g., Acts 20:7) and Jesus' first conflict which also represents his most numerous and intense conflicts with his opponents is based on the week—is it legal to heal the sick on the last day of the week, the Sabbath? We will account for such absence in our second reading through Revelation.

## 5. SOME BASIC INTERPRETATIVE APPROACHES AND PITFALLS

The above naturally brings out the question of the rules of interpretation. A common approach is to lay out all the rules before delving into the real content. Given the obviously symbolic nature of Revelation, presetting some rules without referring to concrete examples will not help the readers. Also, as I have demonstrated before, one has to determine what makes sense within the context, hence also to reject some contrary or untested rules, in trying to get a handle on something as simple as one hour or a thousand years. So we will try to find out what rules apply and what do not as we go along.

Table 2. Units of time in Revelation

| Time unit | Reference | Immediate context of the time unit | Sense determined from context |
|---|---|---|---|
| All | 9:15 | And the four angels, who had been prepared for the *hour and day and month and year*, were released . . . | Appointed time |
| | 3:3 | and you will not know at what *hour* I will come to you | An unspecified future decisive moment or event of significance |
| | 3:10 | I also will keep you from the *hour* of testing, that *hour* which is about to come upon the whole world | |
| | 11:13 | And in that *hour* there was a great earthquake, and a tenth of the city fell; | |
| | 14:7 | "Fear God, and give Him glory, because the *hour* of His judgment has come; | |
| | 14:15 | "Put in your sickle and reap, for the *hour* to reap has come, because the harvest of the earth is ripe." | |
| Hour (hōra) | 8:1 | When the Lamb broke the seventh seal, there was silence in heaven for about half an *hour*. | To be determined in the 2nd reading |
| | 17:12 | . . . but they receive authority as kings with the beast for one *hour*. | An unexpectedly short time or an unexpected arrival of an event |
| | 18:10 | "Woe, woe, the great city, Babylon, the strong city! For in one *hour* your judgment has come." | |
| | 18:17 | for in one *hour* such great wealth has been laid waste!" | |
| | 18:19 | "Woe, woe, the great city, in which all who had ships at sea became rich by her wealth, for in one *hour* she has been laid waste!" | |

# FIRST READING—DIAGNOSING THE HURDLES   17

| | | | |
|---|---|---|---|
| | 1:10 | I was in the Spirit on the Lord's *day*, and I heard behind me a loud voice like the sound of a trumpet, | A specific day in the calendar |
| | 2:10 | . . . so that you will be tested, and you will have tribulation for ten *days*. Be faithful until death . . . . | A complete period |
| | 2:13 | and did not deny My faith even in the *days* of Antipas, My witness, My faithful one, who was killed | A period associated with an event or a person |
| | 9:6 | And in those *days* men will seek death and will not find it; they will long to die, and death flees from them. | |
| | 10:7 | but in the *days* of the voice of the seventh angel, when he is about to sound, then the mystery of God is finished, as He preached to His servants the prophets. | |
| | 11:6 | These have the power to shut up the sky, so that rain will not fall during the *days* of their prophesying; | |
| Day (*hēmera*) | 4:8 | . . . *day* and night they do not cease to say, | Unceasingly |
| | 7:15 | . . . and they serve Him *day* and night in His temple; | |
| | 12:10 | . . . the accuser of our brethren has been thrown down, he who accuses them before our God *day* and night. | |
| | 14:11 | And the smoke of their torment goes up forever and ever; they have no rest *day* and night, those who . . . | |
| | 20:10 | . . . and they will be tormented *day* and night forever and ever. | |
| | 6:17 | for the great *day* of their wrath has come, and who is able to stand?" | A decisive moment |
| | 16:14 | . . . to gather them together for the war of the great *day* of God, the Almighty. | |
| | 8:12 | . . . so that a third of them would be darkened and the *day* would not shine for a third of it, and the night in the same way. | Daytime |
| | 21:25 | In the *day* time (for there will be no night there) its gates will never be closed; | |

| Time unit | Reference | Immediate context of the time unit | Sense determined from context |
|---|---|---|---|
| Day (*hēmera*) (continued) | 11:3 | And I will grant authority to my two witnesses, and they will prophesy for twelve hundred and sixty *days*, clothed in sackcloth." | To be determined in the 2nd reading |
| | 12:6 | ... so that there she would be nourished for one thousand two hundred and sixty *days*. | |
| | 11:9 | ... will look at their dead bodies for three and a half *days*, and will not permit their dead bodies ... | To be determined in the 2nd reading |
| | 11:11 | But after the three and a half *days*, the breath of life from God came into them, and they stood on their feet; | To be determined in the 2nd reading |
| | 18:8 | For this reason in one *day* her plagues will come, pestilence and mourning and famine .... | An unexpectedly short time |
| | 9:5 | And they were not permitted to kill anyone, but to torment for five *months*; and .... | To be determined in the 2nd reading |
| | 9:10 | They have tails like scorpions, and stings; and in their tails is their power to hurt men for five *months*. | |
| Month (*mēn*) | 11:2 | ... and they will tread under foot the holy city for forty-two *months*. | To be determined in the 2nd reading |
| | 13:5 | a mouth speaking arrogant words and blasphemies, and authority to act for forty-two *months* was given to him. | To be determined in the 2nd reading |
| | 22:2 | On either side of the river was the tree of life, bearing twelve kinds of fruit, yielding its fruit every *month*; | A generic time unit in a natural year |
| | 20:2 | And he laid hold of the dragon, the serpent of old, who is the devil and Satan, and bound him for a thousand *years*; | |
| | 20:3 | So that he would not deceive the nations any longer, until the thousand *years* were completed; | |

FIRST READING—DIAGNOSING THE HURDLES     19

| | | | |
|---|---|---|---|
| Year (*eniautos*) | 20:4 | and they came to life and reigned with Christ for a thousand *years*. | A very long time; the more precise meanings to be explained within its context in the 2nd reading |
| | 20:5 | The rest of the dead did not come to life until the thousand *years* were completed. | |
| | 20:6 | but they will be priests of God and of Christ and will reign with Him for a thousand *years*. | |
| | 20:7 | When the thousand *years* are completed, Satan will be released from his prison, | |
| | 1:3 | Blessed is he who reads and those who hear the words of the prophecy, and heed the things which are written in it; for the *time* is near. (*kairos*) | Decisive moment |
| | 22:10 | And he said to me, "Do not seal up the words of the prophecy of this book, for the *time* is near. (*kairos*) | |
| | 2:21 | I gave her *time* to repent, and she does not want to repent of her immorality. (*chronos*) | Opportunities |
| Time (*kairos* and *chronos* only) | 10:6 | and swore by Him who lives forever and ever, who created heaven . . . , that there will be delay (*chronos*) no longer | Delay |
| | 11:18 | And the nations were enraged, and Your wrath came, and the *time* came for the dead to be judged, and the *time* to reward Your bond-servants the prophets . . . (both *kairos*) | When things are completed |
| | 12:12 | . . . because the devil has come down to you, having great wrath, knowing that he has only a short *time*." (*kairos*) | Brief period |
| | 20:3 | after these things he must be released for a short *time*. (*chronos*) | |
| | 12:14 | where she was nourished for a *time* and *times* and half a *time*, from the presence of the serpent. (*kairos*) | To be determined in the 2nd reading |

Note: The occurrences are grouped according to the sense they convey rather than the order they appear in Revelation. Only the relevant portion of the verse rather than the whole verse is given.

Having rejected a priori Procrustean rules for Revelation, I would suggest a general proximity or concentric principle in interpreting Revelation as a first *common sense* guidance. When any author writes a book, divine inspiration notwithstanding, he/she would want the readers to understand; otherwise, why write? The readership the author has in mind determines the information he/she wants to put into the book—what do the readers already know and what does the author need to add to what they already know through the book. Based on this consideration, the author would try to make the book *totally comprehensible* to the intended readers. This means that the information in the book would largely be sufficient for the target readers to grasp the book's message *without much outside knowledge.*

In the flow of the author's presentation, he would do the utmost to guide the readers logically through the book. The clear implication is that each unit (sentence, paragraph, chapter . . . etc.) is to be understood best within the immediate context. In this way, interpreting any passage in a long piece of writing would need to start from the passage itself, and then seek greater and greater contextual understanding by expanding outward to put the passage into perspective of the entire writing. It is only until these are exhausted that one should go outside the piece of writing being studied. In practical terms, this means seeking understanding from Revelation based on the internal information in Revelation first, and if necessary, go out to other New Testament writings (when Revelation was written down, no formal New Testament existed, but the teachings prevalent within the Christian community at the time eventually made it into the New Testament), then to the whole Bible, then finally to the outside world. Reversing this order not only violates common sense, but can lead to disastrous expectation of cosmic proportion. Such can be likened to reading one's fate in the alignment of the remotest objects—the stars—rather than first seeking explanation of the present from one's actions and situation. Thankfully, the Bible teaches moral responsibility, but condemns astrology!

Yet an equally important context must be accounted for. Revelation concludes the Bible, hence it would naturally respond to its introduction, Genesis. In so viewing the Bible as one narration, *Genesis must be taken as Revelation's immediate context*, injecting itself into Revelation's message by default. As we will see, reading Revelation and Genesis side by side illuminates key passages.

Another principle to keep in mind is that Revelation is highly symbolic and such must be respected. This has two implications. First, the details of each symbol must be preserved without collapsing it to what is familiar to us. We have already seen how time is symbolic, but this applies to other "entities" as well. In Revelation, a number of length scales are used, e.g.,

144 cubits, being the wall thickness of the holy city in 21:17, conveys two messages, one through the number "144" signifying efforts from the chosen (twelve tribes coming forth from Israel which have similarly multiplied; section 11 of the second reading) and the other one through the unit "cubit" which is the length of a human forearm from ankle to fingertip, signifying the wall of the holy city to be the fruit of humans' labor. But in some English versions (even the NASB from which I quote here), it is collapsed into its modern equivalent—72 yards. The two symbolisms in the original text are lost in this totally unjustifiable rendering. Unfortunately, many more can be found. This can only be overcome by checking out the original Greek text or comparing other translations, a job made easy by the helpful material on the Internet.

Beguiling may be the intention of these "conversions" to make the Bible more relatable to modern readers, these renderings hide a more disturbing assumption: As opposed to putting oneself into the shoes of the author to grasp the message, such collapsing assumes that the Bible can and should play by our rules, just like a boat demanding a lighthouse to move out of its path!

The second implication, following from our previous analyzes, is that one should first treat everything in Revelation as symbolic unless absolutely compelled by contrary evidence. Mixing "literal" and "symbolic" interpretations endlessly confuses. Such also betrays another egocentric (and haphazard) attempt to Bible study: since taking the Bible literally feels more concrete and comfortable to me, I will try to make sense of what I can grasp as literal first, and only failing that, resort to symbolic interpretation. But the Apostle John did not know what modern readers, or readers down the ages, can and cannot make sense of literally to cater to their reading needs, even if that were desirable. Not surprisingly, the outcome of such an unnatural attempt would be a human concoction alien to the flow of the Bible. A more respectful approach would be to treat everything as symbolic, since many passages obviously demand that, and to note the internal peculiarities and connections of the symbols therein.

Finally, one should also guard against extraneous conditions. A clear example is found in some "equivalence" principles of time. Desperate to concretize Revelation's symbols, some have demanded a "day" in Revelation be read as a year or some other familiar time units (jarringly contradicting the intent of 2 Pet 3:8), thus the 1,260 and 3.5 days in chapter 11 are read as 1,260 and 3.5 years. But none of these desperate attempts have pried open the enigma of Revelation by one iota.

In the following reading, I will show how a natural contextual understanding would.

# 2

# Second Reading— Gathering the Gems of Revelation

## 1. JESUS' SELF INTRODUCTION (CHAPTER 1)

LOGICALLY, THE FIRST CHAPTER of Revelation introduces the whole book. But this introduction, apart from mentioning briefly where John was when he received the revelation (Patmos, 9) and what he should be doing (writing to seven churches), is totally focused on one person. And that person is none other than Jesus himself.

Among the many things that happened to Jesus and the works he performed, which aspects stand out here? Jesus has been portrayed in exotic out-of-the-world symbols—white head, blazing eyes, burnished feet with soothing sound, mouth with a two-edged sword, hands holding seven stars, glowing face . . . etc. (12–17), but the *only event* that links him to the worldly happenings is Jesus' self-proclamation at the end of the chapter: "Do not be afraid; I am the first and the last, and the living One; and *I was dead*, and behold, *I am alive* forevermore, and I have the keys of death and of Hades" (17b–18). Jesus' death and resurrection thus link his earthly works and teachings with the Jesus who is no longer physically present with his followers. This though does not mean that all that Jesus taught and did are no longer relevant in comparison with the central importance of the resurrection event. On the contrary, because of Jesus' resurrection, all the other events making up his life, works and teachings have now been validated, hence important.

Precisely because of the resurrection event, Jesus can repeatedly claim to be the one "who is and who was and who is to come" (1:4, 4:8) as well as the Alpha and Omega in various forms (1:8, 1:17, 22:6, 7, 13). It is only fitting that at the very end of the book, the Alpha and Omega comes along again to remind the churches who he is. No one should doubt Revelation's cosmic implications.

Why then did Jesus ask John to write to seven churches? To tell them about a future that will materialize soon: "Blessed is he who reads and those who hear the *words of the prophecy*, and heed the things which are written in it; for the *time is near*" (3). But how is the future communicated here? Is it in the form of a timetable with epochs demarcated by sharp boundaries in between and the main actors in each epoch well spelled out, or is it in the form of a grand vision with no fixed milestones and the same cast of characters from beginning to end? In other words, *is it a movie or a timeless portrait?*

The precise time keeping enabled by better clock-making in the scientific age has somehow dominated our understanding of time. Such can easily lure us into thinking of "time" in Revelation as linear (*chronos*). But as pointed out in our first reading, Revelation's focus is on *kairos*, that momentous, significant, and appointed time. In other words, it is "high time" that is referred to here when John says "the time is near." Coming to grips with this time concept is closely related to the other term used here—words of prophecy—which together with "the time is near" is also repeated at the end (22:10). What goes between these two verses, that is almost all of Revelation, must then be seen as this words of prophecy. What then is the meaning of prophecy here?

In the Old Testament, prophecies have at least two intertwined elements: forth-telling and fore-telling. Forth-telling speaks more of the consequence of one's action should one persist without changing course. The said outcome may not be directly brought about by God but is more a natural consequence of God's ordained laws (e.g., if you drink and drive, you will claim innocent victims and harm yourself). On the other hand, when the actor in question is too far gone in one direction, then his/her fate is sealed regardless and no present actions can alter that end, fore-telling may take over. Often, these two elements are mingled. Well-known examples are Jonah's prophecy to Nineveh which did not come to pass because his proclamation, though being the result of his rueful skimping of God's message through omitting the condition "if you do this," was heeded as a warning resulting in genuine repentance of all in Nineveh from the king down (Jonah 3:4–9). Yet, Israel repeated flouting of YHWH's warning (e.g., Isa 6:8–13) has locked it into a way of no return, hence the prophecy of Jeremiah (chapter 38) that Jerusalem's wall would be breached and the remnants taken captive. In this case, hope is still not lost, but lies beyond the inevitable and the prophesied (now fore-telling) immediate ruin. That leads to more prophesying in terms of forth-telling (how man should respond) and fore-telling (what God would bring about).

John speaks here of what *must shortly take place* (1:1, 22:6), seemingly placing his prophecy into the category of rigid fore-telling. But on the other hand, significant time, *kairos*, being free from the specifics and strictures of linear counted time points more towards forth-telling: since people are behaving like this, something great is coming, be prepared, or . . . As such, it would be wrong to permit ourselves to be guided by only forth-telling or fore-telling as we try to make sense of Revelation. Just let the text within the context first speak to us. This we will do as we go along.

But what is the true purpose of Revelation? Or what effect should proclaiming what must shortly take place have on the recipients? It is reassurance. "Do not be afraid" sums up the expected reaction of the listeners. This then serves as an unconventional (and somewhat unscholarly) guide to unravel Revelation. So if we have our wits scared out of us upon reading Revelation, then we have to ask whether we are understanding Revelation properly, or alternatively, whether we belong to the intended recipients. Our answers can be any combination of "yes" or "no" to both. Revelation is meant to reassure true followers of Jesus. As we shall see, Revelation also calls the wayward to repentance.

John sees himself as participating "in the tribulation and kingdom and perseverance in Jesus" which he shares with all his readers—contemporaneous or those to come. If Revelation is meant first for followers of Christ throughout all generations, then this mixture of sufferings from persecutions (tribulation), the hope of the full advent of the kingdom and the long-suffering (perseverance) kindled through faith in Jesus would be the common experience, to varying degrees and in various forms, of all believers that make up the churches. "Tribulation" (*thlipsis* in Greek) then refers not to any specific period of intense persecution just as involvement in the kingdom through persecution is the unchanging call down the ages.

Jesus greeted John on the Lord's Day (1:10). By the time John recorded the revelation towards the end of the first century, the Christian community has institutionalized the practice of remembering Jesus on the first day of each week through the breaking of bread (Acts 20:7). Unlike the Jewish Sabbath celebrated on the last day of the week to recall God's completion of his creative activities in six days and resting on the seventh, the Lord's Day signifies looking forward to a new creation initiated by Jesus through his resurrection on the very first day of the week of creative work. John's encounter with Jesus on this conspicuous day *neatly introduces what follows as the new works of Jesus and his followers which are yet to come.* This new beginning belongs to the Lord. It is his day because the final victory has been won through his death and resurrection.

## 2. SEVEN CHURCHES IN ANTICIPATION (CHAPTERS 2–3)

Revelation's introduction and conclusion make clear that the entire book is addressed to seven churches (1:4, 22:16). If we take the narrow view that these seven churches only represent those in the specific location mentioned, then most of Revelation's messages are history since all of those churches have since vanished. Revelation would then be deprived of a target audience. But no one holds this untenably narrow view. Instead, two interpretative grids are used to make the messages to the seven churches relevant. One holds that the seven churches represent seven periods in the history of the spread of Christianity. The other holds that the particularities of the seven churches together represent the advantages and challenges the universal church and the individual churches face in history to varying degrees and in different combinations, hence each of the messages to the seven churches would always be relevant to the Christian communities scattered throughout the globe.

Regardless of which view is more in line with the true import of Revelation, an issue which we will take up in section 2.4 of the fourth reading, one must not ignore the fact that despite the particular message(s) addressed to each church, *the entire message of Revelation is for each and every church*. John's address to the churches has not ended after chapter 3, but indeed only starts in earnest in chapter 4 and runs to the end of Revelation. The particular messages in chapters 2–3 are just the menu to whet their appetite for the full and rich banquet prepared for them. Of course, many applications can be drawn from the specific messages to the seven churches, but they mostly follow two lines: 1. continue to be faithful in what you have done well, and 2. repent of what you have fallen short, with a promise that Jesus would recompense swiftly and eventually.

John had the benefit of living in the era of the seven churches and understood their specific situations. We do not, and hence have to rely on patchy research of history to establish the historical setting of each church in order to situate the specific messages addressed to her. Most of the historical details of these churches have been lost in time, and efforts at reconstructing them are sometimes not a lot better than backward projections from what is described (because the church is asked not to do this, they must be practicing it . . . ) with little new insights gained. To do justice to the obvious universal character of the Book of Revelation, I have chosen to bypass the historical settings of Revelation, which is also that of the seven churches, and attempt to understand Revelation's message through its own narration.

## 3. THE HEAVENLY WORSHIP

### 3.1 First Heavenly Worship (chapter 4): The Eternal God and His Creation in Praises

Grandeur opens the full message of Jesus to the churches when John is invited, then ushered, in spirit to an otherworldly scene of heavenly worship. Two episodes of different emphases unfold in heaven, one each in chapters 4–5.

The first episode features a throne which was attended to by worshipful beings. Scant and beyond-frail human expression is the description of the one sitting on the throne (*like* a jasper stone and a sardius in appearance, 3) which is only appropriate for the inapproachable God who must be at the center of everything. What comes out of the throne takes on more concrete shape—flashes of lightning and sounds and peals of thunder, seven lamps of fire burning before the throne (seven Spirits of God) and something like a sea of glass, like crystal. The end of this episode sees four living creatures and twenty four elders praising God, not for any redemptive act in Jesus yet, but *simply that they owe their very existence to God's creation*: "Worthy are You, our Lord and our God, to receive glory and honor and power; for You created all things, and because of Your will they existed, and were created." (11). Sufficient for praising God is the fact of creation through God. Sentience, that is the awareness of one's existence, is its own purpose before God and is ground for worship; nothing extra is needed. This sentience is the absolutely private realm of its possessor, yet it opens him/her to God and other sentient creatures. Reinforcing and perhaps undergirding this basic praiseworthiness is the rainbow's permanent presence around the throne (3) which constantly reminds God of his covenant with Noah, that is his commitment to his own creation.

An unchanging eternity is the sense conveyed since praises are heaped on the creator who lives forever and ever, day and night unceasingly. Nothing seems to intervene to disrupt this eternal worship except for a hint of his temporal involvement with his creation expressed in the worship song in (8)—"who was and who is and who is to come." This paradoxical expression can be construed as the Old Testament name of God, YHWH (Exod 3:14), translated (with some difficulty given its indeterminate form) alternatively as "I am who I am" or "I will be who I will be" with the former emphasizing the eternal unchangeable self-sufficiency of God while the latter the dynamic involvement of God in his creation to shape a future. The former meaning neatly fits into the emphasis of this first heavenly worship episode in chapter 4 while the latter the next episode making up the heavenly worship in chapter 5.

Two types of beings are also introduced for the first time in Revelation—twenty four elders and four living creatures. The twenty four elders find no precedence in the Bible, and John simply states their existence without further explanation of who they are and wherefrom do they come. The mystery of the twenty four elders will be revealed in chapter 21. On the other hand, the four living creatures in different forms were first encountered in Ezek 1 when Ezekiel was commissioned. While the elders sit on thrones, the living creatures have no such support. Though many features of Ezekiel's four living creatures are beyond common human comprehension in three-dimensional space and time, *they all have human form* (1:5). On top of that, they each have four faces (of a human, a lion, an ox, and an eagle) together with wings and human hands. John's much shorter description has nothing of the 3-D-space-defying features in Ezekiel, but retains the four distinct facial appearances of these creatures except that each of John's creatures only has one face rather than four as in Ezekiel. John's living creatures each has six wings rather than four as in Ezekiel's. Given the similarities and dissimilarities between the two accounts, a judicious reading of these four living creatures against Ezekiel's account is necessary. And since revelation is indeed progressive, such unraveling would be done when we encounter these living creatures doing their works in the first four seals later. But for now, based on Ezekiel's basic datum, we can at least say they are human-related. Elders as used in the Bible are also humans.

## 3.2 Second Heavenly Worship (chapter 5): The Redeeming Lamb and Creation's Forward Movement

Breaking from the picture of ceaseless worship conveyed in the first episode, this episode opens with a question, the first in Revelation. A timeless eternity is finally interrupted by temporality: movements, changes, and progress or regress, and above all, even doubts (in form of questions) are now in view. While this is still a heavenly scene, the eternal heaven has condescended and broken through to the earthly to entertain the doubts of mere mortals.

After seeing the scroll that is written on both sides, the question raised by an angel is: "Who is worthy to open the book (scroll) and to break its seals?" What does the scroll signify and why does John weep bitterly when no one was found to be able to open these seals?

The meaning of the scroll seems to lie in the earlier promise of the angel to John: "I will show you what must take place after these things" (4:1). John was promised a glimpse of the future, the meaning and end of history, sealed up in the scroll. After witnessing the ceaseless praise the living creatures and elders are heaping on God, but still fully aware of a broken creation, John wonders if the final victory of good over evil, order over chaos, praises over curses, beauty over ugliness, honor over sordidness, purity over filth will materialize at all if no one can take history by its rein and move it forward to that envisaged and sought-for eternity. The current pathetic earthly picture cannot stretch into endless eternity without God losing praises from his creatures. The ground for praising God in the first episode—that creation exists because of God's acts of goodness—is insufficient in an order now marred by corruption and lawlessness. If history is left to run its course without divine intervention, then what would happen does not have to be left to speculation at all. John has seen enough, and so have we, to draw a definite conclusion. If the lofty eternal God does not lower himself to embrace transience, if the boundless eternity does not come into contact with the finite, then the temporal and the limited might as well fail the expectation of the "I am." The seven churches together with the cosmos have no future. Such frustrated expectations cause John to weep bitterly.

How then does this creator of the cosmos who lives forever and ever embrace the temporal and limited? In the most extreme opposite one can imagine—*by being slain*. When the Lamb that was slaughtered, standing between the throne and four living creatures (i.e., between God and humans—see section 4.1 for meaning of these living creatures) and among the elders (being fully human), finally comes along to take the scroll out of the hand of the one on the exalted throne, rejoicing and praises break out from every quarter in creation! As opposed to previously praising God all by themselves, the twenty four elders and four living creatures are now leading a choir that sings a new song that eventually engulfs all creation. This new song breaks with the ceaseless praises of the first worship scene. Its dynamic contagion spreads concentrically.

New in this song is the praise not only of the creator and his act of creation in the first episode, but of the Lamb that was "slain, and purchased for God with Your blood men from every tribe and tongue and people and nation. You have made them to be a kingdom and priests to our God; and *they will reign upon the earth.*" (9–10). Over God's creation is now established the reign of a kingdom with priests. God has not abdicated his throne, but is now reigning through the intended intermediary of his agent—humans. This achievement elicits praises. When the choir conductors (twenty four elders and four living creatures) sing their praises, they draw in other singers like themselves (living creatures and elders also) that are simply too numerous to count—myriads of myriads, and thousands of thousands—to continue with the wider praise (12). Subtly, this version of the song is modified from the previous with "men from every tribe and tongue and people and nation" omitted because they themselves are the fulfillment of the first version.

But now in the third and final round of singing, the human boundary is burst. The choir conductors draw in uncountable humans to the choir who in turn draw in all creatures in creation without exception to the singing, resulting in *all of creation resounding in a new song* (13). As if to make sure that nothing in creation is left out, John points not only to "every created thing which is in heaven and on the earth and under the earth and on the sea," but emphasizes "and *all things in them*." This final song of praise from the entire created order in the heavenly worship now goes beyond the previous two rounds by including the one sitting on the throne, together with the Lamb. The creator God has now joined the redeeming Lamb as the one worthy of all ultimate praises. When every nook and cranny of God's creation is filled with the song of praise, the most the first conductors could do is to say "Amen" and fall down to worship.

The two episodes in heavenly worship now throb together in unison. The rainbow constantly around the throne of God is now more than answered in the mighty chorus of all creation. What emanated outward from the throne is now echoed back in praises from the outermost reach of creation. "I will be who I will be" has now redounded back to the "I am" producing the finality in "who was and is and is to come" (4:8).

Our modern sense may be rattled when John describes every created thing singing a new song. How can non-sentient things praise God? Is this symbolic or has John indulged in poetic license? The two are not the same. Symbol admits much latitude in interpretation, but all those symbolized must share in some basic nature for them to be subsumed under the symbol. Poetic license has no such constraints. If John strays into unchecked poetic license, then Revelation cannot be interpreted and fails to live up to its name. Unless proved otherwise, we have to assume that John is employing proper symbols. In this case, is our modern sense of things, which cannot freely sing and praise, right?

Both Old and New Testament passages show nature communing with the creator (Ps 104; Matt 6:26). Some of these may indeed be understood as human perception (Ps 19), but others demand a more straightforward understanding like what we encounter in Revelation. Two understandings are possible. First, *God does count* the proper workings of his creation as singing praises to his wisdom, power, and might regardless of whether the parts in the creation are sentient or not. Such is totally plausible but in this case the Lamb's redemption would play no role had there been no corruption of creation. In the two heavenly worship episodes, all of creation *only comes into praising God after the Lamb has redeemed the uncountable multitude, signifying that non-sentient creation only joins or can only join the singing chorus after or through "sentient" humans.* If so, with the Lamb redeeming humans, the parts of creation these humans can offer up to God by way of proper restoration, nurture, care and utilization are indeed in praise of God's wonderful creative and redemptive works. This is the second understanding. Finally completing the original mandate in Gen 1 for humans to rule over all of creation would eventually allow all creation's praise of its creator to be properly *channeled through the sentient humans*. Thus is fulfilled the proclamation in the very first song sung by the four living creatures and twenty four elders: "you have made them to be a kingdom and *priests* to our God; *and they will reign upon the earth*." Priests act as a go-between for God and creation. What godly humans creatively fashion out of non-sentient matter—all the techno-scientific, artistic, and cultural fruits of humans, and what he can tend well resulting in the lion and the lamb grazing together . . . etc.—is now echoing human's praise of his creator through the priest-kings. Creation's "anxious longing," that is, it "waits eagerly for the revealing of the sons of God" (Rom 8:19) is now satisfied.

## 4. SEVEN SEALS: STARTING WITH THE CUSTODIANS (6:1—8:1)

In our familiar spatial perception, John could not have determined that the scroll in the hand of the one sitting on the throne is written on the front and back before the seal was broken by the Lamb. He just knew it because he was given this sense by whoever reveals this to him. Thus demanding conformity to our earthly perception is a no-go for understanding Revelation.

Writing double-sided on the scroll can mean what is superficial (on the outside) has another side which is known only to God. With the Lamb breaking the seals, what was known only to God is now revealed to humankind, true to this revelation.

Seals on the book may signify a foregone end or a determined fate. Breaking the seals opens up a new future and provides an alternative to those whose fate has previously been fixed.

### 4.1 The First Four Seals

Opening each of the first four seals follows the same pattern: the Lamb opens, then John hears one of the living creatures calls out "come" and there comes a horse followed by what seems to be the consequence. Each horse has a different color. The order in which each seal is broken corresponds to the ordered description of the four faces of the living creatures encountered earlier in the first heavenly worship episode in chapter 4 since John orders them in both passages. This is summarized in table 3.

Table 3. A summary of the opening of the first four seals

| Seal | Face of creature* | Phenomenon unleashed | Consequence |
| --- | --- | --- | --- |
| 1st | Lion | white horse with bow and crown | repeated conquering |
| 2nd | Ox | red horse with great sword | peace taken away with mutual killing |
| 3rd | Human | black horse with a pair of scale | scarcity of daily necessities |
| 4th | Flying eagle | ashen horse with death | kill through disasters |

* Inferred from the order given in the first heavenly worship (4:6–7)

Ezekiel's vision that these creatures all share human form suggests that each of their faces represents a human trait or an aspect of human nature.

The consequences of opening the second to the fourth seals are undoubtedly destructive and undesirable. While the word conquer (*nikaō*) in the first seal simply means to overcome without conveying a definite positive or negative sense (e.g., Jesus overcomes the world, John 16:33), inferring backward from the rest of the seals, it is reasonable to suggest that the consequence of opening the first seal—repeated conquering—should also be undesirable.

To fully understand these four seals, let us answer two questions. First, why is conquering (resulting from opening the first seal) bad and undesirable? God has given humans both the mandate and correspondingly the majesty (like a lion) to reign over creation just like his own household (subdue and rule over (Gen 1:28)). By its very position, creation is subject to humans' godly and beneficial reign. But the interjection of sin has disrupted that order, first with the land bringing forth thorns and thistles to thwart humans' effort, then the fear of humans has come upon the animals after the flood (Gen 3:17–18, 9:2). The original respect that humans should receive from each other and from the rest of creation because of their given position has since been lost through their disrespect of God. God's created order is also out of whack because of humans. To compensate for that loss, conquering now kicks in to fill the void in a sinful world. Humans now have to *impose* their will on creation and each other through threats and violence, i.e., conquering, and not only once, but repeatedly. An undesirable warped power and violent relationship now takes hold within humankind and between humanity and the rest of God's creation. The same corruption of a godly endowment is seen in the other three attributes that follow.

Second, what does the flying eagle signify in the light of the above understanding? Observe that in the first seal, what is meant to be majestic and beneficent rule turns into its opposite: violent imposition of one's authority; in the second seal, the loyalty, power, and diligence innate in human nature, as symbolized by the ox, has been corrupted to bring about its opposite: strife and mutual hurt; in the third seal, ruling creation with the intelligence and wisdom that only humans can exercise and have been charged to do is intended to bring abundance to all and sundry, but its very opposite—scarcity—prevails, at least for the majority.

If we just take natural characteristics as our guide as I just did above, we may be led to assume that the flying eagle has a lofty perspective or perhaps powerful eyesight and hence should represent an all-discerning spirit. Yet John has already described the four living creatures as "full of eyes in front and behind" (4:8), hence a repeat is unnecessary. Based on the observation that each preceding living creature brings out its opposite in the first three seals, the eagle signifies life since it brings out death (see end of section 4.2 of the third reading for an explanation of the destruction of one fourth of the earth). But why? Ps 103:5 ("Who satisfies your years with good things, So that your youth is renewed like the eagle") uses a well-known biological fact—the eagle renewing its feathers in old age—to illustrate the continual renewal of life. Had humans and their communities been living out the aspects of God's image in them without corruption by sins, then there would be continual renewal of life like the eagle, and not any eagle, but one capable of soaring powerfully into the sky. But very significantly, not only will humankind be renewed, everything intended to be under his charge and care will similarly be in harmony, with famine, pestilence, and killing by wild animals absent from the world's dictionaries. A form of life everlasting ("It is like the dew of Hermon coming down upon the mountains of Zion; For there the Lord commanded the blessing—*life forever.*" Ps 133:3) would result. This is God's promise in the tree of life, now barred to humankind. Yet such is repeated by Moses in his concluding speech to the Israelites before they entered the promised land: "See, I have set before you today *life and prosperity, and death and adversity*; in that I command you today to love the Lord your God, *to walk in His ways . . . that you may live* and multiply, . . . But if your heart turns away and you will not obey, but are drawn away and worship other gods and serve them, I declare to you today that you shall surely perish . . . So choose life . . . for this is your life and the length of your days . . . " (Deut 30:15–19).

Not surprisingly, the essence of these four living creatures can be traced further back to earlier teachings. When Moses summarizes YHWH's instructions to the people towards the end of his life, he commands: "You shall love the Lord your God with all your heart and with all your soul and with all your might" (Deut 6:5). The loyalty from the heart (ox) guides the exercise of wisdom in the soul (human) and his majestic might (lion) to bring about life eternal for "you" symbolized by the flying eagle. Jesus' message is also life for creation (Matt 22:37; Mark 12:30; Luke 10:27).

A careless reading of the first four seals could easily have started with trying to understand the meaning of the horses and their riders rather than the four living creatures. But these horses and horsemen come from nowhere in the Bible and with very minimal information—color and what they carry, whereas the four living creatures have an immediate introduction that traces their origin to around the throne of God in chapter 4 and an even richer description of heaven in Ezek 1. (Four horses are mentioned in Zech 6:1–8, but they differ in colors to Revelation's four horses and have scant provincial description, hence are not related to Revelation's four "universal" horses and as such offer no clue in understanding Revelation's four horses even if John had used similar symbols.) Importantly, the horses here are *only called forth by the living creatures*, indicating that these horses are merely instruments (or workhorses) for the living creatures. Their colors are merely used to highlight the consequence—white-victory; red-slaughter; black-scarcity and famine; grey-partial (one-fourth) death.

Logically, the seals start with the lion-faced living creature. It is supposed to reign over other creatures, and if done according to God's intention, would end in the renewal of life like the eagle. Also, since these living creatures are manifestation of human nature, they are neither accorded thrones to sit on nor crowned, as for the elders who are truly created beings. God's intention for all creatures—humans or otherwise—to praise him according to their true, rather than perverted, nature in the previous worship scene now flows into the seals.

Objections may be raised about taking the four living creatures as aspects of human nature. Common categorization demands that the nature of an object is not the object itself just as the hardness of a rock is not the rock per se.

Such objection is certainly valid in our everyday existence since we do live in an established order with clear categorical differentiations. But here in both Ezek 1 and Rev 4, we are brought into the very existence of God who created, hence above and precedes, the order familiar to us. We live in the "finished" product of God's work, but how God created this order is not part of the order. The difficulty in conveying the very existence (not just presence) of God is acknowledged when Ezekiel haplessly summarized his vision: "Such was the *appearance* of the *likeness* of the *glory* of the Lord" (1:28b). The unapproachable brilliance of God has to be qualified again and again, somewhat clumsily.

What is certain is that these living creatures emanate from God directly, but reach to the level familiar to us humans. The allusions to these creatures having human form, hands and face (Ezek 1:5, 8, 10; Rev 4:7) owe their origin to God himself: "and *in the center and around the throne*, four living creatures full of eyes in front and behind" (Rev 4:6b). The center is God, but around his throne are twenty four elders who sit on their thrones. By contrast, the four living creatures just shuttle (Ezekiel's version), or occupy a position (John's version), between God and the more familiar human figures (the elders who by default are humans—see section 11 of this reading). What are the nature and "mechanism" of the "things" between God and humans is forever off limits to us, but what is clear is that God made humans in his image, wiring into them some of his attributes. For the lack of a better description, what Ezekiel initially had difficulty categorizing and describing ("within it there were figures *resembling* four living beings" 1:5) was later reluctantly called the four living creatures and taken up by John to inform his readers of how they are all made in God's image, hence possessing godly attributes which though can be perverted. Here, our taking the four living creatures as attributes is also reluctant, but necessitated by data.

By this meaningful ordering of the four living creatures, John systematically presents how when the godly majesty of humans is corrupted, the ensuing vigorous violent conflicts and bloodshed would impact on the very support that people depend on to bring out scarcity and famine which lead to widespread death. All these contradict God's intention and are open for all eyes to see. Through his nuanced use of the symbolic seals, John is conveying this message *from a universal perspective*. Also, these living creatures are the first set of "four" encountered. In Revelation, four conveys entirety, and in our context means that the whole of human nature is corrupted. We will encounter more fours later.

In a specific way, Revelation lives up to its claim to reveal God's mystery: the four enigmatic living creatures in Ezekiel are *finally explained* in John's received visions.

## 4.2 The Fifth Seal

Opening the fifth seal does not follow the formula of the first four. No living creature is there to call forth anything. Instead, slain souls are seen crying out asking God to judge the world and avenge their sufferings, but they were told to be patient until the number to be killed like them would be complete. After we have understood the first four seals, this fifth one follows logically: in the midst of humankind's wholesale perversion of God's good image in them, a remnant, despite the twisted human nature, holds fast to God's word to prevent themselves and creation from being corrupted further; they suffer the consequence of their unyielding faithfulness to God and are persecuted; in their persecution, they cry out to the just God to put an end to these perversions. Not only do they stand against the tide, they want to turn the tide. God's response to these supplicants does not make sense (there needs to be more persecutions and martyrdom!) unless there is a purpose in all these.

## 4.3 The Sixth Seal

God's short reply to the persecuted souls in the fifth seal is elaborated in the sixth. Two types of people are contrasted in this one seal which has the longest description among the seals. This seal consists of three episodes. The first type of people is described in the first episode (6:12–17) and is introduced by great and terrible turmoil (earthquake . . . stars falling . . . etc.) while the second type is associated with arresting harm to creation as a result of their being sealed (second and third episodes, 7:1–8, 7:9–17). Fearful is the first type of people who shows no specific trait (from all walks of life—kings to slaves) except their attempted avoidance of God's wrath at extreme costs (to be buried alive by mountains and rocks). As opposed to fleeing the wrath of God, the second type in the remaining two episodes is described as being sealed by God and enjoying his protection. These two types are echoing what the previous seals have been describing: 1. that part of humanity which has twisted God's image in them in bringing death to themselves and creation in the first four seals, now elaborated in first episode of this sixth seal; 2. the other part of humanity which provides a counter weight to the preceding perverted masses in the fifth seal, now expanded on in the last two episodes of this seal (explained further in section 3.2 of the third reading).

What makes up this second type which has two descriptions—144,000 equally divided among the twelve tribes of Israel and an uncountable multitude from all peoples regardless of background? Two readings of the composition of this type are possible for the 144,000 and multitude, they are: 1. two distinct constituents, or 2. one and the same group.

From the context, the latter interpretation is correct. Note that the descriptions of the 144,000 and multitude are mutually exclusive. The 144,000 are sealed, and this sealing has the effect of halting the work of the four angels with authority to harm the earth. On the other hand, the multitude seems to be reacting to God's action in praise and they are from the most diverse ethnicity ("every nation, all tribes, peoples and tongues"). They have embarked on and completed a perilous journey ("come out of the great tribulation") in partnership with the Lamb ("washed their robes and made them white in the blood of the Lamb") and in return God will protect them ("spread his tabernacle over them") where their former sacrifices will all be deemed worthwhile since they can serve God day and night without their former tears and hurts brought on by a hostile environment. Life everlasting (reaching the springs of the water of life—echoing the flying eagle of the fourth seal before the sickly ashen horse is called forth) is their lot.

Taken in isolation, the descriptions of the 144,000 and multitude are incomplete. Yet when they are seen as two aspects of God's work, a logical story that spans God's salvation history emerges: God heeds the call of the saints in the fifth seal, so he calls (seals) his people to make good on his promise through Abraham to bless the families of the earth (Gen 12:1–3). These people respond to God with praises and commensurate works which end also in them being rewarded for their sacrifices. God's promise to Abraham—uncountable descendants—is fulfilled symbolically through each of the twelve sons of Israel multiplying similarly (by 12; see section 11 of this reading for a further nuanced understanding when the New Jerusalem arrives), then each of them multiplying immeasurably (by 1000—an indefinitely large number) to become the multitude.

With this horizon, not only do the second and third episodes of this sixth seal make sense, but the whole series of seals also weaves together a story commensurate with Revelation's universal perspective: ultimately, humanity is not differentiated according to ethnicity (Jews or otherwise), but rather by their relationship to God and his creation. Such is clear from the first four seals collectively and the fifth seal. Apart from being incomplete if the 144,000 are not understood as the multitude, such take would also destroy the clear flow and scope of the Revelation as a whole.

In a self-posed riddle, John is asked who are those robed in white and where have they come from. This is answered in reverse: "These are the ones who come out of the *great tribulation, and they have washed their robes and made them white in the blood of the Lamb*" (7:13–14). The great tribulation has been given fanciful interpretations in the popular literature, most commonly a seven-year period of intense and unprecedented persecution of believers or of great misery upon the non-believers. But all these violate the cardinal rule of interpreting any intelligent writing, not just biblical text: to take things within context. From the preceding passages, what does this great tribulation refer to? Nothing but the sum total of the disasters and miseries brought on through human perversion in the first four seals. Saints have suffered greatly through this because of their loyalty to God. This tribulation started with the first human sins (alienation from God, feeling shame . . . to murder . . . etc.) and lasts as long as humans continue to corrupt their relations with God, among themselves, with others, and with creation. If at no time since Adam and Eve fell are some humans not acting out their sinfulness, then this "great tribulation" has run uninterrupted since our first parents sinned. That is why John also sees himself partaking in this tribulation which he shares with other believers (1:9). All sufferings from human perversions throughout creation's history would constitute the great tribulation. The immediate context is *totally sufficient* to give the "great tribulation" its *full* meaning. Reading more fanciful events into the tribulation only tickles some disaster-craving minds.

## 4.4 The Final and Most Uncharacteristic Seal—An Incomplete One

When the final seal was broken, the shortest "duration" in Revelation is encountered: "when He (the Lamb) broke the seventh seal, there was silence in heaven for about half an hour." The other two Revelation's "events" ending in a series of seven signify a finality that would last forever, e.g., "he will reign forever and ever" in the seventh trumpet (11:15) and "It is done" in the seventh bowl (16:17), but the "completion" in this series of seals (being the first series) conveys the exact opposite. It is short-lived, even halving the duration of all the other counted hours in Revelation (all in chapters 17–18 and always "one hour"). Note that in the sixth seal, while sinners are hiding from God at all cost, *God has neither pronounced their fate nor the fate of his creation*, as he has surely done with the saints. On these God was silent. The poignant use of "half an hour" (an incomplete hour) in this seventh seal says that the fate of sinful humanity is still not finalized or sealed by human perversions and the sins catalogued in the first four and sixth seals. The seemingly appropriate doom that would come upon sinful humankind has now been voided by God's stay of execution ("silence in heaven"). God cannot wait even one hour without taking action to alter humankind's and creation's fate. The trumpets and bowls that follow tell us how. In this is creation's hope.

## 4.5 Testimony of the Scroll—Seven Seals Together

What then does this series of seven seals convey? Seals suggest something fixed and inalterable. Once a seal is set upon an object, especially by one with authority, nothing can further change the fate of the sealed. God has hard-wired certain attributes into humans according to his own image, hence we see the four living creatures proceed from the throne of God in the heavenly worship scene. There God is worshipped because of his act of creation. This episode is the first and foundational. That much also is sealed. Yet coupled with the freedom that God has endowed humans, these attributes can call forth a saint or a pervert depending on the person's choice. (I avoid the phrase "an angel or a demon" given Revelation's use of the word "angel" for both God's and Satan's messengers/servants.) Sadly, the wrong choice was made, leading to disaster after disaster, destruction upon destruction, and if left unchecked, would end in death, not only for humans as a species, but also for God's creation under their charge.

With humankind hurtling down the path towards eventual destruction, and claiming victims after victims in its path, those who insist on faithfully sticking to God's intention for humans made in his image would inevitably question how long this wholesale corruption would be allowed to go on without the sovereign God intervening—the fifth seal. They offer their wish for a quick rectification through their prayers, like smoke from the altar. They were then assured of their acceptance by God through being given a white robe.

Yet quick retribution prompted by justice is averted by divine intervention in the seventh seal. What follows—in the trumpets—tells how this is done.

A natural question is whether the seven seals can represent different periods, sequentially? Since writing is a linear arrangement of words, these seals can only be mentioned one after another, and for marking them out individually, are also numbered. Yet they do not necessarily connote chronology. Aspects of human nature do not wreak havoc one after another, just as the four living creatures in Ezek 1 move in tandem without breaking rank. All kinds of human perversion visit upon creation simultaneously, not separated in time. Saints have been crying out to God from the time of Adam until now. John is describing an ever-valid human phenomenon until the "silence in heaven" breaks into humanity and starts the trumpet series.

## 5. SEVEN TRUMPETS: HOW GOD WORKS IN ALL CREATION (8:2—11:19)

### 5.1 Lead up to the Trumpets

While the seven seals are on the scroll in God's hand and the associated "events" seem to proceed directly from the throne through Jesus (the Lamb breaking the seals), the trumpets are initiated from two directions: 1. the Lamb halting humankind's final retribution in the silence of the seventh seal, and 2. the saints whose prayers are offered together with much incense to God. In place of the reactionary cries of the persecuted souls in the fifth seal is now found the positive prayers of the saints to start the trumpets call. Humankind is a full participant from hereon.

### 5.2 The First Four Trumpets

Each of the trumpets is sounded by an angel rather than by the Lamb. An angel is simply a messenger from God for a specific task and may be any agent, super-natural or otherwise. While angels played only a minor role in the seals, they are now major players in the trumpets. Also, while the natural world provides only the background in the seals where humankind is the protagonist, it now comes into absolute prominence in the trumpets.

When the first four trumpets are sounded, four aspects of natural creation are struck successively by four agents. They seem to be arranged according to the severity of the attack (table 4).

Despite the severity of each attack, the damage has not rippled through the whole created order, but is invariably contained to within one third of the total.

### 5.3 The Fifth Trumpet

Locusts symbolize destruction. They first appeared as one of the ten plagues in Exod 10:1–20 and are used in conjunction with curse on the ground due to God's displeasure (Joel 1–2). Since they destroy the reproductive capacity of vegetation at its bud, they represent a fundamental attack on creation, rendering it forever sterile. Yet, the locusts unleashed in the fifth trumpet assault creation in a most unusual way—they do not damage vegetation, but sting humans. Such mutated creatures, in the hand of the fallen angel, now go about tormenting humans.

**Table 4. Aspects of the first four trumpets**

| Trumpet | Target | Functions in the natural order | Agent of attack | Consequence |
|---|---|---|---|---|
| 1st | Earth | provide food and habitat for all land creatures, including humankind; regulate the weather | hail and fire, mixed with blood | 1/3 of the earth, trees, and grass burned up |
| 2nd | Sea | provide food and habitat for all marine creatures, navigation for humans; regulate the weather, | burning mountain | 1/3 of the sea becomes blood, sea creatures died, ships destroyed |
| 3rd | Springs of water | sustain many creatures, especially humans | burning star | 1/3 of the waters becomes wormwood causing many deaths |
| 4th | Celestial objects | energize and set the rhythm of the whole earth system; navigational reference for all creatures | unspecified, but up to the task | 1/3 of the sun, moon, and stars darkened |

Symbolizing the evil miasma of God's opposition with mutated locusts and describing them grotesquely, John wants to convey that this twisted force of nature has seven (seemingly complete) desirable traits pertaining to its outward appearance:

1. Strong and swift—like a horse;
2. Authoritative and seemingly intelligent—wearing golden crowns;
3. Relatable to and being part of humankind—human faces;
4. Charming and seductive—women's hair;
5. Voracious and powerful—teeth of lions;
6. Tough and well-fortified—scales like iron breastplates;
7. Fearsome and menacing—sound of chariots and war horses.

After the passing of the locusts from the front which conveys all the trappings of worldly desirables—power, respectability, beauty, friendliness, invincibility . . . etc.,—comes something the gullible would least expect. At the rear end of these mutated locusts comes a sting which torments humans, *and only humans*, worse than death. After the sugar coating is gone, the poisonous pill finally dumps its cargo on those who initially happily swallow it.

And who is responsible for this insidious Trojan horse? None other than the ultimate diabolic creature—the angel of the bottomless pit who rules over these mutated locusts. To sum up the mission of the locusts in no uncertain term, John resorts to an unusual and unique description: two converging meanings based on two cultures expressed in one language (Greek). From the Hebrew-scripture's perspective, the mastermind behind the locusts is the angel who rules in hell (*Abaddōn*), but what can be generally experienced from a gentile Hellenist culture is destruction (*Apollyōn*). God's choice of Abraham and his descendants as the carrier of God's message to the world have uniquely enabled them (the Jews) to know that the general destruction witnessed by gentiles and Jews alike can be traced back to the lies of the angel of the abyss. The fundamental cause as well as the result must be made known. John presents here a total picture of the source of creation's predicament.

Now this revelation—the angel from hell is bent on destroying God's creation—clears up the enigma of the "one third" and "five months" in these first five trumpets. While forces aligned with this hellish angel try to destroy God's good creation using increasingly lethal weapons—from fiery hail to destroyer of celestial objects, God and his saints (remember the trumpets are initiated by prayers of the saints) protect creation and limit the damage to a non-overwhelming one third for their continued survival, while their torment on humans is restricted also to a tolerable period (five months being less than half of a very long time of one year). The locusts are not allowed to do irreversible damage to humans, namely to kill a person which would shut the door to his/her repentance. God is very patient with humans. In opposition, Satan would let this tolerable human misery to fester into destructive acts on creation to serve his purpose.

Finally, why are *only humans* tormented when the locusts, following their natural instinct, could have aimed at God's creation at its base? The answer: Satan can only lie, that is his limitation. On the contrary, God has placed humans in between himself and his creation to look after all that he has made. Humans are to stand in the gap for creation's well-being. Destroying this custodian would naturally breach the defense of creation leading to its destruction. Without humans compromising, God's creation stands intact. Viewed another way, only humans have the capacity to buy into or reject Satan's lies, or simply put, to be tempted and fall. Hence humans represent the only vulnerable part of creation open to Satan's attack. Satan can only muster physical force *through humans*, hence he has his followers attacking the only one soft spot in creation.

## 5.4 The Sixth Trumpet—Turning Point of Creation and of History

Editorially the longest, this sixth trumpet consists of three distinct episodes:

1. Angels released from the four corners of the earth bringing violent actions that kill one third of humankind; but this atrocious disaster does not lead the survivors to repentance (9:13–21);

2. An angel holding a little scroll and roaring seven thunders that are forbidden to be written down, and ends in John commanded to swallow the scroll in the angel's hand in chapter 10; and

3. A series of events concerning two witnesses are revealed to John, after being told to measure the temple of God; these events culminate in the resurrection of the two witnesses and people glorifying God (11:1–13).

### 5.4.1 First Episode of the Sixth Trumpet (9:13–21)

With God so protecting humankind from death and unbearable torment that may come from the angel of the abyss, one would expect humankind to see through Satan's lies and learn God's goodness, but instead, it leads to further destruction, this time through material violence.

Though Babylon is not explicitly mentioned, the reference to Euphrates makes this clear. This great river supplies Babylon with her lifeblood—water (Jer 51:61–63). Before travelling very far shortly after coming out of Noah's Ark which had been their shelter and protection, survivors of the great flood came to the plain of Shinar and collectively made a monumental decision: "They said, "Come, let us build for ourselves a city, and a tower whose top will reach into heaven, and let us make for ourselves a name, otherwise we will be scattered abroad over the face of the whole earth."" (Gen 11:4). First, they decided to replace the name God gives to humankind—*Adamah*, meaning from the soil—with another one. Whatever the new name may be, which is still unknown, it openly defies the original mandate from God to rule over God's creation. This mandate necessitates people to go to the ends of the world (to scatter) to exercise their rule over God's creation. To put their rebellious intention into practice, they consensually decided to build a city and a tower that would reach up to heaven, equaling or even better than God in stature. Before they could agree on a name for themselves,

God frustrated their plan by confusing their tongues and the name Babel (Babylon) stuck by default or by divine design to symbolize humankind's organized defiance of God.

This episode is initiated through a voice from the four horns of the golden altar to release what had hitherto been restrained—human organizing power. Unlike the saints petitioning God for judgment on the world from a *humble position under the altar in the fifth seal (6:9), the voice here comes from the horns above the altar*. Horns signify power and people have made unreasonable demands or drawn a false sense of security by holding onto these horns (1 Kgs 1:50–51, 2:28). The context suggests that this voice represents rebellious people demanding autonomy from God, according to the lies of Satan. Importantly, this autonomous power is not for the building up of creation. After flouting their God-given name to rule over creation, humankind takes on the de facto name of *Apollyōn* and turn against each other in the most gruesome way.

Who can be these four angels? Matched with these four angels are four timescales which are also *all the time units* used in Revelation: hour, day, month, and year. These angels are destructive agents to organize people in complete disregard for what God intends. They operate on *every conceivable timescale* known to humans. In other words, these miscreants are ever-present and inescapable. Note for now that the most important timescale—the week—is absent here, and indeed from Revelation (see section 4.2 of the first reading). Why? Let us wait for the revelation in the third episode of this sixth trumpet to find out.

While the number of saints praising God in 5:11 is described as myriads of myriads (or ten thousand times ten thousand), the number of horsemen on horses here is twice myriads of myriads (9:16), conveying the message that the saints are in the minority, outnumbered by the opposing, hence destructive, forces.

When God destroyed the sinful cities of Sodom and Gomorrah, fire and brimstone were rained down from the sky resulting in smoke covering the land (Gen 19:24–27). The natural destructive forces unleashed by God through nature are now domesticated and harnessed (like using horses) by humans to unleash on each other (17).

Unmistakably contrasted with the fifth trumpet of mutated locusts are that: 1. The origins (bottomless pit and Euphrates), hence natures, of Satan's and humans' assault on God's creation are very different; 2. Violence unleashed by humankind does not stop after the first attack as it perpetuates itself from the tail back to the head endlessly (the horses have heads in their serpent-like tails) whereas the mutated locusts only sting once from the tail after each pass-by; 3. Human violence is glorified since the attack is frontal (wearing flaming colors on breastplate and through their lion-like heads) whereas the locusts have to attack by stealth in presenting an appealing façade while hiding their true nature to sting in the tail as scorpions do; 4. Falling into the violent hands of humans is much worse than the torments of Satan himself since in the latter God forbids killing and limits the duration of the torment, but humans' violence sees no such restraints; 5. Humans have amplified Satan's scorpion-size lies to monstrous physical violence (their warhorses) against each other.

Since the Euphrates supporting Babylon points to humans organizing themselves to supplant God, it is wrong to read the one third of humankind being killed or creation being destroyed as resulting from God's direct action or judgment on his organized opposition. This passage tells us clearly that humans themselves are responsible for their mutual cannibalization. Equally unwarranted is to read a final confrontation between God and his opponents into this passage: the climax of the narrative is yet to come.

God's limiting all these destructions to one third should have been more than enough to wake every survivor of the catastrophe up to seek an alternative path. But instead, they do not repent of these practices. There seems no alternative human route after they reject God's naming.

### 5.4.2 Second Episode of the Sixth Trumpet (chapter 10)

Is God at his wit's end with this seemingly final rejection? This episode tells us that God is wiser than our cry for revenge in face of rejection.

A strong angel now appears. He has three outstanding features, among others: 1. a rainbow upon his head, 2. holding a little open scroll, and 3. with feet on both land and sea. We will see the significance of the third feature in chapter 13. For now, the rainbow that surrounds God's throne is conferred on this pivotal angel to remind him of God's concern for his own creation. With his roaring cries come seven peals of thunders. John heard the intelligible (since he intended to write them out) voices of the thunders, but was commanded not to record them. This is the only time in Revelation when something is revealed, but then sealed up, never to be mentioned again. Two interpretations can be considered. First, an important revelation is hidden for some unspecified reason, leaving the reader to speculate what it is. Yet this contra-revelation is highly unlikely given that it goes against the expressed intent of Revelation (22:10, "Do not seal up . . . "). The second is that the thunders are effectively cancelled by God and God wants to tell us why he has voided them. Indeed, this is the straightforward interpretation fully supported by the context.

In response to not writing down the thunders, the angel swore to the ever-living creator of all that there would be no more delay in finishing the mystery of God. The clear impression is that had the thunders been recorded, there would have been no delays. In the previous episode, the time is fully ripe for judgment on those spared death, yet still reject God one last time. The thunders—the final and complete destruction of the recalcitrant—must come swiftly to bring justice to a fitting conclusion. But at what collateral cost? The clear answer is the destruction of creation along with rebellious humans, since the demise of the steward would spell chaos and destruction on those under his charge, if a replacement is not found.

*To God, creation is much larger than its assigned steward and indeed it encompasses all,* as is emphatically stated (6) that he is the one "who *created* heaven and the things in it, and the earth and the things in it, and the sea and the things in it." God making humans is not even mentioned here. This emphasis on creation, together with the previous trumpets where damages to aspects of creation are repeatedly circumscribed, marks a sharp departure from the seals in which God is never once described as creator. In the seals, humans fail God and God calls some to reverse the consequence of their failures. But here, for the sake of creation, God directly charges his strong angel with the "rainbow mission," i.e., to avert the destruction of creation, on the condition that the final wrath on the rebellious would not be delayed.

God's promise to himself in Gen 8:21b is now made good: "*Never again will I curse the ground because of humans, even though every inclination of the human heart is evil from childhood.*" (NIV). Creation is to be saved *despite humans' waywardness.*

But if things proceed "business as usual," then the same cycle of "God's-kindness—humans-rejection" would be repeated endlessly without progress, and indeed would only go from bad to worse. Something novel will have to come in. That novelty is right in the hand of this angel—the little open scroll—which John, after swallowing it Ezekiel-style (Ezek 2), is asked to "prophesy again concerning many peoples and nations and tongues and kings" (11).

The wrath that is the seven thunders is not concealed, but cancelled. The "silence in heaven for about half an hour" of the seventh seal is now finally broken by an unimaginably creative plan in the little open scroll when the last episode of this sixth trumpet opens. Creation is rescued from its seemingly sealed fate by the message in the open little scroll. What then does this pivotal scroll contain?

### 5.4.3 Third Episode of the Sixth Trumpet (11:1–13)

Given the many enigmatic symbols and "events" described in this last episode of the sixth trumpet, it is beneficial to lay out its salient features:

1. John is told to mark out the temple from its outer court;
2. The nations will be allowed to trample the holy city for 42 months;
3. Two witnesses are to prophesy for 1,260 days;
4. These two witnesses will be empowered to resist harm and wield punitive power;
5. After their witnessing, the two witnesses were killed in the great city without burial;
6. People rejoiced over the death of these two witnesses for 3.5 days;
7. The breath of life from God resurrected the two witnesses at the end of the 3.5 days;
8. The witnesses went up to heaven to the consternation of their enemies;
9. An earthquake happened with partial destruction of the city and the people therein;
10. Those who witnessed the resurrection gave glory to God.

In this passage are mentioned some enigmatic "durations": 42 months, 1,260 days, and 3.5 days. As mentioned in the first reading, months and days are the only two time units used in Revelation intermediate between the longest and the shortest. Both the longest (year, and always with 1,000) and the shortest (hour, and always with 1 or half) time units are only used in an indefinite sense. Note further that counted months are only used on God's adversaries (e.g., five months of torment of those who do not have the seal of God on their foreheads by the mutated locusts) and counted days (in plural) are always used to mark the time which people on God's side are going through. Counted months and days are never used interchangeably on different people.

Note also that 1,260 days is equivalent to 42 months based on a 30-day month which is idealized without the complications of longer and shorter months and leap years. Why then does John want to convey the same "duration" using two separate time units? The fundamental reason harks back to God's design for his creation: God made two great lights; the greater light (sun) to govern the day and the lesser light (moon) to govern the night. These are designed to separate the light from the darkness (Gen 1:16–18). Moon is further the basis of the month. Through measuring time by days for

God's people and by months for God's opposition, Revelation is assigning these two camps to their respective abode, of light and darkness.

Another possible and complementary answer may be that God cares for his own people *moment by moment*, but that phrase cannot convey any sense of "duration" for comparison with other periods, hence the best choice is to use the shortest common time duration that has not been used for another purpose in Revelation. This leaves "day." John wants to assure his readers that God cares for his people as often as is needed—day by day. The menace from the opposition seems to recede to the background and is counted in months without the detailed and intense attention conveyed by days. Thus the suffering brought to God's chosen by the opposition is depicted as a drawn-out background drone of low intensity that pales in light of God's ever-present, always-ready protection.

But why the numbers 42, 1,260, and 3.5? When we go through the time units in Revelation in the first reading, we notice a very conspicuous omission—the week. All the explicit time units in Revelation are derived from nature's rhythm—hour tracks the sun's position across the sky to regulate events; day marks out one complete solar cycle for nature's rhythm; month to follow the lunar cycle to break the year into manageable chunks for human activities, particularly agriculture; year marks the return of the season . . . etc., but a *week stands apart from nature*. Though it comprises seven natural days, the week is not pegged to any natural events. It is the "seven" that makes the week unique. In nature is neither found a seven-day nor a seven-year rhythm anywhere. The week traces its origin to God who worked six days and rested on the seventh, thereafter giving humankind the seven-day work-rest model to punctuate their living. This is intended for the nations as well as individuals on earth. At the end of six days of meaningful labor, God saw the fruits of his work and was satisfied. In his seventh-day rest, he enjoys, loves and is enamored of his work in creation. In the same way, humankind is to find their satisfaction and love in the works of their own hands. This constitutes the Sabbath day teaching given to the Israelites in the fourth of the Ten Commandments (Exod 20:8–11; Deut 5:12–15).

But God is not satisfied with humankind just mimicking him in enjoying whatever they do while being self-absorbed in appreciating their fruits. Specifically, each person is to bring nature into fellowship with God and with himself through his own hands, hence the Old Testament goes on to command the Israelites, when they were about to enter the promised land, to observe a Sabbatical year. Loving what God loves concretely in creation would be an expression of the love for the invisible God. This is done explicitly for the land (Lev 25:1–8). Not to be confused with fallowing the land for it to recuperate its fertility to serve humans further, the land in the

Sabbatical year is to *have a rest of its own*. Whether humans benefit is not the focus. During one year in every seven years, humans (represented by the Israelites) are to stop all farming activities for that full year throughout their entire land (not just one among a number of plots of land as in crop rotation). To survive the long hiatus, humans will eat the Sabbath crop of the land, that is whatever nature produces on its own, thus continuing their learning about the natural world initiated by God through the naming of animals (Gen 2:19–20). *Sabbatical seven-year cycle observance is thus properly humans' work on behalf of God's creation which is also the very first and only task God has assigned all humankind through Adam.*

Eventually, in the fullness of this Sabbatical year practice (after seven cycles of seven years), God would be pleased with humans' work on behalf of his creation and accepts the fiftieth year as his favorable year—the Jubilee.

Within this Sabbatical framework comprising three institutions—Sabbath day, Sabbatical year, and Jubilee year—which should be (and should have been) central to Jewish living in Old Testament times, God can be understood to work, symbolically, seven days in his creation; humans to work seven years to fulfill his divine-yet-earthly mandate to rule over God's creation; and God and humans together would celebrate the Jubilee when their works resonate in harmony.

*Together, the Sabbath day, Sabbatical year, and Jubilee year would form a divine calendar* directing humankind and God's creation to the intended destiny. Repeatedly observing these hammers home the ultimate towards which all creation strives.

The focus of Revelation is the victorious Jesus. This victory is Jesus' resurrection which Revelation takes to be cosmically relevant. Jesus' resurrection must then be understood as the center of creation and history. Together with humans, the Lamb moves God's entire creation forward, creating history. Such is abundantly clear in Revelation's introduction when John encounters Jesus, then in how Jesus addresses his seven churches, and is further brought to a climax in the second episode of the heavenly worship when only the Lamb is found worthy to take the sealed scroll from the one sitting on the throne and open its seals. The narration continues. Within the above Sabbatical framework, where would Jesus' resurrection—the very acme and climax of his labor—fit into God's work of seven days and humans' work of seven years?

The obvious answer is: the mid-point (*the symbolic center*) of a week and the mid-point of a Sabbatical year cycle, namely 3.5 days and 3.5 years from the beginning, respectively. But "3.5 years" is nowhere found in Revelation. Indeed, years are only counted in 1,000. John has tactfully converted

3.5 idealized years into days and months to set it apart from the intended symbolic meaning of a year being a very long time.

Taking Jesus as the fulfillment and embodiment of the Law and Prophets, John *symbolizes Jesus by two witnesses for God* (section 2 of the third reading discusses why the two witnesses should be taken as Jesus). With an eye for the entire span of God's work, John places the resurrection of the two witnesses at 3.5 days (since creation) based on the biblical Sabbath (also creational) reference. Since in this framework, time is not historical time and has a different starting point, Jesus is not understood as resurrecting on the third day after his crucifixion, but after 3.5 days since creation. Moreover, Jesus' resurrection is also the center of human history. 1,260 days and 42 months since creation are both 3.5 years. The end of this period marks *the center of a seven-year Sabbatical cycle of humans' work*. By placing Jesus' resurrection at the center of both God's and humans' history, *John asserts Jesus' duality as the unequivocal Son of God and son of man*. John has nuanced the days and months to inform his readers that even the opposition cannot escape Jesus' reign, which would result in their judgments.

In this theological framework, the 3.5 days, 1,260 days, and 42 months are indeed *of the same duration*, i.e., since creation of the world until Jesus' resurrection for the first part, and from Jesus' resurrection to the completion of God's work in creation for the second part which is covered from chapter 12 onward. As such, they are also concurrent, but viewed from the different perspectives of the parties involved in this description. Needless to say, such unconventional, but biblically significant, accounting of time (*kairos*) forever dooms any attempt to relate these durations to any human linear timescale (*chronos*).

Coming this far, we see that the Holy Spirit has reserved the only time units of concern, i.e., God's creative week and cooperative (with humans) Sabbatical years for narrating God's work. Both units are set by God *according to his calendar* for people emulation. While many people operate on the natural timescales (hour, day, month, and year (9:15)) for mutual destruction in the first episode of this sixth trumpet, we will see below how God counters and reverses this destruction through his creative and cooperative timescales.

Two places are first mentioned: the temple-altar precinct and what is outside, with the former measured and the latter not. God has chosen (measured) the temple and altar as where people can meet him and receive his words, but outside, people do whatever they feel like (trample on) as if God does not exist or is dead. Significantly, this outside area, the court, is also referred to as *the holy city* (*hagios polis* in Greek) which reappears in chapters 21–22, when it is fully transformed and manifested. The trampling of the holy city has happened from the beginning of time (for 42 months). In the midst of all these, God sends two witnesses—the Law and Prophets—to call people back to him, sometimes with powerful demonstrations. Elijah, one of the most outstanding prophets of action, brought fire down from heaven to kill the false prophets of Baal (1 Kgs 18); Moses, another great prophet, but also messenger of the Law of God, turned water into blood (Exod 7) in confronting Pharaoh. Whatever actions they took, the Law underpins their actions as the constant witness. They were the two persons Jesus conferred with in his Transfiguration on the mount (Matt 17:1–8; Mark 9:2–8; Luke 9:28–36). In the broad sense, they represent all the people who have been standing with God since creation and their works symbolize the sum total of what God was doing in the Old Testament, now fully taken up by Jesus.

John witnessed how Moses and Elijah passed their batons to Jesus during the Transfiguration. He also witnessed how Jesus, symbolically bearing the Law and the Prophets, was crucified and died on the cross in a *great city*. But by another symbolization, this great city (Babylon), which God judges in 18:10, now epitomizes the apex of human oppression (as happened to God's people in Egypt), and depravity (as seen in Sodom), both ripe for God's judgment. The wickedness of these two human establishments now bears down on the two witnesses, killing them.

Using representative people, deeds, and moments to subsume many events scattered over a large span of time and locale is not new. Jesus himself uses this, e.g., Matt 23:34–35, "Therefore, behold, I am sending you prophets and wise men and scribes; some of them you will kill and crucify, . . . so that upon *you may fall the guilt of all the righteous blood shed on earth, from the blood of righteous Abel to the blood of Zechariah . . .* "

John has further nuanced his narration to teach important lessons. Consider the two timescales assigned the two witnesses:

- "And I will grant authority to my two witnesses, and they will prophesy for twelve hundred and sixty days, clothed in sackcloth. . . . *Whenever* they have finished their testimony, the beast that comes up out of the abyss will make war with them, and overcome them and *kill them*" (11:3 & 7; Note: most translations use "when," but the Greek word *hotan* can equally be translated as "whenever" and is adopted here to show a sensible in-context rendering).

- "Those from the peoples and tribes and tongues and nations will look at their dead bodies for *three and a half days*, and will not permit their dead bodies to be laid in a tomb . . . But *after the three and a half days, the breath of life from God came into them*, and they stood on their feet; and great fear fell upon those who were watching them" (11:9 & 11).

The first, *the death of the two witnesses, which can happen anytime during the "period,"* is reckoned by timescale of human work of 1,260 days (half a Sabbatical year cycle). The exact time of their death is not specified, regardless of whether the first word in 11:7 is translated "when" or "whenever." 11:3 only says that authority is given them when they prophesy, and 11:7 does not say that they will die at the end of the period. This period also parallels the 42 months given to the nations to trample on the holy city described in the immediately preceding verse (11:2).

In contrast, *the resurrection of the two witnesses happens precisely 3.5 days after their murder.* 3.5 days can only be interpreted as half of God's seven days of work-rest (a week which is not used explicitly in Revelation), hence is not converted. Unlike the human timescale above which is converted into their two equivalents—1,260 days and 42 months, *God's timescale here has no equivalence or parallel.*

These subtle descriptions say that people are responsible for the death of countless messengers of God throughout history which the two witnesses—Jesus—now represent, but *God alone is responsible for bringing about Jesus' resurrection* since the 7-day time-line by which Jesus' resurrection is reckoned (at 3.5 days from creation) is exclusively God's. Humans can never make the resurrection happen. Only God can. And he does.

Gloating over the death of the two witnesses ("will not permit their dead bodies to be laid in a tomb") and encouraging others ("rejoice over them and celebrate; and they will send gifts to one another") to continue their hostility is not made to further insult the two witnesses because their death has immunized them from further humiliation, but to defy God himself. God has borne the pain of these attacks on himself throughout the 3.5 days. These days are exclusively his. This period covers the time since Adam and Eve sinned until the arrival of Jesus. Throughout, humans have been defying God as if he is dead or simply not there—openly displaying the dead bodies of the witnesses. The same defiance, seen from the opposition's perspective, is trampling on the holy city for 42 months, which parallels the living witnesses' 1,260 days.

Since righteous blood has been shed left, right and center throughout history, Jesus' death would be but one episode that would pass and be forgotten in time and the beast that comes up out of the abyss would win one more battle in the long span of history. But the resurrection exploded with a force that shatters the complacency of these murderers throughout history. Those who thrive on murdering (eliminating righteous opponents) to extend or retain their hold on power are completely shaken (as if by an earthquake) and their enterprises shattered (a tenth of the city fell) with casualties (seven thousand killed).

If the resurrection of Jesus has shattered the foundation of Babylon, it seems logical to see the great city collapsing completely. Why has only a tenth of the city fallen and what does that imply? A tenth probably recalls the first of the ten plagues which once started would unstoppably bring in the rest of the plagues, or it could simply mean a significant, but not-yet overwhelming breach. In either case, the *message is that Jesus' victory in his resurrection is seminal*. Building on this sure foundation, humans led by the Lamb are to complete the destruction of the great city which is the subject matter of chapters 12–19.

What the death of one third of humankind through mutual slaughter fails to do in the first episode of this sixth trumpet, the resurrection succeeds: the remaining people "*were terrified and gave glory to the God of heaven.*" The casualties in this victory are also much smaller than before.

In this human-calendar-twisting passage is also found a unique literary rendering. In the narration, the "events" making up this episode seem to come one after another (e.g., "When they have finished their testimony . . . " (7); "But after the three and a half days . . . " (11)), but the tenses used invert this "sequence." The nations trampling on the holy city and the two witnesses given power are in future tense; the works of the witnesses are in present tense (1–10). Greek present tense conveys something that is continued and repeated without specifying the exact time. On the other hand, the events that happen afterwards are not given in future, but past (Greek aorist) tense (11–13). Obviously, the Holy Spirit is trying to make a striking point through jarring our senses.

From human's perspective, that past cannot be changed. Jesus' resurrection, the epicenter of God's work is totally beyond doubt. Relative to the absolute certainty and immovability of Jesus' resurrection, even other past events are cast into the open-endedness of the future. From this iron-clad, rock-solid, unquestionable, divine-guaranteed . . . center of Jesus' work in the past, all of creation's history will have to be re-interpreted and thus cast as future. What seemed like failures in the past are now sealed as successes in Jesus' resurrection and will contribute to creation's glorious future. God's unceasing work in Jesus throughout history is present—ever-relevant. Another way of appreciating this logic in the inversion of tense is that Jesus will create a totally different destination and destiny for all his creation past, present, and future. As such, even the imprisoned past of creation is set free into Jesus' future, hence the present and future tenses in describing events that took place before that absolute anchoring point in history.

Regardless of how the inversion of time is to be taken theologically, the narration in chapter 11 *cannot be interpreted as chronologically linear*.

The most prominent Jewish, and indeed biblical, time unit—week (*Sabbaton*)—which was found inexplicably missing in our analysis (section 4.2 of the first reading) now takes center stage to anchor all the histories of his creation and of humankind therein. Breaking into the mundane natural calendar with his own calendar, the creator has entered forcefully into human history. Jesus has now filled in what lies between the Alpha and the Omega by working through the whole creative week of God and the seven cooperative years of God-human partnership day after day.

*Jesus' resurrection redefines time Sabbatically and shatters linear time with its trans-temporal significance.*

## 5.5 The Seventh and Last Trumpet (11:15–19)

The seventh trumpet sounds immediately after the resurrection of the two witnesses. For the first time in Revelation (and in human history since Adam and Eve fell), the kingdom of the world is declared to have become the "kingdom of our Lord and of His Christ, and He will reign forever and ever." As such, it would be utmost inappropriate if these two witnesses are taken to be some human agents other than Jesus himself. Only the Lamb who took the scroll out of God's hand can bring this victory about.

Two verses later (18), this picture of instant transformation of one kingdom into another is further nuanced by the twenty four elders in their unreserved praise: "You have taken Your great power and *have begun to reign*." But extending the reign is not without opposition since "*the nations were enraged*" and would resist, which would bring about God's wrath and judgment of the dead. These few sentences neatly encapsulate the struggle in the next nine chapters of Revelation (12–20).

Within a span of three verses (15–17), the paradox of the already-but-not-yet inherent in Jesus' triumph is brought out in stark relief. Resurrection from the dead means that the hitherto unbroken and all-pervading power of decay, destruction, chaos, lawlessness, darkness, meaninglessness, nothingness, empty void, and ultimately death has been punctured and shattered. Despite its seemingly miniscule numerical beginning with only one person resurrecting among the millions upon millions who have seemingly perished and its seeming irrelevance to the rest of creation, a beachhead has been established and progression to the end unstoppable, just as the morning star (22:16) inexorably ushers in the dawn and eventually the full brightness of the day. Declaring victory is not premature despite the hard slog and sacrifice which are yet to come (fifth seal) because it is certain and unalterable. Symbolic this victory may be, but non-substantive it is not, because those who see the final victory will live by the unshakable hope of this victory and transform the kingdom of this world completely into the kingdom of our Lord. High sounding this victory may be, but detached from reality it is not, because the actions of those who heed this high calling are real and constructive in this holy city waiting to be fully born. Far into the distant future this full victory may be, but despairing it is not because each person mindful of the total victory is content with playing his/her part in the long history of creation's journey that God is writing with humans. Humanly impossible this victory may be, but impossible it is not, because God has done it in Jesus and will do so again with his people and his creation in his good time.

Before turning to the details of the struggle in chapters 12–20, John fittingly brings the seventh trumpet to a close by declaring God's judgment: "the time came for the dead to be judged, and the time to reward Your bond-servants the prophets and the saints and those who fear Your name, the small and the great, and *to destroy those who destroy the earth*." Whereas those who will be rewarded are described in different ways, those eliminated here have all committed the same crime—destroy the earth. This succinctly encapsulates all those who have rejected God's name for them—*Adamah*, from the soil and is to rule over creation—but seek another name which inevitably leads to the earth's and their own destruction. Fortunately for us, God has unrelentingly circumscribed the works of *Apollyōn* through calling his followers to preserve his earth. Such is the blaring message of the seven trumpets, centered upon the Lamb that was slain and is alive forever.

When the seven trumpets are understood together, a puzzle can now be solved: What causes the destructions described in the first four trumpets? The fifth trumpet clearly attributes destruction to the angel of the abyss while the first episode of the sixth trumpet sees humans as killing each other by harnessing the forces of nature. Reading these back into the first four trumpets, the unspecified sources behind the destructive agents should then be understood as an interplay of Satanic and human factors, while the damages to creation are repeated calls (as if by trumpets) for humans to repent.

God's work is incomplete (silence of the seventh seal) if it is only humankind he is dealing with. The constructive part of God's work is now completed when victory is proclaimed to all of creation in the seventh trumpet. The completion of God's wrath is still to come.

## 6. THE SHAPE OF AN INTENSIFIED AND FOCUSED WAR (CHAPTER 12)

Chapter 12 introduces two new prominent characters—a woman and a dragon. The woman is pregnant with a male child while the dragon stands before the woman readying itself for infanticide. The struggle that ensues sees the male child transported to God and his throne and the woman protected twice, for 1,260 days and "time, times and half a time." The saints also overcome the dragon which enrages it further to redouble its effort to destroy the woman. Eventually, the dragon settles for warring against the other children of the woman.

The point of contention in this epic struggle is the male child being born of the woman. Despite his earthly origin, seen in his mother remaining on earth fleeing the dragon, this male child is "to rule all the nations with a rod of iron; and . . . was caught up to God and to His throne," leaving no doubt that he is Jesus.

Sun, moon, and stars have been used to describe collectively one aspect of the natural world (fourth trumpet, 8:12), but here as opposed to them being damaged but protected, they are related to the woman in very specific ways. There are precisely twelve stars. As such, a different interpretation to nature has to be sought.

Before this passage are mentioned two time units—days and months—specifically counted for each party according to whether they are for or against God. Day is regulated by the sun and is also associated with those belonging to God (both in chapter 11 and here in chapter 12), but month is regulated by the moon and is the time unit for the opposition (in both chapters 11 and 13). Thus the context suggests that sun and moon represent God and his opposition, respectively. Twelve recalls God's promise to bless the nations of the earth through choosing Abram. Together, this woman represents the godly humanity which is protected and glorified by God (clothed with the sun) who will make their enemies a footstool of their feet (foot on the moon; Heb 1:13, 10:13, both quoting Ps 110:1) according to God's promise which is first fulfilled in Jacob (twelve stars).

In this sun-moon-twelve-stars description of one woman, *the entire course of the ensuing struggle is presaged.* Also, the opposition's identity and work are also laid out: he is "the serpent of old who is called the devil and Satan who deceives the whole world and he accuses them (the saints) before God day and night."

The struggle between the woman and Satan devolves into a trial of strength between Michael and the dragon, both leading some angels, with Michael's camp winning and casting the entire opposition from heaven down to earth. With that comes the announcement of the arrival of "the salvation, and the power, and the kingdom of our God and the authority of His Christ," the complementary and logical extension of Jesus' victory in the seventh trumpet. Appropriately, the saints are now affectionately addressed as our brethren, rather than just souls under the altar or the white-robed multitude coming out of the great tribulation. The three weapons they use to win the war are also quite factual: 1. "the blood of the Lamb," 2. "the word of their testimony," and 3. "they did not love their life even when faced with death." The context makes it clear that the angels in Michael's camp are none other than these brethren.

Michael is the enigmatic chief prince mentioned in Dan 10 & 12. Here again, the context of Revelation finally reveals who this Old Testament figure is. First, he must be the godly counterpart to Satan's leadership since Michael and Satan (in the guise of a 7-headed, 10-horned dragon) are leading their respective camps against the opposition. Second, Michael appears abruptly after the male child who is to rule all the nations with a rod of iron has been taken up to God and his throne, strongly suggesting that Michael is this male child, just as the 144,000 is the multitude in the sixth seal. Finally, as we shall see, no one except Jesus has been described as leading his saints in the struggle elsewhere in Revelation. Together, these are sufficient in-context evidence to conclude that Michael is another representation of Jesus.

Heaven and earth can take on different meanings depending on the context. The Greek word for heaven (*ouranos*), and for earth (*gē*) is of no help to nail down the exact meaning. *gē* is sometimes even translated as land in contrast to the sea (e.g., 10:5). Before this chapter, taking "earth" as our planet generally makes sense. In the context of chapter 12 here, heaven is the abode of the saints, solidly dwelling on the surface of this planet, from which the lies and accusations of Satan have been expelled through the brethren's three weapons, and concentrated onto the community whose abode is symbolized as earth where Satan's falsehood still finds an audience, hence the comments: "rejoice, O heavens and you who dwell in them. Woe to the earth and the sea, because the devil has come down to you, having great wrath, knowing that he has only a short time" (12). The history of Satan (in 4: "his tail swept away a third of the stars of *heaven* and threw them to the *earth*") can be similarly understood. Yet even before chapter 12 closes, earth reverts back to its old meaning when it is seen as helping the woman (16: "and the earth opened its mouth and drank up the river which the dragon poured out of his mouth"). It is inconceivable that this "earth" is the repository of Satan's lying followers as in (12) since Satan would ensure that the woman is not assisted by his underlings. Rather, it is an allusion to how the earth dried up after the great deluge to enable Noah and his offspring to repopulate the earth as God promised in Gen 8–9. In Revelation, *earth's basic meaning is the good material home God created for humans.* Nevertheless, it has been polluted and damaged by Satan and his cohorts, hence also taken as the symbol for the temporary abode of Satan's followers. God remains committed to his earth, to save it from destruction. As such, *it has become a battle ground for the grand struggle.* Until the final victory is complete, i.e., when the new (cleansed) earth appears, it remains ambivalent, hence its fluid depictions in Revelation.

In the sixth trumpet, 42 months, 1,260 days, and 3.5 days run parallel to each other to give the perspective of human (God's opposition and the saints) and God, each having the same "duration" and each symbolizes the first half of creation's history until the resurrection of Jesus. Here when the post-resurrection history of creation is prophesied, 42 months (later in 13:5) and 1,260 days (which appears here for the second and last time) run parallel to another period—time, times and half a time—during which the persecuted woman is protected. In the first instance (6), "the woman fled (*by herself*) into the wilderness where she had a place prepared by God, so that there she might be nourished for one thousand two hundred and sixty days," whereas towards the end of the chapter (14) "the two wings of the great eagle *were given to the woman*, so that she could fly into the wilderness to her place, where she was nourished for a time, times and half a time." (Eagle symbolizes life (see fourth seal); great eagle is the supreme life or source of life and represents God, and its two wings, power.) Describing one post-resurrection episode from both the human (1,260 days) and divine (time, times and half a time) perspectives, as done in the sixth trumpet, is evident here. The final piece completing the time puzzle is that "time, times and half a time" corresponds to 3.5 days.

Daniel in the Old Testament has first used "time, times and half a time" to prophesy events in his immediate future. John has recycled the symbol. But the meaning of this symbol is no longer bound by its first use in the Bible. In this case, the immediate context of Revelation 11–12 has invested this Old Testament symbol for a local situation with its own meaning that it has shed its Old Testament associations and constraints. For Revelation, we have to ask: is the 3.5 days in chapter 11 the same as the time, times and half a time in chapter 12? It seems that the symmetry that exists before and after the two witnesses' resurrection for the 1,260 days and 42 months would strongly suggest that this symmetry would be extended to the remaining specific timescales in chapters 11–12, namely 3.5 days versus "time, times and half a time." If so, our next quest is to establish a link between "day" and "time." Note that for counting, Revelation only deals in whole numbers and simple fractions. After matching the fraction (half) and the whole number (one for time) for the two expressions, simple arithmetic dictates that "times" means "two times" with "day" corresponding to "time." This matching is no doubt circular and proves nothing, but its message is that the "day" of the Lord is his appointed time. Further, Revelation, true to its name, is self-explaining; any information brought forth from Daniel or other sources is superfluous. Forcing Daniel's meaning onto Revelation only distracts.

But why does the Holy Spirit not convey the message with 3.5 days instead to preserve the symmetry centered on Jesus' resurrection? 3.5 days, despite it being symbolic, still conveys a fixed duration, but the word time used here (*kairos* rather than *chronos*), being "appointed time," is in the hands of the God who alone can appoint it and bring the moment to pass. Stringing together "appointed times" even jars at the very basic rule of human communication, and is forever outside our feeble calculus, thus leaving the decision of when the post-resurrection 3.5 days is up entirely in the hands of God. The "time" will come, but it may be in two "times" or half a "time." This serves as a stern warning against any effort to fit God's work into our timetable (*chronos*), be it out of good intention or not. Similarly, when Satan knows "that he has only a short time" (*kairos*), he is not counting his hours, days, months, and years, but lives under the unrelieved fear of God's sovereign decision and shudder (Jas 2:19). As such, this war that breaks out in heaven after Jesus' resurrection is new since Satan is playing his own end game of self-destruction in constant fear.

Wilderness is the place the woman repeatedly goes to when persecuted. It no more symbolizes a withdrawal from the world than Jesus would closet himself from his creation in any dimension without ministering to its hurts and pains. Instead it recalls the place where Jesus would go and commune with God (closest context) and where God provides manna for his people during the Exodus (wider context).

Ultimately, the message here is a fulfillment of God's verdict on the parties involved in Adam and Eve's fall from grace: "And I will put enmity between you (the serpent) and the woman, And between your seed and her seed." Despite the dragon's ferocity, God triumphs, and he protects the woman and her offspring from harm, in fulfillment of his prophecy: "He shall bruise you on the head, And you shall bruise him on the heel" (Gen 3:15). Though Satan has conceded defeat to God, collecting trophies to mark his downfall is the last game this loser is determined to pursue to the bitter end.

## 7. TWO OPPOSING CAMPS

### 7.1 Anatomy of Satan's Camp (chapter 13)

Completing the victory that Jesus has seminally secured requires understanding the nature of the opposition and its tactics. So the readers are now treated to a tour of the enemy's camp. Three major players are introduced. Continuing from the previous chapter is Satan, but he quickly disappears from the scene after delegating his authority to one of the first two main players—the beasts. These beasts then ply their trade on the third player which is described in different ways around the commonality of living on the earth (13:8, 14). Satan is fighting a proxy last-ditch battle again the creator.

Satan now stands on the border between land and sea: "the sand of the seashore." From the sea rises one beast and from the land rises another. The beast from the sea is grotesque, with multiple heads, horns, and profane markings. Their meanings are not immediately apparent until it is revealed later in chapter 17. What is apparent here is that it combines the characteristic of three ferocious animals (leopard—agile, bear's feet—powerful, and lion's mouth—destructively voracious) and impresses the beholders to the extent that the whole earth worships it in amazement ("Who is like the beast, and who is able to wage war with him?"). Unwittingly, this worship is in effect directed towards Satan as it is only through Satan's delegated authority that this first beast possesses such seeming invincibility. Blasphemy against God and violence against the saints follow from wielding Satan's authority.

Completing the symmetry of the Sabbatical timescales in Revelation is the second and final use of 42 months, which, consistent with our expectation after Jesus' resurrection, is the time allowed the beast to exercise its received authority, just as God's opposition was allowed to trample the holy city before Jesus' resurrection. This 42 months run concurrent to the 3.5 days, and "time, times and half a time" encountered in the previous chapter, but is not identical in *chronos* to the pre-resurrection "duration" given how God exercises his absolute sovereignty through the humanly incomprehensible "time, times and half a time."

From the other side of where Satan stands—land—arises another beast, the second main player. The brief description of this beast's appearance—"two horns like a lamb" (in mimicry of Jesus)—contrasts markedly with that of the first one, but together they exercise the same authority from Satan. As opposed to wielding military might like the first beast, this land-born beast performs soft deception through signs—"makes fire come down out of heaven to the earth in the presence of men" (in mimicry of the Old

Testament prophets (11:5)), and tries to propagate the same deception through its adherents—"telling those who dwell on the earth to make an image to the beast."

Sea is always understood to be fluid and tempestuously unreliable while land provides a firmer ground for people to stand on. The first beast is a politico-military animal rising out of the fickle arena where power can be won and lost overnight while the second beast is a religious animal rising out of the more stable land where various deities have trans-generational hold on their adherents. But God is determined to call both the political and religious arenas to account, hence the strong angel from God in chapter 10 "placed his right foot on the sea and his left on the land" to voice out the seven peals of thunder, and when that were cancelled, "swore . . . that there will be delay no longer." The land and sea on which the strong angel stands (10:3, 5) are now echoed to underscore God's concern with both the political and religious. The two beasts are now tackled.

The major rallying point for these two beasts is the seeming resurrection of the first beast to mimic that of Jesus. On the first beast, "one of his heads looks as if it had been slain, and his fatal wound was healed, and the whole earth was amazed" (3). Fully supporting the first beast, the second beast tells "those who dwell on the earth to make an image to the beast who had the wound of the sword and *has come to life*" (14). Such is a direct mimicry of the resurrection of Jesus though the first beast was not crucified for any cause, but was simply slain. Nevertheless, this fake "resurrection" is sufficient to impress the whole earth, *except* those in heaven since blasphemies have to be uttered and wars have to be waged against the heavenly saints who do not buy any of these at all.

What then is this "resurrection" of the first beast? The description here leaves no doubt that both the politico-military and the religious beasts are united for the purpose to defeat the saints in heaven while holding those on earth under their control. Jesus' very appearance on earth is a contest between the truth of God (sharp sword coming out of Jesus' mouth, 19:15) and the deceptions of Satan. Satan was obviously behind the religious powers (the Jews being swayed by their religious leaders) that colluded with the political powers (the Sanhedrin, local power of Herod, and Roman military might) to bring about Jesus' crucifixion, prompting the earlier description in 11:7 that "the *beast that comes up out of the abyss* will make war with them (the two witnesses symbolizing Jesus), and overcome them and kill them."

The contest Jesus initiates is in the very real sense a life and death struggle. The angel of the abyss would have won if death is the last word. Both good and evil, justice and injustice would have been buried by death if death is indeed final. There is no ultimate reckoning of anything that exists in any way, shape or form, period. But such uniform nihilism is punctured by Jesus' prototypical resurrection. The death that Satan wishes on Jesus and all of his creation would have won eternity and the contest would have been finally over, were it not for Jesus' resurrection. Jesus' resurrection reverses the positions of the contestants. Life is now on Jesus' side and death on Satan's cohorts. Goodness and abundance belongs to Jesus, evil and void to Satan. The politico-military beast that killed the two witnesses (Jesus) has instead suffered a fatal blow. The undeniable reality of Jesus' resurrection, the sword of Jesus (1:16, 2:12, 16, 19:15, 21) has dealt a fatal blow to this beast (14). Facts against facts, hardware against hardware, the beast has lost!

*One would then expect the immediate fall of all the ungodly human authorities everywhere.* Yet the immediate appearance betrays this claim of ultimate reality. The powers that be have not only not fallen, but they have persecuted those who believe in and live according to the ultimate victory of Jesus over decay and death.

The seeming continued wielding of power by the politico-military machine opposed to God gives room for both beasts (the second being the religious establishment) to deceive people through suggesting that the wound suffered by the first beast is just a glitch in the ongoing triumph of evil, *hence the beast has survived the fatal blow from Jesus and will live forever.* As opposed to Jesus resurrecting, it was the beast that *appears* to have resurrected! This sounds true to those who reject God. *After Jesus' resurrection and ascension, this contest morphs into a choice between accepting the ultimate defeat of evil versus conniving with the waning power of evil while it lasts, buttressed by the two beasts' resurrection claim. This is the nub of the whole struggle and also determines how the final victory will have to be claimed, or the weapons used in this fight.*

With strings pulled by Satan from behind, the two beasts would not stop at persuasion. A stranglehold has to be put on the people who buy into Satan's falsehood (those on earth), so that maximum destruction will be wrought on God's creation. These people constitute the final major player in chapter 13 which has to be totally subdued, now symbolized by all those on earth being "given a mark on their right hand or on their forehead, and he (the religious beast) provides that no one will be able to buy or to sell, except the one who has the mark" in a diametric contrast with the seal being put on the 144,000 of God's chosen first encountered in the sixth seal (7:3–4).

The mark of the beast is explicitly given a numerical value—666—which is explained as the number of a man and requires wisdom to decipher. Revelation portrays God and humans as working through one Sabbath cycle to complete their work, hence the previous enigmatic use of 3.5, 1,260 days, and 42 months. Based on this preceding Sabbatical focus, 666 is simply the mark of all human pursuits without God which inevitably fall short of entering the Sabbath of all creation since God rested on the seventh day. Specifically, humans were made on the sixth day of creation, hence the number 6. Satan has delegated his authority to humans in the political arena (first 6) who collude with the humans bent on worshipping anything other than the true creator (second 6) which together impose a totalitarian sway on all other humans that do not worship the true God, including those who do not worship anything at all (third 6). Correspondingly, God's intention is for every sphere of his people (1. political, 2. religious and 3. all other mundane activities like economics) to enter the final Sabbath which would then be 777. But this will not happen with those people in Satan's camp since 666 is their very limit and final destiny.

Subsuming the above human 777 intended by God would be another level of 777 in which 1. humans, 2. God's creation, and 3. God himself would enter into the grand harmony pointed to in the Jubilee year. Humans are intended to lead God's creation to the final Sabbath. Yet the humans' 666 also leads to creation's 666—humans are not in harmony among themselves which spills over to damage creation and in response creation grows thorns and thistles to make people's life miserable. Neither humans nor creation can enter the Sabbath of God. But God would not rest until all his creation would break forth into the final Sabbath, hence the teaching in the remainder of Revelation.

Immediately after describing the first beast's ferocious attack on those in heaven, Revelation gives a very serious admonition to the saints since it is underscored by Jesus' own formula ("If anyone has an ear, let him hear" (9)) and marked at the end with a touchstone ("Here is the perseverance and the faith of the saints" (10b)). The admonition is: "If anyone is destined for captivity, to captivity he goes; if anyone kills with the sword, with the sword he must be killed." This statement is ambiguous as even the above translation shows: the first part on captivity is passive (destined for) whereas the second part is active (kills). Yet the original Greek is consistent for both parts, meaning that both parts can be translated as passive or active. Given the parallel structure of the two parts of this sentence, they should be consistently translated. To break the stalemate, let us invoke our familiar rule of context.

In the chapters we have covered, there has not occurred a single teaching that the saints should passively accept a fate. The churches are to respond to Jesus' words; the saints cry out under the altar and pray fervently; and the chosen praise God. This continues in latter chapters. As such, understanding this statement as "accept your fate" is not only out of character with the whole book, it is also totally meaningless, for why should one be told of something that no one has any power to change except to be scared? And is the purpose of Revelation to make people afraid or its very opposite as we hear from Jesus in 1:19? Also apart from Jesus' statement in the Gospel against violence ("for all those who take up the sword shall perish by the sword," Matt 26:52) is the contrast between the fifth trumpet which exposes the legacy of Satan's sugar-coated poison, and the sixth trumpet, that the violence of humankind would perpetuate itself endlessly—the horses hurt from their heads, but their tails are also headed! This teaching constitutes the immediate context in Revelation. To break this cycle of violence, the Holy Spirit is warning: despite the violence of other humans which ends in 666, *do not retaliate with violence, otherwise this evil will blow back on you, in keeping with your Lord's teaching.* A better translation is thus: "He that leads into captivity shall go into captivity. He that kills with the sword must be killed with the sword" (KJV).

Interestingly, the works of the first beast are described in past tense whereas that of the second beast are always in the present, suggesting not that the first beast is now irrelevant (since (8) says: "All who dwell on the earth *will* worship him . . . "), but that the second beast is *continually trumpeting the lie of all lies that the first beast had won.*

## 7.2 Anatomy of God's Camp (chapter 14)

In contrast to Satan standing on the interface between land and sea to pull strings on the two beasts, the Lamb now stands on Mount Zion to lead his camp, solidly and directly. Three scenes are portrayed: 1. The Lamb with his 144,000, 2. An angel proclaiming an eternal gospel to all, and 3. Harvesting the earth.

Once the equivalence of the 144,000 with the uncountable multitude is established in the sixth seal, this equivalence is not repeated here. (Were there a distinction between the 144,000 and the multitude in the sixth seal, then the Lamb would only be leading an unspecified portion of his followers to claim his victory over the beast, thus contradicting the cosmic scope of the two previous chapters. This last use of 144,000 clinches the equivalence of the 144,000 and the multitude discussed in section 4.3.) Instead the 144,000 are unmistakably contrasted with the entire camp of Satan which operates through violence, deception, and coercion. The chosen of God are engraved with the name of the Father and the Lamb on their forehead to include them into the family of God (rather than shoved into a herd with a mark) and they spontaneously sing a new and absolutely exclusive song known only within the family (rather than acquired through learning or mimicry) before the throne amid joyous music of harps (rather than being threatened with military violence and trade embargo in a cheerless existence). Ironically, these people were not naturally born into the family, but are snatched from Satan's camp ("purchased from the earth") to be reborn and in response have kept themselves pure ("not been defiled with women") and are open to every leading by the Lamb. In anticipation of their union with the Lamb, these people, both male and female, have shunt other pursuits that may have a claim on their lives with a fierce intensity that can be likened to shunning marriage. As in the other use of symbols throughout Revelation to convey a specific point, there is no question that the union of a man with a woman originally blessed by God for enjoyment and procreation is not practiced by these 144,000 chosen by God. Being *defiled* with woman is the point (4); conjugal relationship is not defilement. Being upright becomes their character and despite their former origin (from the earth), they are now considered blameless through the Lamb's redemption.

The second scene opens with an angel flying in mid-heaven, proclaiming an eternal gospel to those on the earth. Earlier on in 8:13 at the end of the first four trumpets, an eagle is flying in mid-heaven announcing woes to those who dwell on the earth. In the war described in chapter 12, Satan's camp was cast down to earth while Michael and his angels retain occupancy of heaven. Who then are the eagle and the angel flying in mid-heaven? No one but the saints dwelling in heaven trying to reach those on earth with the double-edged message of God's goodness open to all and the woeful end if the hearers do not repent. For these people (eagle and angel), their work involves going out as far as possible to others in the enemy camp (on earth) without compromising their own abode (in heaven), hence they have to be flying (rather than living) in between heaven and earth.

The eternal gospel preached by the flying angel is surprisingly simple: "Fear God, and give Him glory, because the hour of His judgment has come; worship Him who made the heaven and the earth and sea and springs of waters." The urgency and seriousness of this good news are reinforced respectively by the two negative messages (or dimensions of the same eternal gospel) proclaimed by two other angels: 1. a big-picture that says "fallen is Babylon the great," and 2. a personally poignant warning that worshippers of the beast will be tormented forever and ever, or to echo the previous chapter, will remain in their 666s with no rest. No one is exempted from these three proclamations as this is preached to "every nation and tribe and tongue and people."

Yet given Revelation's focus on the slain Lamb, how does he factor into this eternal gospel that points only to the creator God? Here, reading Revelation as one unified logical argument rather than as disjoint episodes is paramount. Jesus has already been confirmed as the central figure of all creation in the resurrection of the two witnesses in chapter 11. Springing from this immoveable center is the eternal gospel which presents God successively as creator, then victor and finally judge, all encapsulated in Jesus as the Lord of the Sabbath in chapter 11. The call to fear the creator requires repentance from the wayward, and also forgiveness by the creator.

This gospel, being centered on the Lord of the Sabbath and hence eternal, reminds people of the never-changing goal of God: they should know that the maker of the heaven, earth, sea, and springs of waters wants creation to be recognized as his wonderful handiwork to reflect his glory. His judgment will be based on how we honor him as creator. By contrast, baseless is a gospel that does not preach the ultimate harmony between God, humans and God's creation to be ushered in by the Lamb described in the second heavenly worship scene in chapter 5. Empty is a gospel that ends in the stewards of creation without the creation itself. Emasculated is a gospel that has forgotten the very first biblical command for humans to rule over God's creation. Woeful is a gospel that does not tell of the judgment when humans fail in the first and never-cancelled command of God to all humans. Sterile is a gospel that calls humans to worship a god who abjectly fails to protect his creation from the diabolic destruction of Satan.

But the gospel preached by those chosen and redeemed by the Lamb here is biblically right on the mark, full, abundant, complete and eternally true, when it is founded on the Lord of the Sabbath, the resurrected Jesus.

Further contrasted with the state of mind in Satan's camp is the ultimate fate of those inside: the Sabbath. In Satan's camp: "they have *no rest* day and night" (11). For those persevering in God's camp, dying in the Lord is blessed because "they *may rest* from their labors, for their deeds follow with them" (13). In this is the ultimate Sabbath for humans revealed: those who labor six days in the Lord will enter the seventh and last day of God where his/her works in the Lord are remembered by God to resonate in God's creation. More so, their works are endeared to them just as God is endeared to his creation and finds ultimate fulfillment in his Sabbath rest.

Now that the internal workings of the Lamb's camp and the message they are conveying are laid out, the output of this camp has to be shown. In the last leg of this tour of the Lamb's camp, four characters appear: son of man and three angels. The latter are an angel from: 1. the temple, 2. the temple holding a sharp sickle, and 3. the altar having power over fire. In response to the call from the first angel, the son of man reaps the earth with his sickle. Likewise, in response to the call of the third angel (altar), the second angel also reaps the earth with his sickle. Together, the double harvests are put into God's winepress and out of that comes blood.

This is a most beautiful description of how God and humans work together to complete the cleansing of the earth. In the place where God meets humans (the temple), Jesus (son of man) is petitioned by his saints (the temple angel) to cleanse his creation (harvest the earth). And so he does. In the same temple, saints desirous of a cleansed creation (angel from the altar having authority over the refining fire) pray to God to send his angel to cleanse the earth and again God does, sending his saints (the sickle holding angel) to do the job *in parallel* to what the son of man is doing. The synergism of the praying and working saints and the Lamb completes the cleansing of God's creation.

The work of God and his saints is completed and converges into a torrent of blood measuring 1,600 ((10+6)×100) stadia: 1,000 (a hundredfold of ten which recalls the ten plagues *God unleashed* on the Egyptians to punish them for their recalcitrance) plus 600 (a hundredfold of the *number of a human*—six) stadia (biblically the largest distance measure to indicate its universal scope) up to the horses' bridles (as high as humans can achieve with all his tools, symbolized by the domestication of the horse with bridles).

Despite the fierce combined wrath of God through humans on the unrepentant, God is not overwhelmed by his anger since it is *only multiplied one hundred times* whereas his chosen is enlarged by self-multiplication (12×12) then *expanded a thousand fold* to form the 144,000. Also, the perseverance of the saints, raised separately with each tour of the two camps (13:9–10, 14:12–13), clearly spells out the extent of human actions: *no violence must be used even if one is to be killed by the opposition*. This death in the Lord is blessed. The gory imagery of the river of blood betrays an utterly creative and non-violent approach enjoined on the practitioners. Vivid symbols must never be cut off from consistent and core teachings.

## 8. SEVEN BOWLS OF WRATH—THE END GAME (CHAPTERS 15–16)

So far, Revelation has offered a number of zoom-ins: the second heavenly worship, centered on the slain Lamb in chapter 5, is expanded on in the seven seals with the last seal (silence in heaven) being elaborated in the seven trumpets and when the seventh trumpet precipitates conflicts, the resulting war is portrayed in vivid details in chapter 12 and each camp involved there is dissected further in chapters 13 and 14 which end with ridding creation of its deadly parasites (harvesting the earth). One would then expect the cleansing works of God to have ended, but here again is offered a further zoom-in view of the wrath of God.

Introducing the last seven plagues is no longer prayers (symbolized by the altar and incense) since this wrath is itself answered prayers, but a song of praise sung by the victorious. Appropriately this victory consummates God's righteousness which also echoes the desire of all saints throughout history, hence the song is that of Moses and simultaneously of the Lamb which *resonate to proclaim God's righteous and truthful acts* among all the nations. God deals justly; godly humans desire justice; the Bible teaches God's righteousness throughout.

Echoing the last scene in the tour of the Lamb's camp in chapter 14 where the son of man works together with his saints to harvest the earth, the seven angels about to pour out God's wrath here are clothed in white robes (symbolizing humans purchased by God (7:14); hence these angels are all humans needing and having received redemption) with golden sashes around their chests (representing the son of man (1:13)). Handing over to these angels the seven bowls of wrath is *one of the four living creatures*. Purposely un-specifying this living creature, John is saying that since humans have misdirected every godly attribute that shows forth the image of God, any one attribute—majesty (lion), loyalty (ox), wisdom (human) and continual renewal of life (flying eagle)—would be an appropriate standard to judge their perversions.

The first four bowls are poured on four spheres of nature (earth, sea, river and celestial objects) which are identical to that in the first four trumpets and also in the same order. Yet the effects and purpose are quite different. Protection from damage is clearly the intention of the first four trumpets with God limiting the extent of the destruction to one third of nature while the bowls are all-out unrestrained destruction, yet only aimed at those "who had the mark of the beast and who worshiped his image."

This difference between the trumpets and bowls parallels that of the verdicts God handed down to the first deceived (Adam) versus the first criminal who intentionally killed his brother (Cain). To Adam, God said: "*Because you have listened* to the voice of your wife, and have eaten from the tree about which I commanded you, saying, "You shall not eat from it"; *cursed is the ground* because of you; in toil you will eat of it all the days of your life . . . ," but to Cain: "*What have you done? T*he voice of your brother's blood is crying to Me from the ground. Now *you are cursed from the ground*, which has opened its mouth to receive your brother's blood from your hand. When you cultivate the ground, it will no longer yield its strength to you; you will be a vagrant and a wanderer on the earth" (Gen 3:17, 4:10–12).

Cursing the ground is intended to remind humans through hardship that nature is designed to produce abundantly for all so that the entire creation can praise and glorify God. *Man is not cursed.* If they henceforth reject the deceiver's lies, which Adam must realize he should, the land would still yield to them through their extra toil. Such hardship through nature's thorns and thistles is portrayed in the first 4 trumpets. This would keep humans focused on the land as they were first instructed and not spend their lives in other devious pursuits, hence is God's protection. He still has the majority two thirds working for him. Yet, when *man is cursed from the ground*, humans are put on the opposite side of God's protection—for destruction through nature. Such is the fate of those who, despite knowing the lies of Satan, initiate and persist in their crimes. Appropriately, Revelation describes their punishments: "Then the third angel poured out his bowl into the rivers and the springs of waters; and they became blood. And I heard the angel of the waters saying, "Righteous are You, who are and who were, O Holy One, because You *judged* these things; for they poured out the blood of saints and prophets (as Cain did to Abel, who are representative humans), and You have given them blood to drink. *They deserve it.*"" (16:4-6). God's patience and grace have run out for them.

Stepping back, we find that introducing God's wrath is not just physical suffering, but first being expelled from the glorious presence of God—"no one was able to enter the temple (to meet God) until the seven plagues of the seven angels were finished" (15:18). This also echoes the fate of the first human cursed by God: "Then Cain *went out from the presence of the Lord*, and settled in the land of Nod, east of Eden" (Gen 4:16). Other sufferings follow.

Parallel to the unleashing of Satan's torment in the fifth trumpet ("the sun and the air were darkened by the smoke of the pit" (9:2) which brings forth mutated locusts to sting humans) is the darkening of the beast's kingdom in the fifth bowl, which provokes a reaction that seals their fate—the citizens therein blaspheme God. By contrast, the victims in the fifth trumpet only seek death, but do not curse God. The kingdom of the beast is marked out by people flouting God's mercy, and God's punishments come at their consistent and final rejection of God's overture, which is also when God's patience runs out.

Echoing the sixth trumpet when four angels bound at the Euphrates are released is now the sixth bowl, which when poured out, dries up the Euphrates. The description "to gather them together for *the war of the great day of God*, the Almighty" gives no indication that these people are warring against God. If we follow the parallel descriptions between the trumpets with the bowls so far, the more likely meaning of this great war is that *these people in the darkened kingdom of the beast have lost all their senses and turn on each other for complete mutual destruction*, out of desperation because the river that supports them is dried up. These would be in keeping with the people, the two myriads of myriads horsemen, fighting each other to death, rather than against God, in the sixth trumpet before God reverses that. Such is also in line with the self-cannibalizing of Satan's camp which will be made clear in the next chapter.

Unlike the destruction in the first episode of the sixth trumpet, when humans *deceived* by the angel of the abyss turn against each other, here in the sixth bowl, *people take instructions directly* from: 1. Satan himself, 2. the first beast who receives Satan's delegated power, and 3. the second beast, now revealed as the false prophet (13). While God prevents humans from further tearing at each other's throat in the sixth trumpet with a message centered on the resurrection of his two witnesses, the grand collusion of the willful opposition, having rejected this message, and now led by the three unclean spirits in the sixth bowl proceeds appropriately to the bitterest end, namely, in the seventh bowl.

A triumphal transformation of the kingdom of the world into the kingdom of God caps the trumpets; destruction is the outcome of the bowls. Under the just demand of God, love and mercy must be completed by commensurate wrath on the unrepentant, thus the ultimate announcement—"It is done," first seminally proclaimed by Jesus on the cross—is not made from the apocalyptic perspective of Revelation *until* this seventh and last bowl of God's wrath. The seventh trumpet is now completed in the seventh bowl.

Given the correspondence between the trumpets and the bowls, one can understand the seventh bowl to be a fulfillment of the proclamation (prophecy) in the seventh trumpet: *"to destroy those who destroy the earth."* How this is done depends on how we understand the last two bowls.

The sixth bowl speaks of the *Euphrates* being dried up to prepare the way for the kings from the *east* who will gather at *Armageddon*. The seventh bowl sees an unprecedented *earthquake* that destroys *Babylon* and *the cities of the nations*. Given the unique concentration of geographical references in this short passage (16:12–18), do these two last bowls point to a real physical earth-shattering event of gargantuan proportion or are they a theological description?

Let us now try to see how geographic names are used in Revelation.

Cities are named in the letters to the seven churches out of necessity to locate these communities in chapters 2–3, yet they are not part of the main narrative of Revelation which starts only with the heavenly worship in chapter 4 and runs to the end. Within the body of the main message, the first geographic name is Euphrates (9:13) which is set in the universal description of God's protection of his creation in the seven trumpets. The flow in the trumpet series suggests that Euphrates represents the human self-centeredness supporting Babylon though Babylon is not explicitly mentioned at that point. Thereafter in 11:8, the city in which God's two witnesses are murdered is called Sodom and Egypt. Conflating a defunct city and an extant country that are geographically apart, John states clearly that this city is allegorical. Its meaning is thus to be deduced from their associated Old Testament events. Then 14:1 portrays the Lamb standing on Mount Zion with his 144,000. If the Lamb is a metaphor for Jesus and the 144,000 for his chosen, then Mount Zion must likewise be symbolic.

Jumping ahead to subsequent chapters, one can note a symmetry between Euphrates versus Zion and Babylon versus Jerusalem. Babylon first comes out in 14:8 when the eternal gospel is preached. Tracing all mentions of Babylon in chapters 17–18, one finds it not to be a geographic entity, but rather an evil power pervasively corrupting the whole earth. Correspondingly, Jerusalem, the new city that comes down out of heaven in chapter 21 is not a geographic reference, but a symbol of God's rule on earth. Then finally Gog and Magog in chapter 20, as we will see, is a conflation of two disparate entities—even more jarring than Sodom and Egypt before—and do not convey specific geography.

Consider further Revelation's use of direction. Apart from the "east" here in 16:12, the only other cardinal direction found in Revelation is in the New Jerusalem which has four walls each with a gate facing in one of the cardinal compass points (E, N, S, W) in chapter 21. If this city is metaphorical which I will show to be the case, then the orientations of its gates must also be symbolic, to emphasize its continuity with the restored temple of God in Ezek 47:1. Common sense also suggests that when the sun and moon are not needed in the city (21:23), geographic directions are not the point. Indeed, *the "directions" Revelation is more concerned about are "up" and "down"*: John is asked to come up to see the vision, Satan and his cohorts being thrown down to earth and the New Jerusalem coming down from heaven . . . etc. So from all these, we can conclude that *factual geography (place names, cardinal and spatial directions) is not Revelation's concern.*

Could the description of "east," Euphrates, Armageddon, and Babylon in these last two bowls be an exception to the general observation and be real geographic references? Extremely unlikely, since not only would the resonating correspondence between the trumpets and bowls be broken, it would also puncture the cosmic and trans-temporal scope seen throughout Revelation and destroy the intricately designed logic of the narrative.

With the meaning of Euphrates and Babylon clearly understood from biblical events other than geography, "east" and Armageddon (and an earthquake and the hailstones) remain to be explained.

Consistent with how we have determined Revelation's meaning by referring back to the Bible, in particular from Genesis, we find that shortly after humankind fell from grace, east is mentioned twice: 1. God placed an angel to the east of Eden to bar human re-entry after their expulsion (Gen 3:24), and 2. Cain, after his crime against his brother, settled to the east of Eden (Gen 4:16). Now these kings from the east, symbolic descendants of Cain, are marching back towards the place where God has barred them from entering because of their sins.

Apart from showing their defiance of God's ban, these rebels may have a more practical goal in mind—to retake the tree of life in Eden. Expelling humankind from Eden shows God's plan of salvation: "Behold, the man has become like one of Us, *knowing good and evil*; and now, he might stretch out his hand, and take also from the tree of life, and eat, and live forever—therefore the Lord God sent him out from the garden of Eden . . . " (Gen 3:22–23). "Knowing" conveys impregnation since "Now Adam knew Eve his wife, and she conceived and bore Cain" (Gen 4:1a; RSV). Creation would continually be corrupted by sins if sin-impregnated humans are to populate it eternally, hence God's verdict on the sinner that "by the sweat of your face, you shall eat bread, till you return to the ground, because from it you were taken; for you are dust, and to dust you shall return" (Gen 3:19). Through the resurrection of Jesus, only those found worthy will resurrect to inherit the city, thus preventing re-contamination of the world cleansed of sin.

*But the kings from the east want to gate-crash Eden to re-take the tree of life to achieve immortality and to reign eternally over creation without God.* A human paradise excluding God is dreamed up. Such a plan was conceived on the plain of Shinar along the Euphrates and came to fruition in the tower of Babel, symbolized by Babylon. Eden without God, its impossibility notwithstanding, is Babylon. This attempt precipitates the showdown at Armageddon, a strategic plain to the north of Jerusalem, which is symbolic of militarily decisive battles being fought in history. It is also the only geographic name used in Revelation not found in the rest of the Bible. Armageddon also symbolizes the defense of the holy city since Nebuchadnezzar invaded Jerusalem twice through this strategic point, alternatively known as Tel Megiddo. Now in this final battle, before the army of the beast can reach Jerusalem, they have destroyed themselves here in Armageddon. How they self-destruct is elaborated in chapter 17.

After the kings from the east congregate, an unimaginably fearsome earthquake strikes. Since all the bowls are *targeted only at the opposition*, a physical earthquake that destroys the "great city" (Babylon) together with its vassals (scattered "cities of the nations") would have to be geographically spread out, indeed global. Such would claim many victims among the saints (unless the saints are all in one spot), thus negating the focused nature of God's wrath in the bowls.

On the other hand, Jesus' seminal victory on the cross has shattered the opposition to its very core that the ground they relied on is gone: "every island fled away, and the mountains were not found" (20:16; where would Armageddon fit here?). The eternal empire that the kings from the east wish to establish has completely lost its footing in how the authority structure of the cosmos is shaken up (earthquake) through Jesus' resurrection. As such, a theological rather than a geographic understanding makes better sense, as in all cases throughout Revelation.

John knows his scripture well and it does not escape him that Armageddon is not found in the rest of the Bible (Old Testament and the church's teachings that eventually became the New Testament), hence he uniquely introduces it as "the place which in Hebrew is called" (16:16). John could not be introducing his gentile readers to a Jewish place as he could have used Tel-Megiddo directly if that was what he intended. By pointedly conflating two strands—Jewish root (Hebrew) and an ex-biblical geography (Armageddon)—in his presentation, John is repeating in apocalyptic language how Jesus answered the Samaritan woman in his gospel (4:22b-23): "for salvation is from the Jews (Hebrew root). But an hour is coming, and now is, when the true worshipers will worship the Father in spirit and truth (the ex-tradition but decisive element)." The *unprecedented nature of Jesus' resurrection* has, as never before, focused all choices relating to the cosmic struggle on this one point: accept or reject God's ultimate victory in Jesus' resurrection. This singular ex-biblical exception also highlights John's unspoken rule for decryption: read Revelation with only biblical material, rather than outside sources, as background.

Similar to previous targeting, the hailstones that fall are not on creation, but only on people in the beast's kingdom. The fearsome force of nature is now amplified to unnatural proportion—hailstones weighing about a talent each. This weight unit contrasts sharply with the only other weight unit found in Revelation—a denarius (average daily wage, in exchange for a subsistence amount of food (6:6)). Converting this rough weight (about a talent) to familiar modern weight units (about a hundred pounds as in some English translations) is not as meaningful as reading this symbolically from biblical context, as the average wage paid to a worker in silver equivalent over a very long time (ten or more years since a talent weighs more than five thousand denarii). Those who have consistently hoarded up their evil denarius over a very long time without repenting are now paid for their works. Just as Cain was cursed from the ground (Gen 4:10–12), they now receive the curse of nature on their heads.

Both the system (Babylon and the cities of the nations) and individuals (blasphemers who curse rather than repent at the hailstones) have now been judged. Destroying those who destroy the earth is now fait accompli.

Establishing an eternal kingdom by one's own effort or the kingdom of god without God has been the dream of all Babylons. During the last week before his resurrection, Jesus gave the parable of the wicked tenants (Matt 21:33–44) which speaks to such repeated attempts. But Jesus thoroughly obliterates such illusions with his "cornerstone" assertion that what they rejected—Jesus himself—would be the only cornerstone around which the kingdom of God is built. Any other usurpers—every Babylon—would end in a shattering crash. Revelation now teaches the same.

## 9. PHYSIOLOGY OF THE BEAST AND THE MORTAL INTERNAL STRUGGLE (CHAPTER 17)

Revelation divides people according to the camp they belong to: God's or Satan's, with the possibility of the latter joining the former, hence the call for people to forsake Babylon for the Lamb's camp.

Apart from Satan himself, members of his camp are *exhaustively* catalogued in chapter 13: 1. the politico-military beast, 2. the religious beast, and 3. *the masses, marked* 666, who submit themselves to the authority of the two beasts. After chapter 16 describes how God is judging his opponents, the details of how each of the above parties meets its fate are given successively in chapters 18–19. There, the three parties reappear: Babylon in chapter 18 and the beast as two distinct characters in chapter 19 with the second (religious) beast identified explicitly as the false prophet. Here in chapter 17, the overall picture of how these parties go to their destruction is given, just as chapter 12 gives a synopsis of the conflict between God's and Satan's camp to set the scene for the next few chapters.

If the above observation is correct, namely that chapter 17 describes the roles of the members of Satan's camp play in their own judgment, then it is natural to ask whether the three parties in Satan's camp, being exhaustively enumerated in chapter 13, are found in this chapter.

It is easy to identify the obvious—the 7-headed, 10-horned beast is common to both chapters. Also, it is reasonable to equate the people controlled by the beasts in chapter 13 ("And he causes *all*, the small and the great, and the rich and the poor, and the free men and the slaves, to be given a mark on their right hand or on their forehead . . . ") as constituting Babylon in chapter 17 since "the waters which you saw where the harlot

(Babylon) sits, are peoples and multitudes and nations and tongues." Now, where is the second (religious) beast in chapter 17?

While the two beasts are clearly differentiated in chapter 13, the description of the beast(s) in chapter 17 is ambiguous. Three times, the beast is described in different wordings to emphasize the selfsame identity that he "was and is not and will come" (8a, 8b and 11) together with the twice repeated description that he will "go to destruction."

Sandwiched between and also following the above descriptions is the explanation of the seven heads and ten horns on the beast. Yet an enigmatic remark is made: while the heads and horns are explained to be kings, the beast itself is described as "an eighth and is one of the seven" (kings). *The beast is also one of its own heads* as if it is a separate entity from himself! So how are the one beast, seven heads and ten horns put together?

First, what are the heads and horns described in (9–12)? It is stated that the seven *heads are seven kings in time* with the first five passé, the sixth being current and the seventh is yet to come. Interestingly, 13:3 states that *one of the heads* of this beast suffers a fatal wound. Based on context, this head is the politico-military power that was directly struck by Jesus' undeniable resurrection (11:7, 11–13), hence is the political authority of *Jesus' time*—the Roman-Herod-Jewish power. Yet, Revelation never hints at such association, but thereafter describes the whole beast, with all its heads and horns, as having suffered the wound (13:12, 14). Like symbolizing God completing his creative work on the seventh day, the seventh head (king) would be the very last and is completion *in time*. Before that finality every reader now stands, in the time of the sixth king, and at the threshold of the arrival of the seventh. The reader is not meant to identify any of these heads in history, not even the one that directly suffers a fatal wound in Jesus' resurrection. While the "time of arrival" of this seventh head is not given, it is assured the reader that when this head comes, it will not last long (11), in agreement with the rest of Revelation's teaching that evil and the attendant misery will be short-lived (8:1, 10:6, 12:12, 20:10, 17, 19).

Yet another dimension—*power*—is simultaneously brought out. Identified with the coming of the last or seventh king are the ten *horns* (also kings) who have yet to receive a kingdom, but when they each receive a kingdom in future (clearly not one after another, but simultaneously), they will only have one hour to act, again designating a very short period (12). This seventh head stands out from what existed in the five defunct heads and the current sixth by the fact that its power is unprecedented since the other ten kings (horns), each with his own power, all collude together to yield their power to the beast which now manifests himself as the seventh king (13). The number "ten" rather than being arithmetic, symbolizes completeness, i.e., the seventh king is seemingly complete in power, hence can wield totalitarian control. The "kings from the east" that arise from the drying up of the Euphrates (16:12), taking instructions from the three evil spirits, are now organized to battle and replace God on earth. These horns together echo the two beasts' control of the rest of the 666-marked people in chapter 13.

In contrast to the seven heads, the beast *only has three phases in time*— "was, is not and is about to come." In the last quote in (11), this beast to come manifests itself as the last king and is highlighted by the cryptic reference to it *being an eighth king, but is also one of the seven*. This description makes sense only if this eighth king is of a different nature to the previous politico-military animals since the foregoing picture is already cluttered with political players (whether there are nine, ten or eleven horns makes little or no difference as far as political power is concerned)! But if we take this eighth king, who is also *the beast* (11), as a political power which has amalgamated with the religious deceiver in chapter 13, then this passage is portraying an unprecedented alliance of political power with religious authority to form a super entity which is now called the beast proper.

*The two beasts in chapter 13 have now merged into one beast in the fullness of time in chapter 17*. At least, they stand behind a unified façade. No longer does the first beast have a leopard body, bear feet, and lion mouth (13:2) nor the second beast have two horns like a lamb and speak as a dragon (13:11). Here at the threshold of their judgment (go to destruction together), the anti-creator religious and political entities, which are usually separated, manifest themselves as one unified body with the raison d'etre to oppose the Lamb (14). This corresponds to the seventh king (head) which is yet to come. Working backward, the sixth king (current) corresponds to the "is not" phase of the beast while the first five kings to the "was" phase of the beast. John has no interest in doing a historical analysis of the identity of the first five kings, with Revelation being what it says it is, but only to tell the readers where they find themselves now.

What then are the three phases—was, is not and is about to come—of the beast? On the plain of Shinar by the Euphrates when humankind got together to make a different name for themselves by building the tower of Babel and by implication rejected the name God has given them, *then the beast was*. In other words, the beast manifested itself as a unity. When this anti-God alliance of power was shattered by God confusing the tongues of the people, the *beast is not*. It just lurks in the background waiting. But at the appropriate time when the seventh king comes, together with the ten horns (also kings like the heads) conferring their power on the eighth (but also one of the seven since it is also a political body) king, the beast *will have come* again. It has finally manifested itself in all-out opposition to God, as when they built Babylon (the beast was), creating a wonderful spectacle for the people whose names are not in the book of life. These gullible people (Babylon, the harlot who sits on the beast) will wonder how this can come about and believe that they can finally do away with God (13:4). While there is no vacuum in political power (seven kings, or heads, come in succession), the power to *oppose God in unison* has been temporarily neutralized when God confused the tongues of Babel tower's aspirers by the Euphrates, hence the contrast between the "*is not*" (the middle phase) of the beast and the "*one is*" (sixth) among the seven heads.

A picture is given here of an unprecedented evil power yet to come, but this theme of the diabolical plays second fiddle to the main emphasis, which is the *briefness of the beast appearance*, putting it just one small step away from its final destruction. It will receive power for one hour (the first such usage; see section 4.1 of the first reading) and like all the remaining usages of one hour in Revelation (all in the next chapter), this conveys unbelievable rapidity. The beast's *assured rapid destruction* is repeated twice in quick succession in verses 8, 10, 11 & 12. By contrast, its unity in power is mentioned only once in (12–13). The message: by faith in God's providence, there is nothing to fear from this transient and de facto vanquished power to come.

Yet the ending of the beast and Babylon is more interesting than one would expect. All along, the beast is in cohort with Babylon and they belong to the same camp. When faced with God as their one common threat, one would expect a sense of unity, if not love, to prevail within this camp. Such a sense of comradeship is only natural at least until the two devils have fully crossed the bridge, yet it is also very deceptive. John tells us that God is wiser than anything that can be devised in Satan's camp. He has put into their hearts a spirit of tearing at each other's throat to bring about a final mutual destruction within the camp. Indeed, this has been done before for humans' protection when tongues of peoples were confused so that the tower (Babel) that must eventually fall would not destroy the builders. Now in progressing from trumpets to bowls, God has removed his protection and allowed their destructive intent to fester on the confused tongues to bring about the fall of Babylon. This is Babylon's judgment. "Fallen, fallen is Babylon" rings out loud and clear.

Yet, in hindsight, this is not surprising at all: Satan, the father of lies, deceives for the purpose of destroying God's creation through the people acting out his falsehood under the beast(s). While truth leads only towards creative upbuilding and life, deception pricks and cuts in every direction possible to bring destruction to both the deceiver and the deceived. Hence the angel of the abyss is called the destroyer (*Abaddōn* and *Apollyōn*) in the fifth trumpet regardless of culture.

Now a puzzle still remains: while Babylon (the multitude) was subjugated to the two beasts in chapter 13 (forbidding daily transactions without the beasts' stamp), the same multitude is now sitting on the beast as if the beast is just the multitude's workhorse, reversing the master-subject position. This may even cast doubt on my earlier conjecture that the 666-stamped subjugated multitude in chapter 13 is the proud Babylon in chapter 17. Which picture—the multitude controlling the political-religious machine or the opposite—is true? Does Revelation fore-tell an inevitable evolution of the master-subject relationship?

Remember that all these descriptions pertain to happenings *within Satan's camp*. What is the unchanging message Satan is preaching to his followers? "You surely shall not die! For God knows that in the day you eat from it (the tree of the knowledge of good and evil) your eyes will be opened, and you will be like God, knowing good and evil" (Gen 3:4–5). In humans desiring to be like God, the most these creatures of God could achieve is to exclude the consideration of God from different spheres of their lives. There can be no question of fighting against and bringing about the material or factual destruction of God since God is a spirit and all powerful. Only when God took on vulnerable human flesh could the beasts (all humans) be physically fighting against God. Yet in that very conflict, what seems like Satan's victory turns out to be his ultimate undoing and the beginning of the judgment of his kingdom. Needless to say, God has achieved the ultimate success in Jesus' resurrection!

Those in Satan's camp are people who have bought into and are living out this foundational "you will be like God" nonsense of Satan with foregone consequences. God, the ultimate sovereign, by his very essence, is jealous of any pretension to his sovereignty. Only one being can occupy that position and God is rightfully in that position. Vying for god-like supremacy and dominance at all costs (inevitably destructive) must be the favorite game in Satan's camp and would inexorably lead to mutual cannibalization within the politically (ten horns), religiously (eighth king who is also one of the seven), and economically (Babylon) organized, ending in Babylon's downfall. The flip from politico-religious top-down domination in chapter 13 to populace bottom-up domination in chapter 17 is to bring out the insuppressible conflict that would inevitably erupt leading to the implosion of Satan's camp, whether it be the populace destroying the beast or the reverse. Nevertheless, the outcome is never in doubt: *mutual annihilation*. And it is this outcome, and not how history develops, that is the ultimate concern.

How then are we to take the claim that "God has put it in their (members of Satan's camp) hearts to execute his purpose by having a common purpose, and by giving their kingdom to the beast, until the words of God should be fulfilled" in bringing about the destruction of Babylon? Is it God's work or a natural consequence of people wanting to be God? The answer is that they are two sides of the same coin. By the very nature of God's design, people claiming to be God will destroy each other. Viewed holistically, this is also God's work. These same two aspects can be seen in the confusion of tongues at Babel: humans wanting to be the sovereign cannot accommodate other self-claimed sovereigns and will eventually lead to conflict; but this is no less God confusing their tongues.

When the tongues of Babel builders were confused, God was protecting his people from self destruction (first episode of the sixth trumpet) and eventually brought in true harmony and unity under the Lamb in chapter 14 with one new song for all. By opposing God, people in Satan's camp are *abandoned to their own violent devices* driven further by their exclusion of each other.

Schematizing the above understanding is figure 1.

To complete our analysis, let us try to decipher the "seven hills" and the mind of wisdom needed to grasp the prophecy.

Rome is built on seven hills. Revelation, now in explaining the heads on the beast, identifies them with seven hills. One's gut reaction is thus to link the beast geographically to Rome. Yet immediately, Revelation adds another dimension which cannot be pigeon-holed by geography—time. These hills are also kings, with the first five defunct and the sixth now reigning. Then are readers to take it that five hills of Rome have physically disappeared? Of course not! Yet, this is neither the first nor the last time Revelation has put together two entities of disparate nature (here enduring hills and transient kings) to convey something universal in scope, e.g., Sodom and Egypt in chapter 11 and, as we shall see, Gog and Magog in chapter 20. John is using hills to signify enormous political power and seven for completion in time (i.e., throughout history) to describe the universal dominance of the earthly and ever-present Satanic power represented by the beast(s). Rome's seven hills are just an ex-biblical coincidence which must not distract from our so-far-successful Bible-first approach to interpretation.

That being the case, the wisdom called for now makes sense. Wisdom in the Bible always emanates from God, as Proverbs makes abundantly clear (1:7). It cuts through all the technical complications to arrive at the straightforward essence of a matter that is *the concern of God, hence also to those who fear him*. Understanding "666" is the first call for wisdom in Revelation. Contrary to the esoteric numerologies to calculate which historical person this number may represent, 666 straightforwardly means that the political, religious, and economic spheres cannot enter the ultimate Sabbath which is the *main concern of God*. Such is also in perfect agreement with the context.

God has one over-ridding concern in the history taken up in Revelation. When the judgments in the seven thunders are cancelled in the second episode of the sixth trumpet, the angel has to swear to God that there will be no further delay (10:6). From God's perspective (the angle of wisdom), he wants evil to be eliminated without delay. Wise is thus the mind who sees through the vicissitude of history and global affairs (seven hills, heads, horns, was, is not, to come . . . etc.) that the temporary collusion of diabolical powers in whatever guises will not endure. They remain but one hour, for only a short while, and will speed directly to destruction. This insight (wisdom) is repeated for emphasis. God's Sabbath will arrive sooner than one expects.

Indeed, *by identifying the present as the "time" of the sixth king (one is living), John puts all his readers in the "ever present," always at the threshold of the coming of the seventh king.*

**Figure 1. The Beast(s) in Biblical Perspective.**

|  | Players in the Background | Manifestation throughout Creation's History | | |
|---|---|---|---|---|
|  |  | **Beginning (Genesis)** | **Present (Gen–Rev)** | **End (Revelation)** |
| God | 'came down to see the city and the tower which the sons of men had built' (Ge 11:5) | 'And God blessed Noah and his sons and said to them, "Be fruitful and multiply, and fill the earth.' (9:1) | 'the Lord scattered them abroad from there over the face of the whole earth' (Ge 11:8a) | 'These will hate the harlot and will ... burn her up with fire. For God has put it in their hearts to execute His purpose' (16, 17) |
| Forms of the Beast | 7 heads / 10 horns – political beast in time and power | 'let us build for ourselves a city, and a tower whose top will reach into heaven' (11:4a) | 'and they stopped building the city' (Ge 11:8b) | 'And the whole earth was amazed and followed after the beast...' (13:3b) |
|  | colluding to gain power | '*was*' = 1st to 5th kings  United political and religious power to build the Tower of Babel | '*is not*' = 6th king  Factious political and religious powers | '*to come*' = 7th king + 10 kings, one purpose: give their **power** and **authority** to the beast' (13) |
|  | Religious beast / false prophet, with two horns and speaks like the dragon | 'let us make for ourselves a name, otherwise we will be scattered abroad over the face of the whole earth' (11:4b) | '... Babel, because there the Lord confused the language of the whole earth' (Ge 11:9a) | '10 kings who have not yet received a kingdom, but they receive **authority** as kings with the beast for 1 hour' (12) |
| Relation | innately hostile | Support | Subjugate | Open hatred |
| Babylon – Harlot | 'peoples and multitudes and nations and tongues' (Re 17:15) | 'Now the whole earth used the same language and the same words' (Ge 11:1) | 'no one will be able to buy or to sell, except the one who has the mark... of the beast...' (Re 13:17) | 'she glorified herself and lived sensuously' (18:7a) |

## 10. THREE-WAY SPLIT OF BABYLON EXPLAINED

### 10.1 Downfall of Babylon (chapter 18)

Following the exotic and gory symbols we have encountered so far, the description of Babylon's activities in chapter 18, by comparison, comes out as very mundane and even benign and peaceful.

For the first and only time in the New Testament, one group of people (merchants) and their range of activities (commercial transaction) are elaborated extensively. Five times are merchants mentioned in the New Testament with four times in this chapter (3, 11, 15, 23). An alternate description—"every shipmaster and every passenger and sailor, and as many as make their living by the sea" (19)—gives even more prominence to merchants here. By contrast, the familiar political power—kings—is mentioned twice (3, 9) and only as spectators and collaborators. Further elaboration of these merchants' influence is their wealth and how others have grown rich through them (13, 15, 17, 19). As if these are not enough to show them off, even the commodities they trade are detailed (12–13). These include not only luxurious items (gold, silver, precious stones . . . etc.), but religious goods (incense, frankincense), full range of livelihood consumptions (wine . . . wheat, cattle, and sheep), military hardware (horses and chariots), and even the immoral (slaves and human lives). Right or wrong, nothing that can enrich these merchants through trading is off limits to them.

The way Babylon comes to her end is also detailed: "become a dwelling place of demons and a prison of every unclean spirit, and a prison of every unclean and hateful bird" (2); "her plagues will come, pestilence and mourning and famine, and she will be burned up with fire" (8); "no one buys their cargoes any more" (11); "the fruit you long for has gone from you, and all things that were luxurious and splendid have passed away from you and men will no longer find them" (14); "great wealth has been laid waste" (17, 19). Her end would come quite swiftly and unexpectedly—in one hour or one day (8, 10, 17, 19; note in table 2 that three of the four mentions of "one hour" and the only mention of "one day" in Revelation are all used here to describe Babylon's swift demise). To illustrate the completeness of her end, an angel likens it to a millstone dumped violently into the sea. Needless to say, when the commercial activities stop, the genteel niceties that these support would likewise cease, but here this inevitability is not taken for granted, but emphasized—"And the sound of harpists and musicians and flute-players and trumpeters will not be heard in you any longer; and no craftsman of any craft will be found in you any longer; and the sound of a mill will not be heard in you any longer; and the light of a lamp will not shine in you any longer; and the voice of the bridegroom and bride will not be heard in you any longer" (22, 23).

This time, Babylon's end is final. The evil trapped in her is final; her desire is forever frustrated; her practices will never ever be revived; she will never be rebuilt.

But what are the sins of Babylon that deserve such an ignominious end? None other than all the sins committed by humankind throughout all the ages, for "in her was found the blood of prophets and of saints and of *all who have been slain on the earth.*" Yet this deepens the mystery further: How can seemingly non-violent trading be responsible for these wicked murders of all times? Or has this passage succumbed to irredeemable hyperbole?

The answer is in (7): "To the degree that she glorified herself and lived sensuously, to the same degree give her torment and mourning; for she says in her heart, "I sit as a queen and I am not a widow, and will never see mourning."" Such is reinforced by her being described as a harlot. In the Bible, another description is sometimes confused with prostitution: adultery. Two distinct Greek words are used for these two types. An adulterer(ess) (*moichalis*) has pledged total devotion to a lover through marriage, but then decided to shift the original love to another person (Rom 7:3). Idolatry is the spiritual counterpart of adultery. But the voluntary professional prostitute (*pornē*, 17:1, 5, 15, 16, 19:2) has no such first love. She frowns on adultery. She *loves only herself and does everything to advance her position.* Fornication (*porneuō*, 14:8, 17:2, 18:3, 9, 19:2) is her game through which she corrupts the world. In the end, she glorifies herself and nothing else (persons or things, material or spiritual). Babylon is not an *adulteress,* but *a harlot.*

Babylon would stop at nothing to be the supreme being. To support her ascendency to that supreme position, military and religious forces are just the means. Aggrandizing herself and pretending to be all in all through enrichment of all kinds is the goal. That is why she sits on the beast like riding on a horse—her beast of burden. In her has the lie of Satan, first accepted by Eve and Adam, come to full fruition. This queen does not lament widowhood despite having no king, but rejoices in her seeming eternal invincibility and glory.

In her reckless and ruthless strife to live out Satan's original lie—"you surely will not die! For God knows that in the day you eat from it your eyes will be opened, and you will be like God, knowing good and evil" (Gen 3:4b–5)—she has claimed victims after victims such that all the sins humankind has ever committed can be accounted to her "being-God" illusion, and appropriately so, to the exclusion of every other thing or creature since a god brooks no equal or opposition. In her, the goal of Satan—to destroy—is fully lived out. *Nothing more destructive is the pursuit of humans pretending to be God.*

But even on the eve of Babylon's destruction—God "destroying those who destroy the earth" (11:18)—the call is made for people to come out of Babylon (4), echoing the corollary of the eternal gospel preached by the saints in chapter 14, and apparently many do, since "the earth was illumined with his (the angel coming down from heaven) glory" (1). And despite the violent image of a millstone being hurled down, Babylon ends "*because no one buys their cargoes any more*" (11) rather than being defeated militarily. The *great* (*megas*) city (2, 10, 16, 18, 19, 21) which has laid up *great* wealth (17) is now lamented by former *great* men (23)—merchants of earth who deserted her after the angel with *great* authority (1) illuminates the earth. All the self-claimed greatness of Babylon is totally laid waste, a great waste! Those who refuse to take the side of the victor are forever trapped in the *great* city turned *great* prison. The *great* city in which the two witnesses (Jesus) were murdered (11:8) is no more.

Regardless of what precipitated Babylon's downfall, pride has a way of blinding the eyes to all imminent dangers, thus setting up a sudden (in one hour) and spectacular fall.

In one way, Babylon represents all the people who do not acknowledge the creator God, even those constituting the beasts, for they are also of human origin. John is saying clearly that *no one in Satan's camp* can escape the judgment of Babylon.

About seven centuries before Revelation, Ezek 26:1—28:19 prophesied the destruction of a historical city, Tyre, through the action of Nebuchadnezzar, king of Babylon. Many of the broad features—trading through merchants plying the sea made the city fabulously rich and inordinately prideful; her destruction is final and she is never to be rebuilt; those who got rich through her bemoaning her downfall . . . etc.—are common to John's description of Babylon here. Clearly, John has recycled the content of Ezekiel for his description here. From that standpoint, one can legitimately ask: what has Ezekiel's prophecy contributed to the details of our understanding of Revelation here? The answer: only as one demonstration among many. Babylon in Revelation is global, but Tyre in Ezekiel is local; Babylon is still extant, but Tyre is defunct. This is yet another clear example of how Revelation's symbols should not be yoked to Old Testament prophecies (e.g., "time, times and half a time" in Daniel) which have a very different context and have already been fulfilled. On the contrary, Tyre can be taken as *a Babylon that has fallen*, and as such, one of the numerous Babylons in the past, present and future that must fall miserably. Babylon in Revelation is a general description of the oppositions to the sovereign creator.

## 10.2 Celebration and Judgment of the Beasts (chapter 19)

After the son of man and an angel are seen harvesting the earth at the end of chapter 14, the wrath of God having finished in the seven bowls in chapter 16 with elaboration of the spiritual/moral dynamics that brought down Babylon in chapters 17–18, attention is now refocused on the camp of the Lamb in chapter 19. Appropriately, this starts with a worship scene in heaven, the last in Revelation.

The first heavenly worship scene is in chapters 4–5 with two episodes, each narrated in a chapter. In the first episode, God the creator is praised for his creation. In the second, the Lamb is praised for taking a seven-seal scroll out of the hand of the one sitting on the throne which sets off a series of actions leading eventually to the harlot's judgment. The last worship scene of Revelation here caps such actions of the Lamb. The worshippers respond in praises for his judgment. Such praises are simultaneously universal ("for He has judged the great harlot who was corrupting the earth with her immorality"—earth here means God's creation and is a fitting end to 11:18 where God promises to judge those who destroy the earth) and personal ("He has avenged the blood of His bond-servants on her"). Importantly, it is also permanent and irreversible: "Her smoke rises up forever and ever." Yet unlike in the first worship scene when the praises were led by the elders and living creatures which then spread concentrically outward, to the multitude of people, then to all of creation, the praises here are started by the multitude in heaven to be echoed by the elders and living creatures. The *order of worship is reversed* and all the other non-sentient creatures in creation have been left out. Why?

Two complementary answers are: 1. the actions the Lamb initiates from the throne of God is only completed by the multitude who follows him everywhere, hence the praises of this completion appropriately arise from this spontaneous multitude; and 2. the worship by all creation, sentient or otherwise (see end of section 3.2 of this reading), in the first worship scene still awaits its material completion in the last two chapters (21–22) of Revelation. But the announcement of this still-to-come completion is now made in advance: the marriage of the Lamb.

Holy and otherworldly the bride may seem, she is nonetheless clothed with the downright mundane: "righteous acts of the saints" (8). These are symbolized by the "fine linen, bright and clean" given to her. Yet consistent with 7:14 ("*they have washed their robes* and made them white in the blood of the Lamb"), people not only receive, but also participate in working out their salvation. With God's empowerment, the saints have now responded to God's overture with their own righteous acts which are also considered God's righteousness.

As if John has not been excited enough by all that go on before, the Lamb's marriage announcement dazzles him so much that he mistakes the messenger as a rightful object of worship—an absolute "no" for a Jew. He is promptly redirected by the announcer. This marriage of the Lamb, the hope of all history, is in a class of its own when it comes to exciting and warming the human heart.

Before the arrival of the bride, the groom shows off his many credentials. In a few short verses (11–16) is summarized the many previous allusions to his nature and his works which set him apart from his followers: By nature, he is multi-dimensional (many diadems on his head), faithful and true, penetratingly discerning (flaming eyes), exclusively self-knowing (a name known only to himself). From all these is revealed the Word of God which now descends to intersect and interact with humankind, resulting in the Lamb judging and waging war in righteousness, being clothed with a robe dipped in blood; striking the nations with a sharp sword from his mouth while ruling them with a rod of iron; and bringing about the fierce wrath of God as in treading grapes in a winepress. He rides on a triumphant white horse, and so do his followers who are also garbed in purity (fine linen white and clean). The result of his position and works is that he is fittingly the King of kings and Lord of lords.

When Revelation debuts its white horse, it is called forth by the breaking of the first seal in chapter 6. Destructive conquering ensues, as we infer from the context. But the Lamb striking the nation and his rod-of-iron rule here proceed not from humans' physical weaponry which destroys, and has to be repeated because of ineffectiveness and tit-for-tat response, but from the Word of God that proceeds from the mouth of the slain Lamb. The four destructive and violent horses unleashed by perverted human nature in the first four seals are now conquered peacefully once and for all by this supreme horseman and his army on white horses. The 144,000 mentioned twice before (chapters 7 and 14) are not just idle worshippers, but revealed to be *determined yet peaceful followers of the peaceful Lamb here*.

The way the Lamb wages war is not mentioned until now in this final tier of revelation in chapter 19. Peeling back the apparent reason for Babylon's destruction to reveal the core, one encounters the fundamental or bedrock reason for the defeat of Satan's camp—the Word of God. The life of Jesus embodies, materializes and epitomizes the Truth. Since falsehood grates against the Truth, the defeat of untruth comes through its self-contradiction and resulting internal disharmony. It is just a matter of time. Purely and simply, the Truth kills falsehood.

After the elimination of Babylon, a great supper is prepared for the arrival of the bride. How is the supper prepared? Simply by defeating the beasts-populace alliance formed under Satan which has the satanic temerity to make war with God. From the context, *this human-divine conflict is by nature different from the intra-human conflict narrated in the sixth trumpet and bowl.* The latter involves physical violence on each other whereas the former the overcoming of falsehood with truth. Eliminating the power-center (beast) and its support (deceiving false prophet which is the second beast in chapter 13) is the first step: "these two were thrown alive into the lake of fire which burns with brimstone." The second step, by sharp contrast, involves the majority making up the alliance being *killed* with the sword, leaving much human and horse flesh to be devoured. But reinforcing the peaceful theme to the end, this sword comes not from the powerful arm of the Lord, but from his mouth! It is the truth of God preached by the Lamb's army, not violent coercion as prevalent in Satan's camp, that finally defeats and consumes the opposition.

Birds flying in mid-heaven are now called to the feast of God which serves human and horse flesh in abundance! In 8:13 and 14:6, flying in mid-heaven are an eagle and an angel proclaiming woes and an eternal gospel to those in Satan's camp on earth. The same people in heaven who reach out as far as they can to the enemy camp on earth are now, described as birds, blessed because they have been invited to the great supper of the Lamb. They are now rewarded for their effort. But are we to understand this supper as a cannibalistic orgy of exacting a vendetta as it may seem at first glance? Not if we care to trace the emphasis on peaceful means running through Revelation. Rather, claiming as rightful spoil all that is valuable in the enemy's camp as in an ancient battle is the imagery employed here. Paul also employs a similar metaphor in Eph 4:7–8 ("But to each one of us grace was given according to the measure of Christ's gift. Therefore it says, "When He ascended on high, He led captive a host of captives, And He gave gifts to men.""). Using their God-given talents, even those in Satan's camp have discovered and invented uncountable "good" things (including science and technologies represented by the domesticated horse) that were put to deplorable use for self-glorification (in Babylon) to serve the purpose of the beasts and Satan. Now all these goods are taken over by God's birds for building up God's creation, as originally intended.

## 10.3 A Précis of God's History and Satan's Downfall (chapter 20)

Chapter 20 opens into four parts:

1. Satan imprisonment for one thousand years; his necessary release for a little while (1–3);
2. The first resurrection; a one thousand-year reign with Christ (4–6);

3. Satan's release for a short while and its aftermath; Satan's and the opposition's fate (7–10);

4. Every human judged before a great white throne according to the book of life (11–15).

As noted in the first reading, all (six times) the counted (always by one thousand) years in Revelation occur here within six verses (2–7; one in each verse).

In this chapter, Satan is the only clearly identifiable character left in his camp after all his underlings have perished. As clarified in chapter 13, Satan has delegated his authority to the two beasts and to those who do not resist the mark of the beast on themselves. Yet he remains as the spiritual puppet master, hence on a different plane to the visible politico-religious activities of the two beasts and their followers. How then is this deceiver-cum-accuser being dealt with?

Any understanding of this chapter must fully account for its extraordinary drabness relative to all the other chapters in the book. Such a consistent style is *deliberately taken* to convey an important message. The lack of colors, details, and nuance in chapter 20 (section 4.1 of the first reading) gives us a sense that the description is a super-narrative in which the events and characters can be seen as *transcending* usual mundane chronology, though the order of the happenings is never inverted, thus preserving cause and effect. Indeed, many of the previous "durations" are already narrated from the higher creational/Sabbatical timescales which do not conform to our modern time accounting methods (e.g., 1,260 days, 42 months, 3.5 days, 5 months . . . etc.). Through these timescales, many characters take on transtemporal dimensions (e.g., the two witnesses, the woman giving birth to a male child, the saints, the two beasts, the dragon . . . etc).

As we have seen in chapter 11, the Sabbatical timescales place Jesus at the center of the long span of creation's history, splitting all of history into two halves. Yet, even at this level of narration, Jesus is simultaneously the two witnesses as well as the male child born of the woman who will rule the nations with a rod of iron. Standing at the center of history because of his resurrection, Jesus is also active throughout history from beginning to end, as he himself stated factually in response to Jewish Sabbath's restrictions: "My Father is working until now, and I Myself am working" (John 5:17). From *this vantage point that is even higher than the Sabbatical timescale*, the distinctions between the Old and New Testaments (e.g., Lion of the tribe of Judah versus the Lamb; song of Moses versus that of the Lamb; the twelve tribes of Israel versus the multitude; the destroyer's name in Hebrew versus that in Greek . . . etc.) are no longer evident and *all history is seen as one unbroken and consistent dealing of God who works in Jesus* since he is indisputably the creator of all things, and through his death and resurrection, has also secured for himself the authority to become the prime mover and focal point of history. As such, all those who have followed God, from Abel who was murdered by his brother Cain, but who nevertheless still speaks to us through his blood (Hebrew 11:4), to the many prophets who have been persecuted, to the saints that are still to be slain (described in the fifth seal) are seen as beheaded for following the same Jesus (compare 6:9–11 with 20:4). Just as the Sabbatical timescale transcends natural times punctuated by our planet's position around the sun, the timescale of God and Jesus as active and consistent workers throughout history, that is the *cosmic timescale*, further transcends the Old versus New Testament demarcation. If in this time-accounting approach, even the most exciting and pivotal event of history, namely Jesus' death and resurrection, is transcended and understood as the ever-effective motivating force, the "events" represented therein must necessarily be stripped of the details that would otherwise be apparent on a finer scale description. Such is the perspective of chapter 20. Only *"generic events"* would be recorded. Significantly, the many epithets ascribed to Jesus in previous chapters are now uniformly and plainly replaced by Christ (4, 6).

Revelation's description of its central figure is interestingly nuanced for three levels. This central figure is Jesus Christ. *John only uses this two-word term in the introduction* (1:1, 2, 5). Thereafter, each word is used singularly. At the personal level, "Jesus" predominates as the subject of our faith and is the one the saints, in their perseverance, can relate to through his testimony (1:9, 12:17, 14:12, 17:6, 19:10, 20:4). Then in the very end, this singular Jesus, for the first and last time in Revelation, speaks directly to the churches, eliciting John's call for Jesus' speedy return and a blessing in his name (22:16, 20, 21). In these instances, Jesus is who he was on earth and continues to be present among his followers, rather than the figure involved in cosmic action.

Above this personal level, the Jesus in action is never described by his explicit name—Jesus or Christ. Rather he is the Lamb opening the seals on the scroll in God's hand and guiding the saints to the springs of the water of life; the two witnesses prophesying and who died and resurrected; the male infant targeted for death by Satan but who will rule the nations with a rod of iron; the Lamb leading the saints on Mount Zion; the son of man harvesting the earth with the angels; the rider on a white horse smiting the nations and treading God's winepress . . . etc.

At the highest or divine level, the other singular name "Christ" is only used three times and always with extending God's authority over his world. First, "the kingdom of our God and the authority of His Christ have come"

(12:10) after Satan has been thrown down to earth. *The last two times occur in quick succession here in 20:4 & 6 when Christ reigns with the resurrected for a thousand years.* "Reign" (*basileuō*) used here emphasizes regal authority while the act of ruling (*poimainō*) elsewhere (12:5, 19:15) speaks of the kind action of feeding and caring. Here, Christ is described as reigning by virtue of his divine status while Jesus rules with his actions. This reign occurs on a higher plane than where action is seen.

Previously, Revelation has narrated creation's history starting from the beginning. After God's creation, humans were supposed to be reigning over creation with the majesty of the lion in relation to other animals, but what follows in the first seal necessitates repeated conquering (a perverted form of ruling). Yet with Jesus' resurrection, this lost regal authority has been restored, not only to Christ, but to all those who have suffered persecution for God (beheaded) in the fifth seal, so much so that they are seen as reigning with Christ all along. Dead or alive, *they are exerting their influence* throughout human history (4: "Then I saw thrones, and they sat on them, and judgment was given to them") despite their transience in human time-accounting, just as Jesus Christ is still seen as working actively in history despite his humanly short appearance on earth (~33 years) and even shorter public ministry (~3 years). These dead saints do not participate in the day-to-day administration of the world. How they have responded faithfully to God in their lives would constitute a judgment on future generations (Matt 12:41–42; Luke 11:31–32). Even now, Jesus is reigning in the lives of the believers, surrounded by a great cloud of witnesses throughout history (Heb 12:1). Yet the righteous deeds of these witnesses would have come to nil had ultimate evil not been decisively vanquished, and death not been dealt the irreversible fatal blow by Jesus in his resurrection. But since their testimonies in history have been accepted by God, *their deeds have now been assimilated into Jesus' work. Consequently, they also share in Jesus' resurrection or symbolically seen as having resurrected with Christ.* As such, they become first fruits of Jesus' resurrection, which is the first resurrection. Their eternal destiny has been sealed and secured in Christ and nothing further can alter that fact; the death that comes to some people—the second death based on judgment without Jesus' intervening mercy—will no longer alter that in the universal judgment before the great white throne (5b–6a: "This is the first resurrection. Blessed and holy is the one who has a part in the first resurrection; over these the second death has no power"). John is using symbols to recast the teaching in his Gospel (5:24): "Truly, truly, I say to you, he who hears My word, and believes Him who sent Me, has eternal life, *and does not come into judgment, but has passed out of death into life.*"

This trans-generational description has been used before with the two witnesses in chapter 11 where they represent all the many witnesses for God from the time of Adam to the time of Jesus, but are then taken up by Jesus in his resurrection. These myriads of witnesses for God can then be seen as having resurrected with Jesus to join the whole body of witnesses throughout history, now depicted as reigning with Christ for one thousand years.

Thus is the majestic heavenly worship scene—"You have made them to be a kingdom and priests to our God; and they *will reign upon the earth*" (5:10)—realized in down-to-earth history.

Since the time God pronounced judgment on Satan, represented by the serpent, that he would move on his belly and eat dust (no longer at eye-level with humans to deceive—Gen 3:14), Satan has been restrained, as if by a great chain and imprisoned in the bottomless abyss. Of course, Satan is not idle ever since. The seed of deception he planted in Eve and Adam has eventually brought forth the beasts and Babylon. He still works by delegating his authority to the beast(s) and as such he is sometimes seen as working in history himself, e.g., pursuing the woman and trying to devour her child in chapter 12, but in this high-level cosmic narrative of chapter 20, he is just the dragon who is continuously restrained by God shortly after creation for a very long time—one thousand years. People infected by Satan's lies (fifth trumpet) still run a camp to train adherents in the art of deception, accusation and destruction in chapter 13, but Satan himself is severely circumscribed. One must not lose sight of the intention the one thousand years convey: *God's continuous restraint of Satan to protect humankind.*

For us humans, the one thousand years is to be appreciated through God's assurance—Satan is bound for a long time, but will be released for only a short time. But how short? Remember the shortest time unit in Revelation is "hour" (Babylon is destroyed in one short hour!) and half an hour is mentioned in the seventh seal during which heaven was silent (8:1) which can be taken to mean that the ultimate completion with God judging the world (later on associated with seven) has not arrived, but God is taking very swift action to include all his creation in his work. This "short while" which is meant as a sharp contrast to the "thousand years" can then be understood as even shorter than this shortest definite "duration" of half an hour. In other words, it is unbelievably short, *hence Satan's temptation is bearable and can be resisted with patience.*

Then why *must* Satan be released? Destroying him right in his abyss would wreak much less havoc on earth and from that perspective much more desirable. Yet, if Satan is to be effectively defeated, Satan's very lies that our first parents bought into must be exposed and disbelieved by the descendents of Adam and Eve who have now found a new champion in

Jesus Christ. If the *rule of the game is such that human decisions determine the win-lose outcome*, then the game has to proceed to its end with humans choosing between the intimate experience of good or the first-hand encounter with evil according to what God instructed them about the tree of the knowledge of good and evil (Gen 2:16–17). In the first round, humans chose to disobey God and brought about undeniable and unavoidable experience of evil on themselves and all of creation. In Jesus' resurrection, another possibility is opened up. Choosing to follow Jesus would bring the inalienable experience of goodness on the decision maker. Such would radiate out and percolate down to all of creation because the one charged with ruling over creation has aligned his/her choice with that of the creator. As such, making the choice is unavoidable. Humans would be better off passing the test than never having been tested. That is why Jesus teaches us to pray that we not fail the test rather than avoid the test—"Lead us not *into* temptation, but deliver us from evil."

But choice is meaningless without a real alternative. If Satan is to be defeated this time around while the rule of the game has not changed, humans must make the choice to follow or reject Satan in the light of Jesus' triumph. There is thus no alternative but to let Satan play his trick one more time. Satan *must* still have the freedom to deceive and have his deception rejected for Jesus' victory to be complete.

In this cosmic timescale, even those who had made a decision for the creator before Jesus' historic resurrection, i.e., in Old Testament times, are seen to be included in Jesus' resurrection, hence they have also resurrected.

Let us now jump ahead with the narration before returning to figure out what that cosmic showdown means.

If chapter 20 is intended to convey generic and trans-temporal truth, why then is there *a seemingly specific reference to "Gog and Magog"*? Yet on closer inspection, this points to the exact opposite of being specific. Both Gog and Magog are on the very fringe of familiar biblical personage and geography. Gog and Magog trace their first and only usage to Ezek 38 and 39 where a prince (Gog) hailing from a place (Magog—"the remotest part of the North") is prophesied to conceive the evil thought of attacking Israel, God's beloved, with an inter-national/inter-racial coalition. Gog will eventually be annihilated by God. This final act will be established as a memorial for those who intend to destroy God's beloved. Major elements of this event are used to illustrate the final showdown between God and his opposition here in chapter 20. But "Gog and Magog" here is fundamentally different from their first use in Ezekiel: Gog *the person* and Magog *the place* are lumped together unnaturally which are described as "in the four corners of the earth." As opposed to differentiating between a specific person and his where about, the two separate symbols, Gog and Magog, are merged into one to convey people everywhere generically. This conclusion is further clinched by their target: "they . . . surrounded the camp of the saints and the beloved city." To the extent that the camp of the saints cannot be confined geographically and by time (since true saints must always have gone to every corner of the world to preach to all nations, Matt 28:18–20), Gog and Magog cannot refer to any specific locations or persons, but "they came up on the broad plain of the earth" (which broad plain?) as if they appear everywhere out of nowhere.

Could this Gog and Magog "coalition" come together at a specific time, that is, during the "short time" when Satan is released, to precipitate one apocalyptic universal confrontation? This is highly unlikely, given the flow of the whole chapter. The people being judged before the great white throne should include those besieging the camp of the saints. Every dead person (great and small, in the sea, and death and Hades itself (13)) is summoned before God (according to physical birth registries—books (12)). Progression of thought suggests that these are the same people besieging the saints' camp. It goes without saying that all these deaths have happened throughout the vast expanse of time since creation and are thus generic rather than specific to a certain period, strongly indicating that the Gog and Magog "coalition" is the mass of rebellious humanity scattered in creation's time and space.

Gog and Magog besieging the camp of the saints is thus the cosmic metaphor corresponding to the great tribulation that the saints are seen to be coming out of in the sixth seal.

If this is the proper meaning of "Gog and Magog," then how do we take Satan's deception? On the surface, the passage reads like a final one-off momentous showdown between Satan and God through their representatives—the nations being deceived ganging up against the camp of the saints and the beloved city. Yet the generic description adopted throughout this chapter points to a different perspective: this showdown is played out in the life of each individual throughout history rather than at a definitive universal moment ahead of history's consummation. *Though "nations" were mentioned early on, it is the individuals rather than the nations that are judged according to their deeds in the very end (11–15).* As noted in section 4.1 of our first reading, the Greek word *kairos*, which means appointed and historic time or moment, is used throughout Revelation except in three places where *chronos*, indicating linear time, is used instead. Deliberately using *chronos* here not only indicates complete freedom in making a choice (God has not appointed or determined the moment), but also points to non-orchestrated events (any time would be appropriate). Such an interpretation is further corroborated by comparing 12:12 where Satan is described as "knowing that he has only a *short time*" (*kairos*) with the *short time* (*chronos*) here: Satan's time for work is definitely short because of Jesus' definitive victory, but how one responds to the short temptation of Satan during his/her life on this earth is open to each person and *not determined by God*. Had the showdown been meant to convey a cosmically decisive moment, *kairos would most definitely have been used*. Accordingly, the "thousand years" takes on an additional meaning: a flexible duration appropriate to the person's situation. The thousand years end for a person when he/she has to be tempted by Satan to make a decision (in this instant—a short time) for or against God, just as Jesus was tempted three times in the wilderness by Satan before he started his public ministry, and again through Peter who tried to dissuade him from bearing the cross in Jerusalem (Matt 4:1–11; Luke 4:1–13; Matt 16:22–23).

Yet the "thousand years" of each individual making up the torrent of history also constitutes the cosmic thousand years. From this cosmic perspective, the "thousand years" would signify a very long period, or a humanly unattainable period (given the Bible record of longevity is held by Methuselah who lived short of one thousand years—969, Gen 5:27) to put each of us in our place in history. Such a "period" can be understood to correspond to the previous timescales of 2×1,260 days which are equivalent to 2×42 months which are also equivalent to 3.5 days + time, times and half a time, depending on whose perspective (saints', opposition's or God's) is in view.

The two perspectives of the thousand years converge in this: our individual decisions for or against the creator (and conversely Satan) take on cosmic proportion when Satan's final doom is brought about by our collective individual rejections of his lies after Jesus exposes these lies in his resurrection. Because of the generic nature of the descriptors (1,000, a little) and units (year, *chronos*), one size can and does fit all.

Then the dead were judged according to another book (of life (12)) which records their deeds, again regardless when and where these were done. Here, nothing, not even earth and heaven, can shelter humans from the all-discerning God (11), in a direct response to the naïve who call upon the mountains and rocks to fall on them to shield them from God's wrath (6:15). This metaphor does not mean the end of the material world. Also, in the sixth seal, God has not pronounced a judgment on these naïve wreckers of his creation. Now he has.

Death and resurrection are mentioned here, and the context seems to imply that there are two or more of each, but interestingly, only a first resurrection and a second death are directly mentioned; a first death or a second resurrection are not! Those who were beheaded for Christ are not described as dead, but have participated in the first resurrection. Those dead whom the sea, death, and Hades eventually toss up are not described as having first died and resurrected but simply put before the great white throne. Here, the foci of those two terms—first resurrection and second death—seem to have been singly reserved for what matters: one's final position, either reigning with Christ in the first resurrection which will continue or in the lake of fire which is the second death.

Since both those for or against God have died and none has resurrected since Jesus' resurrection, John is under no illusion that some believers would bodily come back to live to reign with Christ before the final judgment. Consistent with his symbolic description right from the beginning of Revelation, John has portrayed how our righteous deeds for Christ are not in vain throughout the long history of creation. Such is the cosmic version of his previous assertion and assurance to believers in the Lord: "Write, "Blessed are the dead who die in the Lord from now on!" "Yes," says the Spirit, "so that they may rest from their labors, for *their deeds follow with them.*"" (14:13). Not only are New Testament believers the beneficiaries of Jesus' victory, but those who seemed to have perished before seeing the triumph of righteousness over evil are now also taken up in Jesus' pan-ultimate triumph. A bodily resurrection literally one thousand years (or some definite duration) before the final judgment is not taught here.

Let us entertain, just for argument's sake, that these people have indeed bodily resurrected one thousand years before the final judgment and not just metaphorically through their past witnessing. The question then is whether these will still have to stand before God's great white (pure) throne for judgment? Note that the passage does not say that the dead have resurrected to stand trial, rather "the *dead*, the great and the small, *standing* before the throne" (12); "the sea gave up the dead which were in it, and death and Hades gave up the dead which were in them; and they were judged, *every one . . .* " (13). Unmistakable is the universal sense that everyone *without exception* will be judged, as is also asserted by Paul, emphatically even for believers (Rom 14:10–12; 2 Cor 5:10). Remember also that this judgment passage is set in the pan-historical perspective of chapter 20. If these beheaded had been rewarded with bodily resurrection before the final judgment, then they would have short-circuited the final judgment, contradicting its universal scope. Then the books recording humans' deeds and the book of life would be incomplete. Yet 14:13 quoted above promises not a bodily resurrection before the final judgment, but a rest that would see one's life work being affirmed.

In the end, Revelation, and indeed the whole Bible, allows no special passage to a blissful eternity even for those beheaded for Christ. Bodily resurrections have to wait for the final judgment when the sheep and goats will be revealed, but not before.

Indeed, Revelation only says that "over these (those who have a part in the first resurrection) the second death has *no power*," but *not that they can bypass the divine due process* of judgment before entering life. As such, the claim that "the rest of the dead *did not come to life until the thousand years were completed*" (5a) must likewise be taken as the counterpart to those beheaded for Christ: these people who have not made a stand for or against Christ during their lives for whatever reason will not leave their godly impacts on history and have not been affirmed by God in their lives; their eternal destiny is for now hidden in the scrolls awaiting the final judgment together with the believers whose destinies have already been affirmed.

Can the above understanding be supported by the text? Common translations of 5a above and 3b (" . . . so that he would not deceive the nations any longer, *until the thousand years were completed. After these things he must be released* for a short time") are particularly problematic since they seem to convey a chronological order. Yet, John's original choice of words allows for a different rendering.

The Greek word translated here as "until" is *achri* which when applied to space would mean "as far as." Yet in the absence of either a time or space connection, it simply places a limit on the object (e.g., "as long as it is still called "Today,"" (Heb 3:13), hence some versions have rendered it "*while* it is still called today"). The other Greek word translated "completed" is *teleō*. Using this word to convey numerical completion is rare. Examples of more common usages are: "My grace is sufficient for you, for power is *perfected* (*teleō*) in weakness" (2 Cor 12:9) and "If, however, you are *fulfilling* (*teleō*) the royal law according to the Scripture, "You shall love your neighbor as yourself," you are doing well" (Jas 2:8). Further, the Greek word translated as "after" is *meta* which in most cases is rendered simply as "with." If the one thousand years is taken to be a snapshot of history, or simply creation's history, thus putting it above mundane or linear time (i.e., it is timeless), then the above two verses can be paraphrased as:

- 3b: . . . so that he would not deceive the nations any longer, *while (as long as) creation's history is being perfected (completed). With these things he must still be released for a short time.*

- 5: The rest of the dead did not come to life *while (as long as) creation's history is being perfected (completed).* This is the first resurrection.

Understanding the larger context helps to decide between possible translations.

Another puzzle solved through the present take is: Where does the multitude besieging the saints' camp come from after these people have been neutralized together with the beasts in chapters 18 and 19, *if these 'events' are taken as sequential*? They can only originate from the saints that remain. If so, from this saintly community must arise another set of beasts and another Babylon organized to attack the saints since Satan is only allowed to deceive. Such is re-emphasized here in vs. 3, 7 &10. If so, chapters 12 to 19 will then repeat ad infinitum. Then one must question the effectiveness of the previous vanquishing of Babylon and the beasts, and has to swallow the unchristian position that evil is an eternally recurring feature of existence. Our hope is thus bogus; God has failed; Jesus' claim of final victory is hollow; repeated conquering (first seal) is the game; the curse of sin and sting of death will remain. But thanks be to our Lord Jesus, we know better.

A final judgment based on deeds is consistently biblical. Faith in Jesus Christ is only real when fruits are borne according to the profession of faith. Unambiguously, the touchstone of these fruits is in God's hand beyond third party scrutiny (God's books have not yet opened on these people). Mortals read about God's criteria, but how these criteria are to be applied to each person must be deferred to the only God who knows human hearts fully.

In the end, not only are evil doers, but their temporary repositories—the sea, death and Hades—are also thrown into the eternal fire where the unholy trinity (Satan, the beast and false prophet) will be. A common feature of the downfall of all these ugly characters is how unceremoniously they proceed. This stands in diametric contrast to the rich and colorful reactions to Babylon's downfall in chapter 18 that reverberate in every direction. The main feature and the sideshows are clearly delineated: God desires to rid his creation of corruption that originates from the all-encompassing enterprise and totality that humans have constructed to replace God (Babylon); Satan and his direct cohorts (the beasts) are just the facilitators of evil along the way.

Three "entities" will be giving up their dead—sea, death, and Hades. The latter two are thrown *as one* into the lake of fire with Satan, but the first simply finds no further existence in the new order (20:1). What do these entities represent?

The judgment before the great white throne is the final reckoning of every person according to his/her deeds. This reckoning is only made possible by Jesus' victory over death and Hades. Without Jesus' resurrection, death would be the universal leveler, obliterating both the good and the bad, the moral and the immoral. Hades would also continue into the indefinite eternity, snuffing out any hope therein. Together (i.e., death *and* Hades), they form one complete stranglehold on all who know or believe no better. Now that Jesus has resurrected, death and Hades are forced to give up those trapped in them, i.e., those who believe there is no the final reckoning before God. This deception of Satan is completely shattered and destroyed in the lake of fire.

Then what is the place of the sea? Symbolized by the sea is whatever is chaotically uncertain, hence the political beast arises from the sea. As opposed to accepting the firm belief of no final reckoning (death and Hades), those dead in the sea has lived in the twilight between hope and hopelessness, groping for a way out of the uncertainty through whatever means at their disposal—religion, politics, works . . . etc. These people will be answered definitively by the "Father of lights, with whom there is no variation or shifting shadow" (Jas 1:17b) who reigns on a throne before "something like a *sea of glass, like crystal*" (4:6). Placidly clear and certain are God's judgment and administration and the fact of life everlasting.

Despite the various shades of belief in a final reckoning before God (sea or death and Hades), the all-encompassing book of life has the last word on every person's fate.

Since chapter 20 takes an all-pervasive cosmic timescale different to the Sabbatical time of chapters 11–13 and that the intervening chapters (14–19) do not mention a time at all, it can be concluded that the judgment of Babylon in chapter 18, the beast(s) in chapter 19 and Satan in chapter 20 are neither meant to be put on any specific timescale nor ordered sequentially. The judgments on any of these parties will come in God's good time.

Now the last anti-god character in Revelation is destroyed. True to his name and nature, he would be happy to see his own commanders (the beasts) and foot soldiers (Babylon) destroyed—spend eternity with him in the burning lake. His desire to destroy God's entire good creation ends up in destroying only all those who have rejected God. The loop is now closed. Destroying the destroyer (11:18) also serves to cleanse God's creation.

*To avoid misrepresenting Jesus' work as only applicable to those who are born after his resurrection,* Jesus' seminal victory in history is not marked out here in chapter 20, but seen as applicable throughout the entire space-time that exists, in a final validation of and complement to the previous depiction of him as the most important (center) of God's, saints' and opposition's work. Both the past and future which have been inverted in the tense used for describing the two witnesses in chapter 11 are now seen as one and displayed simultaneously. Jesus' fullness fills all in all (Eph 3:23) without being pantheistic.

John's shift to a "background" perspective in chapter 20 also re-emphasizes a subtle previous message: Satan only lies, but does not kill physically, hence remains in the dull background; humans are the prime actor in damaging creation according to Satan's lies (fifth and sixth trumpets). The saints live in the variegated present and must stand their ground rather than off-load their responsibilities down the line to Satan as Adam and Eve did (Gen 3:11–13) when tempted (Satan let out to deceive briefly again). God's judgment is not obviated by Satan's lies. Yet believers are not alone since we "have so great a cloud of witnesses surrounding us" in the beheaded, but resurrected, saints throughout their history. And indeed, "apart from us they (all witnesses in history) would not be made perfect" (Heb 11:40—12:1) when the totality of God's work is viewed in one go as in chapter 20.

The perspective of Rev 20 in relation to earlier chapters (8–19) can be likened to viewing things while ascending from the surface of the earth to space. Within the forest canopy, one sees a wonderful display of activities and colors (flowers, insects, mammals, birds . . . etc. going about their activities). In the ocean, the same variegated hues and whimsical behaviors are displayed among corals and many other marine habitats. Yet ascending above these, one can only see blue waves and green trees, and further up, patches of blue and green. When one ascends further, even these blue and green merge into one monochromatic dot in space. All other colors have faded and the dot seems to be perpetually going around a bright object. Revelation 20 is the theological equivalent of viewing God's work from deep space.

## 11. ADVENT OF NEW HEAVEN AND EARTH (21:1—22:5)

This passage addresses two interlinked questions: 1. Is God's ultimate goal in creation just the elimination of evil, and 2. Does God want to return creation to its pristine past after it was tainted by sin? The answer to these two questions is both a resounding "no."

To start, we do not see the lost garden, Eden, reappearing. A city, rather than a garden, coming down from heaven, appears. From the beginning, a garden was planted by God, but a city in the Bible, unless otherwise specified, e.g., Heb 11:10, has always been a human construct, as is Babylon. Yet, this last city in Revelation comes down from heaven. What distinguishes this city from other human constructs is not only its origin, but God dwelling within it, resulting in things that are humanly impossible—tears wiped away, the disappearance of death, mourning, crying, and pain. These seemingly unavoidable miseries—knowledge of evil—that had inflicted all living creatures are now passé, miraculously.

God once again proclaims, for the second and last time in Revelation that "It is done." God has now reached his goal. Jesus first proclaimed similarly just before he breathed his last on the cross (John 19:30), but things on the ground do not seem to have improved, if at all, since we even see the wrath of the dragon increased with Satan redoubling his destructive efforts before his foregone and imminent demise. Yet, Jesus' proclamation on the cross was not premature, but seminal: the outcome of the war is sealed with Satan's defeat and the triumph of good over evil. This proclamation is only completed with the two proclamations that we now find in Revelation: Babylon is finally destroyed (16:17), and the city of God is finally realized (21:6). Evil is not only eliminated, but God's kingdom has come, as we have been taught by Jesus to pray for. The story is now completed by this last proclamation which sees beauty and goodness pervading the city.

A subtle difference in the Greek word used by Jesus on the cross (John 19:30, *teleō*) and in Revelation (*ginomai* for "It is accomplished/done") teaches a very important lesson. The first word signifies a completion, but the second word goes further—something has been created (e.g., "All *things came into being* (*ginomai*) through Him, and apart from Him nothing *came into being* that has *come into being*" (John 1:3)). Building on what Jesus finished (*teleō*) on the cross, God and humankind have brought about the destruction of Babylon, but also brought into existence (*ginomai*) a city, the New Jerusalem.

Jesus, the Alpha and Omega, works from the beginning to the end. His six days of work is now brought to a completion in the final Sabbath, the seventh (3.5+3.5) day. Yet the end is also a new beginning because he has made everything new. This new creation will be untouched by what were unavoidable with the old—tears, death, mourning . . . etc.

Surprisingly, this ending and new beginning are not the works of God alone. Starting from 21:10, a different picture of the city comes into focus. This city has human names brilliantly written on it—the twelve tribes of Israel and twelve apostles. By chronology, Israel comes before Jesus' apostles. The former should then be viewed as the foundation (according to how we build), but since the Lamb is the center of history and central to the construction of this city (only he is worthy to open the scroll in chapter 5), Jesus' twelve apostles rather than the twelve Israelite tribes are the foundation stones. The solid foundation of the apostle's teaching has replaced the tossing waves of the sea of godless politics, hence the "no more sea" metaphor in (1). On the gates (the first point of entry) are the names of the twelve tribes of Israel. The enigmatic twenty four elders that have been conducting the harmonious heavenly worship before are now revealed to be these leaders of the people in the New and Old Testament (12+12=24).

The city measures 12,000 stadia on each side. By common experience, this size (over two thousand kilometers) dwarfs its gates and foundation stones. Through multiplying the number of the chosen tribes or apostles (twelve) with the generically large (1,000) to count the longest human measure (stadia), the Holy Spirit is teaching us that God's promised city is large enough for all. The wall thickness is no less revealing: 144 (12 Apostles × 12

Israeli tribes) cubits. Such progressive unveiling in Revelation casts a new light on the 144,000 which was taken as the self-multiplication of the twelve tribes of Israel (section 4.3 of this reading), but is now shown to be the resonance between the old and the new, between God's former ethnic choice and his universal choice in the grand finale. Human hands (a cubit being the typical length of the human forearm from finger tip to elbow) from the community of the chosen are instrumental in erecting the high wall. The immense proportion of this city also dwarfs the wraths of God and humans which converge to form a shallow (only up to the horse's bridle) river only of 1,600 stadia long (14:20).

Then something even more profound happens. The city is measured according to angelic (heavenly) standard which is also human standard. Though angels are often human agents in Revelation, the deliberate equating of the human with the angelic here emphasizes that God dwelling among his people is nothing less than God's total acceptance of people in the city and consequently also of their works with the results that any convention they adopt for their own labor and convenience is unreservedly assimilated into God's work. The measure used by humans is established through the exercise of their creativity in freedom. This fruit of human creativity is treasured by God in the construction of the city and stands diametrically opposite to the first fruit of the freedom of our first ancestors, Adam and Eve. Freedom without rebellion, enquiry without disbelief is not only possible, but is now the rule without exception in the city.

Conspicuously absent here are the four living creatures, each having a distinct face (lion, ox, human, and eagle), that have constantly shadowed the twenty four elders since their joint debut in chapter 4. They, being aspects of God's image that humans are supposed to bear (section 4.1), now impel the kings of the earth (majestic as the lion) to faithfully (like an ox) bring glory and honor (fitting for creative humans) into the holy city where death is conquered by life eternal (as the eagle is rejuvenated). The city, now full of the fruits of properly aligned human freedom, is illuminated and powered by God and the Lamb.

Unlike the vision of Ezekiel who envisages the gate of the restored city closed during working days but opened only on the Sabbath and the new moon (46:1), the gates of this heavenly city will never be closed, forever welcoming the glory and honor of the nations. *The cycle of work and rest has now become one unending Sabbath* when human labor is no longer endless unrequited toil. Finally work will yield its glorious fruits forever, safe from worms, moths, and rust. As God rests and unreservedly enjoys his creation, all creation now enters into the same deepest satisfaction that it has always longed for.

As in the vision of Ezekiel (47) who saw a river, now a river of the water of life is found right in the middle of the street in the city. The river of God's and humans' wrath in chapter 14 only flows outside the city. What was once forbidden humans because of Adam and Eve's sin—the tree of life—now reappears, not in a pristine Eden, but inside the city. Not only is this tree of life no longer guarded by an angel with a flaming sword, it even produces fruits every month, apparently spontaneously without humans tending it; nourishment directly from the river of God suffices. The agricultural activities which involve hoeing and pruning, namely mutilating, nature are no more. Amazingly, all these do not happen outside the city, but within the cooperative venture of God and humans. Rather than taking a hands-off stand towards nature and letting it run on its own, godly stewardship brings about a harmony that inter-nourishes all parties.

Yet trying to locate this city in any geography is totally futile despite its mention of the four compass points for the gates: since God has replaced the sun, how then are east-west, north-south referenced? Instead, the truth of the creator, God's Word, which exposes every falsehood, reigns universally.

Progressive revelation has now taken a final leap forward. What was lacking in the last worship scene in chapter 19 when compared with that in chapter 5, namely praises from all of creation, sentient or otherwise, is now completed with sub-sentient creation (tree of life) chiming with the harmonious choir of the cosmos led by the uncountable multitude and the elders. *The bride of the Lamb, this New Jerusalem, is not only the human community, but a city that has, as its thoroughfare, God's creation in harmony with humanity and with God.*

In bygone times, humans were to labor six years and observe one Sabbatical year on behalf of the land, thus bringing nature into harmony with themselves which is to be accepted by God in the Jubilee year. Now within this consummated Sabbath, humans are to enjoy the fruits of nature according to nature's rhythm rather than humans': fruits and leaves of this tree sprout according to nature's cycle—months of the year. The symbolic 2×1,260 days assigned humankind for the completion of his work on behalf of God's creation in chapters 11–12 is now complete and assimilated into God's work. The lost harmony between humans and nature is now more than restored. The only curse—on the ground—pronounced as a direct consequence of Adam and Eve's fall is no more. Nations are restored to vitality and vibrancy through the leaves of the tree of life. What Paul saw in Rom 8:19–22 of creation longing for the revealing of the children of God has now reached its apogee. Freedom for all—humans and creation—is a reality. Under the throne of God in the illumination of God's light, not only will the lamb and the lion graze together in harmony (Isa 65:25), they will furthermore look out for each other's interest, providing for and satisfying each other's needs.

Since the fall of humankind, God has been trying to re-establish his rule over all of creation. Without deviating by one iota from his original intention, God has done so singly through humankind. Now God's presence is a permanent feature on earth, all the nations in their kaleidoscopic expressions—not just one uniform clump of redeemed people—will come under his rule. Various nations would now express their glory and honor according to their particularities and unique situations. Differences in the nations of the earth are not obliterated, but sanctified and accepted by God to complete his wonderfully creative but harmonious, very good creation. Unclean persons with their fruits will be barred entry to the city, though not by shut gates since the city's gates will never be closed, but perhaps by a sanctified spontaneity that comes from the city being illuminated by God and the Lamb rather than by nature's light.

Twice in the last two chapters (21:8 and 22:15), mention is made of those who have rejected God, but always in contrast to those who would be enjoying the unalloyed goodness and unending creativity in the city. They remain outside the city. Their final abode is the lake of fire. This speaks of not a total redemption of humankind. There is still a portion of humans that has rejected God's mercy and love and has chosen to remain in the collapsing Babylon to be imprisoned in her destruction (18:2). Despite human's desire to see a perfect state of existence in the future, God's Revelation is realistic and has not short-changed justice in the light of all the miseries that believers and creation have gone through in the here and now through unrepentant sinners. Despite God's best intention not to see anyone perish (2 Pet 3:19), the freedom ingrained in humans which none of us as-yet-mortals can understand, let alone explain, means that continual rejection of God is real and must come at an eternal price.

One may say that these "outsiders" would tarnish that perfect existence to be realized in the fullness of time.

Yet, if we take the city to be a community in progress, with God peaceably extending his sovereignty over his creation, then these outsiders represent the residual evil that will gradually be diminished with each forward step in the saints' march. Growing to fill spaces where evil once reigns—in individuals and structures—is the hallmark of this city. The ongoing struggle of the city gives it a unique touch of realism that sets it apart from idealistic philosophical projections and longings. Because evil is real, the price Jesus paid is also real and is highlighted (1:5, 18, 5:6, 9, 12, 13:8). His followers' struggle against evil is also real and ongoing. No saint can be complacent to pretend that final evil has been eliminated. *Outsiders within each person and structures remain.*

## 12. CALL TO ACTION (22:6–21)

It is only fitting that Revelation starts with Jesus, but now also ends with Jesus speaking.

While Daniel's received vision left him exhausted and sick (8:27), the much older John is totally dazzled and energized by what he is given to see. For a second time in his awestruck urge to worship, he falls down to worship at the angel's feet and again he is promptly corrected, but not reprimanded. It is only understandable that such a mosaic of the cosmos' future, which can only be symbolized rather than being described precisely, would leave any recipient temporarily disoriented. For those who do not appreciate the shattering and transforming impact of such a received vision, this blunder of mistaking a messenger for the object of worship is an embarrassment, but not to those who have even a slight inkling of the enormity of such a revelation. In comparison, what Daniel saw does not even register on the scale of Revelation.

In contrast to the command given to Daniel to conceal his received vision (12:4), John is commanded not to "seal up the words of the prophecy of this book, for the time is near." In light of the game-changing revelation, people will have to choose between the camp of the victor or the loser. Their choice must not be coerced, even to the point that even Satan would be let loose to deceive for a short time. Nevertheless, a number of points should be made clear to them: 1. the one who takes creation from the beginning (Alpha) to the end (Omega) is coming quickly, sooner than one can anticipate, hence hesitation and postponing decision can be deadly, 2. this Alpha and Omega will recompense everyone without exception according to their deeds that naturally follow from their choice, and 3. the contrast between the two choices is an absolutely stark matter of life and death, eternally.

Is there any evidence that the darkness we see all around will fade? In other words, is there any indication that Jesus and his saints will indeed win the day, the seventh day? Jesus likens himself to the bright morning star that heralds the full brightness of the day. A foretaste of the sweetness of this day is like water to quench one's thirst, water that is free to all in a parched land.

Because this one revelation is so *complete and integral* in its flow and inter-relatedness, as we saw and shall see further in the next two readings, a no-tamper seal is put on it to avoid it being diminished or dismembered by those who do not grasp the whole and central import, but twist it to hijack the revealed agenda for one's ambitions or to satisfy one's fancy. Such tampering will be recompensed according to this revelation!

Before the final arrival of Jesus to satisfy our godly longings, the grace of the Lord Jesus is with all.

# 3

# Third Reading—
# Stringing together the Gems of Revelation

REVELATION IS PROGRESSIVE. As the narrative progresses, previous events, characters, and messages come into sharper focus. Broad descriptions in a passage may be further dissected in the hindsight of a later passage. It now behooves us to go through Revelation one more time, using our initial analyzes in the second reading, to gain a better appreciation of the flow and messages of the whole book.

The word "prophecy" was first encountered in 1:3 where we highlighted its two intertwined elements: forth-telling and fore-telling (beginning of the second reading), to open up the possibility that Revelation not only fore-tells the future. Another element is apparent now that we have gone through the whole book: *re-telling*. Indeed, re-telling is a consistent element in Old Testament prophecies to complete each narration. A beautiful example is Isa 5 which Jesus adopts in his pivotal parable to assert that he is the cornerstone shortly before his crucifixion (Matt 21:33–44; Mark 12:1–11; Luke 20:9–17). In Isaiah, God is portrayed as a loving gardener who intelligently and diligently fashions a vineyard in the hope that it would yield good fruits in response (re-telling God's design and love), but instead it produces only worthless ones (forth-telling their present problem) which leaves God no choice but to reject them (fore-telling their end). Re-telling is thus an integral and foundational part to anchor a prophecy.

John wrote Revelation within this logical, and indeed common-sense, tradition. Revelation's first major re-telling is the grand heavenly worship in which God's act of creation is retold through the praises from all his creatures for their creation. Embedded within are the four living creatures which are then elaborated in the first four seals to constitute the second major re-telling (of God making humans in his image) to form the basis for subsequent narration. Other major re-tellings follow: how Satan lied and humankind was deceived (fifth trumpet), which led to their mutual destruction without repentance (first episode of the sixth trumpet) and how God had responded through the Law and Prophets (third episode of the sixth trumpet). Re-telling continues in how the dragon was waiting for the deliverance of the male child to commit his consummate infanticide in chapter 12. Elements of re-telling are also integral to the whole narration of Revelation (e.g., fifth–sixth seals describing how people and God have been interacting; first four trumpets documenting God's unwavering love of his creation . . . etc.). *But as opposed to repeating these as historical events, they are recast as theological symbols for universal instruction.*

*Not mistaking re-telling for fore-telling in prophecy is crucial to locate the thread that runs through Revelation (e.g., the first four seals do not fore-tell, but re-tell)* and develops the storyline therein. With this perspective, Revelation transcends narrow fore-telling to cover the entire work of God from creation to the New Jerusalem. Re-telling does not only speak of finished acts, but extends these relevantly from the past to form the basis of future actions. Given such, general and broad themes from both the Old and New Testaments, rather than minute correspondence with particular verses, are used in John's narration. I will show the untenable consequences of losing sight of this crucial element of retelling and the broad teachings of the Bible in the second last section of this book when a literature survey is done.

To start this reading, a synoptic run-through would be given to set the stage and give Revelation a structure. Then nailing down a key to my interpretation, namely the two witnesses, is done through debating rival thoughts. This will anchor my argument. Thereafter, we will zoom in on a few passages to find out God's overriding concern in Revelation. To better grasp Revelation's structure, the three series of sevens—seals, trumpets, and bowls, prominently in the middle of Revelation—are then juxtaposed to bring out the whats and whys of these symbols. In the fifth section, some of the major symbols—the woman, the holy city . . . etc.—are traced through Revelation's progressive presentation. Since time is crucial in unlocking Revelation, its timescales are laid over one another to draw out their implications on how time is to be understood in the sixth section. Finally, the few major players in Revelation's cosmic struggle are paired up and the roles they play are gathered from different parts of Revelation and schematized in a diagram. Through all these, John's undeserved reputation of not being a systematic writer would be replaced by that of a focused theologian.

## 1. A SYNOPTIC OUTLINE OF REVELATION

Revelation has a message for everyone. This general message is introduced by Jesus' self introduction in chapter 1, but starts in earnest after the seven churches are individually addressed in chapters 2–3. Chapters 4–22 are the body of Revelation's message. Within this body, we notice that every major section raises some issues which are then addressed in subsequent passages. Though these issues may not be apparent in a first forward scan of Revelation, they become clear once the flow of the book is known.

Taking this cue, eight major issues can be identified that connect the presentation in a logical fashion. This reinforces a basic observation: Revelation is *logically-sequenced rather than time-sequenced*. Perhaps by coincidence, the eighth and last issue identified here signifies a new beginning after one cycle of seven, just like the "first day of the week" after the previous week. These major issues are summarized in table 5.

A summary of each unit in Revelation based on these issues is given below.

A. **Encounter with a mission (chapter 1):** Jesus appears to John on the Lord's Day to reassure him and his fellow saints in the middle of the tribulation that because of his resurrection, they need not be afraid. John is to write to seven churches about this.

B. **An appropriate message for each church (chapters 2–3):** An introduction is individualized for each of the seven churches, with the same Jesus, bearing appropriate epithets and displaying suitable characteristics, speaking to each receiving church.

C. **First thing first—Who God is and what he has done (chapters 4–5):** The very provisional introductions to the seven churches are put into a much broader context, in fact the broadest context possible: the worship and praise of God the creator by his creatures for the fact of their existence and the concentrically expanding worship of the Lamb who redeems and moves creation towards the intended destination. Gen 1–2 is retold in apocalyptic symbols, recalling God's creation and his intention.

**Issue 1. Why is redemption needed if creation was good to start with?**

D. **Expanding on why the Lamb needs to take the reins of creation—the seven seals (6:1—8:1):**
   i. God created humans, but the original unproofed nature of humans is perverted by freely-choosing humans to wreak havoc

Table 5. Major issues raised and addressed in Revelation

| Section dealing with | Issue(s) raised | Addressed in |
|---|---|---|
| Two heavenly worship scenes [4–5] | 1st If creation was good to start with as in [4], why is redemption needed as in [5]? | First six of the seven seals [6–7]—humans have perverted God's image in them. |
| Seven seals (6:1—8:1) | 2nd Are human beings the only concern of God; why is there only half an hour in the 7th seal? | The seven trumpets and bowls (8:2—11:19; [15–16])—God loves his creation and will cleanse it. |
| Seven trumpets (8:2—11:19) | 3rd Is Christ already reigning or is he beginning to reign, after his victory in the 7th trumpet (11:15) | [12]—struggle between God's male child and the dragon continues because Satan still fights on. |
| The war resulting from Jesus' seminal victory in his resurrection [12] | 4th How is the war between God's and Satan's camp fought in reality and what are the weapons used? | [13–14]—superiority of God's camp over Satan's and how the earth is cleansed. |
| The great confrontation between the two camps [13–14] | 5th Jesus and his saints have harvested the earth, what more is needed to end evil? | [15–16]—Saints to live in anticipation of God's goodness precipitates God's seven bowls of wrath. |
| Completion of God's wrath in the seven bowls [15–16] | 6th Why does Babylon split into three (16:19) and what is its significance for the saints' struggle? | [17]—innate contradictions within Satan's kingdom identified in [13] are exploited by God |
| Conflicting and untenable foundation of Satan's kingdom [17] | 7th What is the most important component in Satan's camp and the priority in tackling them? | [18–20]—concentrate on Babylon to destroy the support of the beasts and Satan |
| Vanquishing of all evils by the good [18–20] | 8th and final Completion: In what shape will the cleansed creation emerge after evil's defeat? | [21–22]—In the city where God, the Lamb, the saints, and creation live in spontaneous harmony |

A square bracket [ ] is used to indicate chapter for conciseness.

THIRD READING—STRINGING TOGETHER THE GEMS    107

      on each other and on creation, resulting in death (first four seals). Human's fall in Gen 3 and its aftermath are felt universally.
- ii. Yet the cries of the remnant who cares for God's creation have not gone unheeded (fifth seal).
- iii. God would recompense accordingly; those harming God's creation would face his wrath while those heeding God's call to protect his creation would come out of the great tribulation that is brought on by human perversion, in white garment, unscathed (sixth seal).
- iv. Yet dealing with humans only is not enough since God's other (and main) concerns have not fully entered the playing field in the narration (seventh seal).

**Issue 2. The silent half hour: What are the other concerns of God besides humans?**

E. **Bringing in all the players for the end game—the seven trumpets (8:2—11:19):** Beyond God and humans are the rest of creation and another player—the devil. Seven trumpets now complement the 7-seal starting narration of humans created in God's image.
- i. From the angle of God's protection, all aspects (summarized as four) of God's creation are used to remind humans of God's loving-kindness (limiting damage to a minority) despite the havoc that fallen humans and fallen creation (ground being cursed because of humans' sin) have wrought on each other (first four trumpets).
- ii. Another party is revealed—the angel of the abyss whose sole aim is to destroy God's good creation, through deceiving humans (fifth trumpet). Even here, God limits the destroyer's torment on the unrepentant, and is always calling for repentance.
- iii. An action, an appropriate response, and an elaboration are given in the pivotal sixth trumpet. First, humans turn against each other killing a significant portion of themselves, perpetuating a vicious cycle; second, God responds by sending his strong angel, constantly prompted by his covenant with creation, to take action, resulting in canceling God's immediate wrath through preaching a new message; third, this message is elaborated in chapter 11: through the death and resurrection of the one who has fully taken up the works of God in times past (the Law and Prophets), the center of creation's history is established.
- iv. The singular act of Jesus has transformed the kingdom of the

world to become the kingdom of God and initiated the expanding reign of God on earth, culminating in God rewarding his servants while destroying those who destroy the earth (seventh trumpet).

**Issue 3. After his victory, is Christ already fully reigning or only beginning to reign?**

F. **Aftermath of Jesus' seminal victory for his followers, a synopsis (chapter 12)**: The unfinished business of Jesus' victory is expanded on, first in the trans-temporal struggle between God the creator and Satan the destroyer. This centers on Jesus, the male child born of a woman. Jesus' victory has now divided humankind into two camps, with those in Jesus' camp described as being in heaven while the opposition has been thrown down to earth. The saints (those in Jesus' camp) are helped both by their own efforts and God until the end of history while the opposition continues to persecute them.

**Issue 4. How is the war between God's and Satan's camp fought in reality and what are the weapons used?**

G. **The two great camps laid bare and contrasted (chapters 13–14):**
   i. **Dissection of Satan's camp (chapter 13)**: To prepare the saints for action against the destroyer, the structure of the enemy camp is described as comprising three powers—political, religious, and socio-economic—held together by coercion, deception, and connivance, respectively. This camp may even overcome the saints through physical violence, but no one inside can ever enjoy any rest.
   ii. **Camping with the Lamb (chapter 14)**: By contrast, the family of the saints is held together through a common life with spontaneous worship in an intimacy unknown to outsiders. Yet the saints do not idly worship, but reach out as far as they can to call people out of the enemy's camp (on earth) and are assured that they will enter the final rest with their works. Such is the partnership between the son of man and the action-producing prayers of those in heaven resulting in harvesting the earth.

**Issue 5. Jesus and his saints have harvested the earth, what more is needed to end evil?**

H. **How the end game will be played out from the opposition's angle (chapters 15–16):** The wrath that was canceled because of Jesus' actions in the sixth trumpet would come in a different form. This wrath consummates the longing of all peoples before and after Jesus' resurrection, with God rejecting those under his wrath (chapter 15):
   i. When God removes his protection from these people, different aspects of the natural world become a channel of God's wrath in the first four of the seven bowls.
   ii. In the same vein, the torment from the angel of the abyss in the fifth trumpet, now unchecked by God, darkens the kingdom of God's enemy in the fifth bowl.
   iii. Similarly, the mutual destruction of humans in the sixth trumpet, now unchecked by God, leads to a mass unwitting suicide in the sixth bowl.
   iv. God's triumph in the seventh trumpet issues in Babylon's destruction (a three-way split) in the seventh bowl.

**Issue 6. Why does Babylon split into three (16:19) and what is its significance for the saints' struggle?**

I. **How Satan's camp ends up destroying itself (chapter 17)—a synopsis:** To prevent the saints from taking violent and self-defeating actions against Satan's camp, one more layer of analysis is injected into the prophecy of its destruction, the seed of which is already in chapter 13—the immorality and simmering mutual animosity within the devil's camp would eventually destroy Babylon. Instrumental in this is the beast which has existed throughout history, but would sometimes gain almost total power to oppose God, albeit very briefly.

**Issue 7. What is the most important component in Satan's camp and the priority in tackling them?**

J. Elaborations on how each party in Satan's camp falls (chapters 18–20):
   i. **Destruction of Babylon (chapter 18):** Babylon will be destroyed when people see her reality in the light of God's truth and come out of her. Her sins lie not only in her violence, but primarily in her desire to satisfy herself as if she is the ultimate sovereign like God. As such, all human sins ever committed are attributed to her. She is the most fundamental component in Satan's camp.
   ii. **Cleansing the earth for a wedding (chapter 19):** Now that the foot soldiers of the destroyer of the earth have been destroyed,

the Lamb is establishing his rule on earth with praises from all, echoing back to the throne. The marriage of the Lamb is announced and his wonderful nature and works are enumerated to show his worthiness. Those invited (the saints) to the final feast can indulge themselves in the spoil of the enemy's camp. The leaders of Satan's camp, now deprived of a kingdom, are then eternally tormented in the lake of fire.

   iii. **Standing back to view God's work past and present (chapter 20):** To avoid tunnel vision with the preceding series of zoom-ins, a bird's eye view that spans history from beginning to end is painted with the main characters. Humankind throughout history is now divided as those who have always reigned with the ever-working Christ, and those who have not. In the end, Satan's lies will be rejected and the opposition destroyed. Every person will have to stand before God's judgment seat though those who have committed themselves to God will not be scorched by the second death in the lake of fire which is the fitting eternal abode of Satan and his cohorts.

**Issue 8. Completion: In what shape will the good emerge after evil is defeated?**

K. **Finally comes the bride, and they live happily ever after (21:1–22:5):** Partnership between the God who works the humanly impossible and people resting on the Apostles' foundation and God's promise has ushered in a new city in which evil is resolutely rejected. God reigns unopposed therein. Unbroken harmony through total acceptance and inter-nourishment among God's creation, God's people and God himself is the ultimate. The pristine Eden, after a long and arduous journey, has now been transformed by God and the saints into the New Jerusalem.

L. **Overwhelmed to action (22:6–the very end):** Doubts about the possibility and imminence of the coming of the city are dispelled by Jesus' no-delay promise and the seminal evidence of the arrival of the full daylight when all will be rewarded accordingly. No one can escape being overwhelmingly dazzled, not even the writer of Revelation who already knows Jesus so well.

A schematization of the above understanding is given in figure 2:

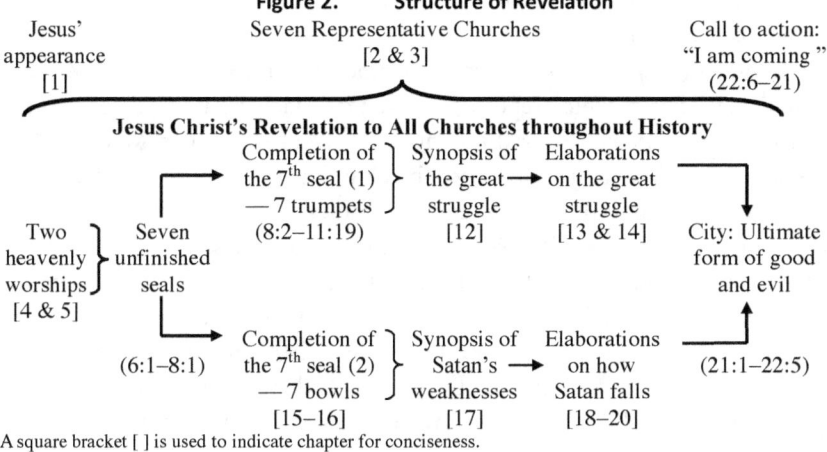

Figure 2. Structure of Revelation

A square bracket [ ] is used to indicate chapter for conciseness.

## 2. WHO ARE THE TWO WITNESSES? A KEY TO UNLOCK REVELATION

Our reading so far suggests that Revelation is built around one central theme which is the core of my interpretation: Jesus will bring his creation from its very beginning (God's creation) to its very end (God's consummation). The way Jesus does this is through his death and resurrection which is the center (focal point) of God's work. This is powerfully conveyed through John's skillful use of time units in Revelation. The key is taking the two witnesses, mentioned only in chapter 11, as Jesus.

Different interpretations of the two witnesses abound. The popular literal understandings see the two witnesses as two real persons or some structure/organization that will appear in the future before some purported events like the fanciful notion of a wholesale transport of believers out of this world. A cursory out-of-context reading of chapter 11 may support this type of thinking because the ministry of these two witnesses is described as future events. But because this future is interpreted as coming out-of-the-blue from the sovereign God without links to the past or present or any preceding biblical teaching, discussing the identity of these two witnesses is nothing more than conjecturing and is as fruitful as trying to figure out who created God. But as we have already seen, most "events" described in Revelation are symbolizations of things and teachings elsewhere in the Bible. To say that the two witnesses, plus a number of other symbols, are an exception to the time-proven approach to the contextual reading of Revelation simply shows the interpreter's failure to find consistency in the narration. This will not be discussed further.

Doing more justice to Revelation's symbols is to relate the two witnesses to biblical teachings which repeatedly state that a fact should be established not by one witness, but two or three witnesses (Deut 17:6, 19:15; Matt 18:16, 26:60; 2 Cor 13:1; 1 Tim 5:19). Since the church is to establish the claim of God's rule through Jesus' resurrection, a sound case involving the testimony of two or three witnesses is needed, hence the two witnesses symbolize the church. Further supporting this take is that they are also referred to as two lampstands before God. Lampstands have been identified as churches early on in 1:12 & 20. Yet the argument is not settled. There are seven lampstands rather than two. Also, throughout the Bible outside Revelation, the number of witnesses to establish a case has invariably been *two or three* rather than just two, casting doubt on the above interpretation.

More so, elsewhere in Revelation, the saints, hence the church, are seen as crying out to God, praying, singing and enduring the persecutions of the beasts while preaching an eternal gospel to those on earth. *Militaristic and violent symbols are reserved for describing God's wrath* (1:9, 6:10–11, 7:14, 8:3–4, 12:5, 13:9–10, 14:1–13, 19:15–18) and never used for human actions. If the witnesses, doing what they are described as doing in chapter 11 (breathing destructive fire on their opponents and shutting up the sky . . . etc.), are indeed the church, then the message conveyed by such deliberate separation of symbols and of roles ("vengeance is mine, I will repay" Rom 12:19; taught throughout the New Testament) is completely neutralized.

Another hurdle to the two-witnesses-as-church interpretation is the resurrection which the two witnesses are described as undergoing. What does this resurrection symbolize? One take is that the church testifies to the hope of the resurrection in Jesus and this unwavering hope is so real that the church is perceived as having resurrected. But this event is not described by one word "resurrection." Rather "after the three and a half days, the breath of life from God came into them, and they stood on their feet; and great fear fell upon those who were watching them. And they heard a loud voice from heaven saying to them, "Come up here." Then they went up into heaven in the cloud, and their enemies watched them. And *in that hour* there was a great earthquake . . . " (11:11–13a). Difficult it is to fit these into the church's experience. More difficult it is to explain why these happen *exactly at 3.5 days* after the witnesses' death.

Deciding whether the two witnesses symbolize the church or Jesus as the fulfillment of Law and Prophets (my interpretation—section 5.4.3 of the second reading) cannot be based solely on finding the strongest correspondence from other parts of the Bible, as each interpretation has a seemingly reasonable case to make. Tracing the flow of the immediate context leading up to the two witnesses would be another start: Satan's lies (mutated locusts in the fifth trumpet) torment but do not kill humans; acting out Satan's lies brings pandemonium—humans killing each other without repenting; God could have brought about judgment (seven thunders), but has chosen instead to transform his final wrath through a *new message* to be preached to all nations (John swallowing the little scroll). *Then comes the two witnesses' ministry* for 1,260 days while the nations are allowed to trample on the holy city for 42 months.

If the two witnesses are taken to be the church, then the new message to be preached is not elaborated on in this narrative, leaving the reader to guess what is in the little scroll John swallowed. The church is then to preach an as-yet-unspecified message. What follows in the next chapters is then an elaboration of the church's work *without first introducing the central figure and content of the message. The most important point in Jesus' revelation is not spelled out.*

On the other hand, if the two witnesses are taken to be Jesus, then the death and resurrection of these two witnesses *lay the foundation of the message to be preached to the nations*—God has been patient with people abusing his rule, but in Jesus' death and resurrection, the seminal yet decisive victory has been won and the kingdom of the world will inevitably become the kingdom of God (seventh trumpet). After identifying this central figure, the ministry of the church to live out this message is taken up in subsequent chapters. The eternal gospel to be preached by the saints (14:6–11) can only make sense with Jesus' resurrection as its foundation.

But even here, the argument is not clinched as the church (if represented by the two witnesses) can just as well be seen to have played its decisive role in the final (not seminal) victory of God. What finally clinches the debate is the intricate symmetry John has skillfully built around these two witnesses. Immediately before the death and resurrection event are found the 42-month, 1,260-day, and 3.5-day periods, signifying half a Sabbatical period of opposition's, believers' and God's work. After the decisive death and resurrection event is found the same: time, times and half a time (replacing 3.5 days), 1,260 days, and 42 months, completing the other half of the period making up a week and a Sabbatical year cycle for the believers and the opposition. When almost *all the specific timescales* (as opposed to generic timescales of 1 hour, 1000 years . . . etc.) of Revelation revolve around this point, the singular importance of this center is unmistakable (figure 3). So is this center Jesus or the church?

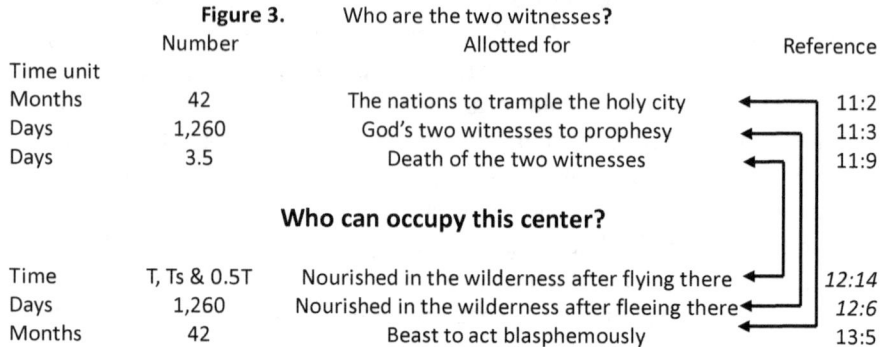

The symmetry starts with the opposition, then moves inward to the saints' and God's work. Note from the order of the biblical reference that the second half of the symmetry is not exact. This may have been done to highlight the fulfillment of Jeremiah's prophecy (31:33) when the saints' will follow the Holy Spirit to take initiative for God, *then* God comes in to help.

Placing the church, rather than Jesus, at the center of this symmetry, thus claiming that the church is the focal point of the opposition's, of the saints' and of God's work, hence also creation's history, *goes against every assertion in Revelation and the Bible*. No one, not even the heavenly church, is able to break the seals on God's scroll in the second heavenly worship scene in chapter 5. Only Jesus, the son of God, the prototypical perfect human, who claims lordship over not only God's work, but even over the opposition for judgment, is worthy to be this focal point. To knowingly say, now that the symmetry is clear, that the church or something else, including the popular speculation of some future figures or structures, would take this center stage is, to me, utmost inappropriate, if not blasphemous.

If the church is understood as the community of believers that only comes into existence after the historical fact of Jesus' death and resurrection, then it (or the two witnesses) can at most only represent half of the entire history of God's creation. How then can it be portrayed as the center? Clearly, both the seal and trumpet series have no less than a cosmic scope which jibes with Jesus as Alpha and Omega. They are also relevant throughout creation's history, with God preventing destruction and bringing humans back to him. God's work does not start only in AD 33, but *in the beginning* (Gen 1:1; John 1:1). The church is not up to this description.

Logically reading Jesus as Lord of the Sabbath also overcomes another difficulty in interpretation. The specificity of the resurrection of the two witnesses—exactly after 3.5 days—suggests a very decisive moment in history. The two-witnesses-as-church thinking has to understand this very specific death and resurrection event as symbolizing how the testimony of the church to Jesus' resurrection is so real because of her determination that the world is like beholding Jesus' resurrection directly. Her martyrdom is recruited to support this argument. But this latter understanding can ill-fit into the preciseness of the time description, let alone explain why the church is left dead and unburied for 3.5 days.

Popular fancy treats this death and resurrection as a future event (contradicting the past tense), thus degrading a wholesome biblical prophecy to a flat prediction devoid of relevance or moral for the present. Such is only fitting for diviners rather than responsible believers.

The church, or some future figures, *will not* go through a decisive death and resurrection, but Jesus already *had*. The practical implication of this firm foundation in Jesus is to disabuse our feeble minds of the heresy in believing that the church, through its own power or determination, can move creation forward without Jesus at its center, and also of the opposite fancifully fatalistic notion of God's supernatural intervention. Surely God can do all things, but he has "made known to us the mystery of His will, according to His kind intention which He purposed in Him *with a view to an administration* suitable to the fullness of the times, that is, the *summing up of all things in Christ, things in the heavens and things on the earth*" (Eph 1:9–10). Dare anyone try to match Jesus Christ?

Having established the two witnesses as *centrally* Jesus, one can now see the implications of this focus in a broader light. Since Jesus continues the missions of Moses and Elijah during the Transfiguration, in fulfillment of his declaration that he has come to complete the Law, and that the church is rightly the body of Christ living out the true Law and Prophets in a new person, the two witnesses, being centrally the resurrected Lord Jesus, *encompass both the Law and Prophets of the Old Testament and the church of the New Testament*. In this very specific sense, the *cosmic Jesus Christ* has disclosed himself throughout creation's history. The upshot: each side of the arguments (two witnesses being Law and Prophets and being church) sees one side of Jesus; both are right, but without Jesus as their lynch pin, both are woefully incomplete.

## 3. REVISITING SOME KEY PASSAGES TO GRASP THE REAL STRUGGLE

In the jubilation of God's victory, let us ask ourselves: If God triumphs, what does that mean? Will all those who follow him be "saved"? Revelation certainly teaches that. But is that the ultimate goal—human glorification?

Are the saints fighting only for their own future with God, somewhat self-servingly? Or could they be fighting for something grander, something that is uppermost on God's mind? Let us reread Revelation for answers. Grasping a few key passages would answer this.

## 3.1 The Enigma of the Saints' Prayers from Under the Altar (5:8, 8:3–4)

After the silence in heaven with the seventh seal, an angel offers incense with prayers of the saints to God. *These prayers mark an important turning point—the transition from seals to trumpets.* Incense is burnt to produce a pleasant aroma to rise up to God. In the Bible, Noah was the first person who performed a burnt offering, with clean animals, and resulted in God, after smelling the smoothing aroma, saying to himself: "Never again will I curse the ground because of humans, *even though* every inclination of the human heart is evil from childhood. And never again will I destroy all living creatures, as I have done. As long as the earth endures, seedtime and harvest, cold and heat, summer and winter, day and night will never cease." (NIV, Gen 8:21–22). From this seminal event, all subsequent offerings that are burnt are first and foremost a reminder to God of the goodness of his creation. This is the *only normative meaning the Bible provides* for fragrant burnt offerings. Incense even stands out among other burnt offerings in that it has nothing but fragrance. It is true that Cain and Abel made offerings before the time of Noah, but theirs were not burnt and God recompensed them as persons. By contrast, *Noah's burnt offering represents not the attitude of the person*, but the wonders of God's creation in its prodigious beauty and awesomeness. God did not turn to humans. Rather, when the soothing aroma of the earth reaches God, *God speaks to none other but himself, and then he makes it known to humankind what he has determined all by himself.*

Before the trumpets sound, prayers of the saints rise together with the soothing aroma of incense (incense is always burnt; offering strange incense is punishable by death—Lev 10:1–2) to God. In Revelation, prayers are never mentioned separately from offered incense. When they are first mentioned (5:8), incense is simply the prayers of the saints. In the remaining two, incense either goes with prayers (8:3) or is the carrier of saints' prayers (8:4). In line with the main thrust of Revelation, the message from the incense-prayers is clear: the prayers of the saints are *always made on behalf of God's creation* and these are what God finds pleasing.

As if God would forget, he sets the bow in the cloud to *remind himself* of his commitment to his creation! This rainbow established in God's material creation now surrounds the throne of God (4:3). Such must have been an addition put in after creation since before Noah, a rainbow had no meaning. Yet, it now is a constant reminder before God, much more so than humans are reminder. Because of the eternal God entering into his own creation which rebounds back with fragrance together with human prayers, *even the makeup of his "eternal, everlasting" heavenly setting has changed* and taken on elements of his material creation. God, who is a spirit (John 4:24), is now inextricably bound up with his very material creation. Reminding himself with the temporal sign of the rainbow is perhaps appropriate for the never changing, immutable, and inscrutable God of how he has tied his future inextricably and irreversibly with his creation in its manifold temporality and mutability. From here on, God cannot and will not go back.

## 3.2 Why are the 144,000 Sealed? (6:12—8:1)

"One hundred and forty four thousand" has been encountered twice in Revelation, the first time in the sixth seal and then in chapter 14 when these stand with the Lamb on Mount Zion. In the sixth seal, immediately after the 144,000 are sealed by God, an uncountable multitude of people appears seemingly out of nowhere. They are revealed to be those who come out of the great tribulation. The 144,000 have suddenly morphed into the multitude who is now dressed in white linen. Further on, all these people are promised guidance to a blissful destination where nothing further will be able to harm them.

What needs to be answered is *why* are these people (144,000 and the uncountable multitude) chosen: to receive protection and blessings from God, or to serve God? From the immediate context, the answer is clear. Those sealed are described as *servants of God rather than saints* (7:3). Servants are to do their master's bidding.

In the sixth seal, we see two groups of people. The first group is fearful of God's wrath saying "to the mountains and to the rocks, "Fall on us and hide us from the presence of Him who sits on the throne, and from the wrath of the Lamb; for the great day of their wrath has come, and who is able to stand?"" But why are they fearful—*because they have seen signs of God's wrath or because they know they have done evil?*

Four symbols from *natural phenomena*—lightning, hail, thunder, earthquake—have commonly been taken as symbolizing divine acts or attributes. Within the context of Revelation, comparison of 4:5, 8:5, 11:19, and 16:18–21 shows that lightning is used exclusively for divine majesty; hail for divine punishment while thunder can be both. Earthquake (seen from 11:13) simply means an earth shaking event of any origin. Strikingly,

*6:12–14 here in the sixth seal have no lightning, thunder or hail*. Instead, very *unnatural* happenings are narrated. To help readers relate to these unprecedented happenings, John has likened them to familiar objects or incidences: "the sun became black *as sackcloth made of hair*, and the whole moon became *like blood*; and the stars of the sky fell to the earth, *as a fig tree casts its unripe figs* when shaken by a great wind. The sky was split apart *like a scroll when it is rolled up*." The last clause goes straight to the point: *every mountain and island were moved out of their places*. In a nutshell, cataclysmic *disruption to the created order* is conveyed in typical apocalyptic language.

Who then is the author of these disruptions? God, Satan or humans? Making God the author of this disruption makes no biblical sense since we have seen in the trumpets that God is the relentless defender of his creation. Up till this point in the narration of the seals, Satan has not made his debut. That leaves humans, which is in line with the first five seals and the rest of the sixth trumpet since they all focus on humans.

Objections may be raised about understanding these phenomena as precipitated by humans rather than God since some of these phenomena seem to have been taken from other biblical passages indicating divine action. The most prominent is how Jesus talks about the fate of the temple. There Jesus uses the passage in Joel (2:30) to say that immediately after the Jewish tribulation, "the sun will be darkened and the moon will not give its light" (Matt 24:29; Mark 13:24). Though one can point out that the wordings and context between Revelation and the other writings are different, the most important criterion must still be that Revelation cannot be held hostage to previous uses (see section 1 of the fourth reading). Revelation has the 20–20 hindsight to re-interpret the symbols cosmically which other writings do not have. And unless we hold that Revelation is just a collection of unconnected passages or sentences, which would make it largely unintelligible, then allowing Revelation to explain itself first must take precedence over reading it through the aid of outside sources, other parts of the Bible notwithstanding.

Recognizing how they have messed up the created order, these human wreckers of God's creation from all walks of life are under no illusion of how their actions would inevitably bring about the wrath of God in recompensing the destroyers, hence their pleading to the mountains and rocks to fall on them. Though damage to the created order redounds to humans as God's judgment on the destroyers, it is only part of it. The full wrath to come from God is expected to be much worse and more painful, and the destroyers know it, hence their very natural but futile plea to be buried under rocks and mountains. The guilty party knows their guilt. Repenting is a different matter.

From the above, the instruction of the angel ascending from the rising of the sun, having the seal of the living God, to the four angels to halt exercising their power to damage God's creation (7:1–3) makes sense: Let us call (seal) people (servants) "from every nation and all tribes and peoples and tongues" to protect God's creation from harm. Remember that sounding each one of the first four trumpets damages one aspect of the created order, hence each trumpet could be associated with one of four angels granted power to harm the earth and the sea here in the sixth seal. In most cases, angels are simply people. Yet the resulting calamities that come upon each aspect of God's creation are limited to one third of the total, with the larger part (two third) protected so that renewal is possible. Who then could the agent that beats back the destroyer (*Abaddōn* and *Apollyōn* in the fifth trumpet) be, but the servants (the multitude or 144,000) sealed for God?

Reading 7:3 as sequential in time gives an untenable sense: hold off the damage (through some unspecified means) *until* the angel sealing the 144,000 has done his job. To start, who harms God's creation, God himself or God's opponents? To make God the author of destruction of his own cherished creation is against Jesus' teachings and the whole Bible. Revelation cannot be saying that. Hence the angels (or simply messengers) given the power to harm the earth and sea must be from Satan's camp, the real opposition rather than an actor in God's self-directed theatrics. Let us now focus on the struggle and ask again: in the sixth seal, what are these people sealed for, *to be protected* from the collateral damage when the earth and sea are harmed, or *to protect God's creation*? The first answer suggests that God is leading a retreating army after losing the fight to Satan. His plea to the winner is: don't attack until we are fully gone! Snatching a half-burnt twig from a forest fire and euphemizing it as a glorious triumph is all God can muster. Poor god! But this is not what the Bible says from beginning to end, let alone what Revelation concludes.

On top of being sealed, these "servants" of God are the same 144,000 standing on Mount Zion with the Lamb in chapter 14. The context of this chapter conveys the unmistakable message that God would work together with his chosen to complete his wrathful cleansing in the winepress (14:14–20). These chosen of God have not been spared the collateral harm on the earth and sea, but have borne the full brunt of the conflict, suffering unimaginable harm throughout this struggle, described as *the great tribulation*, hence the patience urged on those who have already suffered—under the altar in the fifth seal and also as "servants"—is that more of their spiritual progenies will have to sacrifice themselves before the victory is won (6:11). But looking back, this victory is sweet when no further harm will be done to them and they will arrive at the spring of the water of life through the guidance of the Lamb.

Indeed 7:3 supports the above take. The word translated "until" (*achri*) can also be rendered "as far as" when applied to place; context would decide (section 10.3 of the second reading). Clearly the usual indications of time (e.g., day, time, moment . . . etc.) is lacking in this verse to clinch its sense. It can just as well be translated as "Do not harm the earth or the sea or the trees *as far as* we have sealed the bond-servants of our God on their foreheads." In more vernacular rendering, *"as far as"* can simply read *"when and where,"* conveying a limit rather than a real physical location. In either case, God's servants are stopping and reversing the damage to creation by their very presence. If so, this equally valid rendering dovetails coherently with the narration.

Corroborating this interpretation is the developing storyline: God intends creation to be continually renewed through humans' care, but they have perverted God's image in them with sordid consequence (first four seals) leading to cries for justice in the fifth seal. Continuing with the theme of human responsibility, the sixth seal responds to the first four seals to show how the human struggle for creation will be played out between the destroyers and the defenders and their respective final destinies.

Clarion then is the message that this uncountable multitude of 144,000 is sealed for the *explicit purpose* of holding back the damage to creation aimed at by God's opposition. Revelation's teaching must then not be short-circuited to go directly from God's sealing to the bliss that would result in the end. Human efforts and sacrifices in partnership with God must stand between his calling (being sealed) and his final destiny of being with God. It is not that Revelation leaves room for humans in the face of God's "pre-determination" (sealing his people), but *that saintly servants following the Lamb constitute the central narrative*. God only determines in so far as what that victory is. He will work through the labor and unyielding dedication of his servants to claim the full victory already won by the Lamb.

Strung together logically, the six seals give a clear message: The mess in creation left behind by humans corrupting God's good image in them is to be mopped up by none other than humans, called, washed, and transformed in the blood of the Lamb, to stand in the gap for the Lamb. Expect no short-cut.

## 3.3 Seven Forbidden Thunders . . . Jesus . . . Seven Outpoured Bowls of Wrath

Previous contextual readings suggest that the seven thunders (10:3–4) that were not written down are judgments of God on the world or on people who refuse to repent despite his unrelenting protection and care for their wellbeing. The bowls that follow (in chapter 16) are unrestrained wrath of God on the obstructionist remnant, after all has been done and said to reconcile his creation to himself. Naturally, one would ask if the seven bowls are not just the seven thunders delayed.

To answer that, let us ask simply: what purpose do judgments serve? Are they just to avenge the pains God has suffered from his opponents (these indeed are very real and concentrated on his son Jesus Christ) or are they to protect his creation and lead it to the final Sabbath?

The affirmative answer is the latter: to complete the glorification of his creation. What useful purpose does venting one's anger serve if it does not result in bringing about the reversal or elimination of what causes the anger in the first place? So God's wrath—though laden with emotions, humanly speaking—serves to cleanse his creation of undesirables. Such is illustrated in the son of man harvesting the earth which is simultaneously God's wrath (14:14–20). The goal and the process must be clearly distinguished, especially for the creator God who has created purposefully, rather than aimlessly as in the theories of biological evolution.

Next we ask: between the thunders and the bowls stand the victory of Jesus in chapter 11 and all the ensuing ramifications in chapters 12–15; do these change the thunders at all, and if yes, how are the thunders transformed into the bowls?

Logically, it is quite inconceivable to take that the pivotal work of Jesus serves only to delay the inevitable or to buy a little time and nothing changes further. Such would suggest that Jesus has accomplished little. It is obvious from the flow of the seven trumpets that when creation, under the perverted stewardship of humans, has hit rock bottom, that is when those bent on mutual destruction after drinking the bane of Satan do not repent, Jesus' triumph through his resurrection has brought about a total reversal, to the extent that the kingdom of the world has been transformed into the kingdom of God. Ironically, the former kingdom of the world wants to destroy the earth, bringing about God's avowed destruction of these destroyers!

So for a start, the *scope of God's judgment has been substantially reduced* through the preaching of the triumphant message in Jesus' resurrection. In the first five trumpets and first episode of the sixth trumpet, the intent of the destroyer is universal in scope, but God successfully contains that destruction to a minority. The seven unwritten thunders follow immediately in the second episode of the sixth trumpet should represent God's unrestrained wrath. Those judgments would be extended to all humans who do not repent and according to the first episode of the sixth trumpet the non-repentant are almost universal. However, with Jesus' victory and the resulting *transformation, rather than destruction, of the kingdom of the world*, judgment would only come to a minority who still holds out: "And in that hour there was a great earthquake, and *a tenth of the city fell*; seven thousand people were killed in the earthquake, and *the rest were terrified and gave glory to the God of heaven*." A tenth of the city is much smaller than the one third that even God has tolerated to be destroyed previously and seven thousand recalls the remnant in Israel that God told Elijah have not bowed their knees to Baal (1 Kgs 19:18) against the overwhelming opposition. Now in the triumph of Jesus, the ratio of God's followers to opponents has been decisively reversed. The diehard rebels are in the minority. Consequently, damage to creation has also been significantly curtailed.

Since the seven thunders are shouted out by the angel from heaven and they appear abruptly after the people's non-repentance previously, one can only surmise that they *come directly from God*, which would be a repeat of what he did in the deluge of Noah. Yet in subsequent elaborations of the implications of Jesus' victory in the seventh trumpet in chapters 12–15, the *saints are instrumental in struggling against the beasts and their followers*, sometimes even taking great loss in life, so much so that the seven bowls of God's wrath are introduced by the saints singing a bi-testament song of praise prior to the angels pouring out God's wrath in the bowls. Also, these bowls are given by one of the four living creatures and all these living creatures represent human nature in its godly form. Note these angels are attired as those coming out of the great tribulation in the sixth seal (white robe (7:9–14)) and conferred priesthood by Jesus (golden sashes (1:13)) which together point to them as the saints.

All these are put into perspective when we realize how *God was protecting his creation despite humankind* ("Never again will I curse the ground because of humans, *even though* every inclination of the human heart is evil from childhood" (Gen 8:21b, NIV)) and how *he is now glorifying his creation because of humans* (7:1–3, 14:14–20, 21:24 & 26). God has found a partner in some humans.

Through the resurrection of the two witnesses, creation is first saved from the void and formlessness that the seven thunders would bring directly from God. Only those who persist in denying Jesus' victory through commensurate actions would be judged. God's creation would be cleansed rather than destroyed. Then in a colossal reversal through Jesus, this salvation of God's created order is accomplished *through the ministration of the saints*. People are not bypassed, but enlisted through Jesus. Consummating this partnership is that the saints, led by the Lamb, will even bring on God's bowls of wrath on the non-repentant.

## 3.4 From Ark to Ark

Noah's Ark and the Ark of the Covenant are two different objects in the Old Testament, described by two different Hebrew words. The latter is what the Israelites made according to God's instructions and carried with them during their sojourn in the wilderness. Yet in the New Testament, the same Greek word (*kibōtos*) is used for both and appear together in the Epistle to the Hebrews (9:4, 11:7). In Revelation, when the time comes for God to reward his servants and destroys those who destroy the earth, the Ark of the Covenant appears (11:18–19). Noah's Ark is God's preservation and protection of his creation which is solemnized in his rainbow covenant with his creation. In a first fulfillment of this covenant, Abram was then chosen to bring blessings to all the peoples and nations. Later on, the twelve tribes of Israel came forth from Abraham. They were then commanded to carry the Ark of Covenant wherever they went and pitched tents. Just as before for the 144,000, we ask whether these Israelites are chosen just to receive blessings or to bless. The answer is that they are servants of God to labor for his creation. Following this unbroken and unchanging line of God's concern, from the first Ark (Noah's) to the last Ark (Covenant's) in the Old Testament, it would be logical to surmise that though the Ark of the Covenant which contains the golden jar of manna and Aaron's rod which budded (Heb 9:4) constantly testifies to God's protection and sustenance of his people, its full and ultimate intent is to remind Israel of her real mission, i.e., to bless all the families and nations. Helped by the happy (or perhaps divinely designed) co-incidence of having the same Greek word for both Arks, the Holy Spirit is recapitulating this Ark-to-Ark lesson in the last two trumpets: Noah's Ark ends in the *covenant* of the rainbow (on the angel's head, 10:1); the Ark of the *Covenant* (11:19) carries on from Noah's Ark until the New Jerusalem arrives. God has finally fulfilled his covenant.

## 4. THE THREE SERIES OF SEVENS

Seals, trumpets, and bowls (thunders) seem to form the backbone of Revelation. Why and what does that mean?

## 4.1 Why are there Three Series of Sevens?

Revelation narrates three series of sevens—seals, trumpets, and bowls. Though seven churches are also addressed, they are not numbered, hence do not form a series. Within the seven trumpets are also seven peals of thunder, but they are not written down, so only three series are meaningfully recorded.

Based on God's work in bringing creation to completion in six days and himself resting on the seventh, seven means completion. This is beyond doubt. As such, it is biblically consistent for the Holy Spirit to choose seven items strung together to convey God's continual work in his creation, with the seventh being the very last act, the ultimate, the consummation of all.

But from where should he start? The awesome act of God's creation has already been impressed upon the readers in chapter 4 and the centrality of Jesus' work in all things in chapter 5. These paint two successive pictures of the grandeur, majesty, and beauty of God's work and the Lamb's redemption. With that divine preamble, what is the next logical area of concern? Naturally, it is the turn of the custodian of creation whom God has charged with caring for his handiwork upon completion of his creation. But had there been no problem with God's commissioning of humans, then there is no need to write anything further. It would have been a happily-ever-after account immediately following Gen 1–2. But having genuine and humanly inexplicable freedom is what being made in God's image means, among other things, and this freedom can be used as intended or in some other directions contradicting God's original design. As events unfolded, humankind decided against following God's design. This prompted God's response and continual work, making up the rest of the Bible. So the next logical step is to tell what has gone wrong and the consequences. The message in the seven seals is clear: humans in their freedom have put God's good image in them to undesirable use, leading to twisted relationship, conflicts, misrule and finally to death (i.e., the first four seals successively). Very human response, together with God's dealings, follows in the next two seals, thus completing six of the seven seals.

Yet, perverted human nature, hence also actions, is just the beginning. *God's intention does not start and end with humans.* People are only the workers for something far greater. Rather, God created everything and will bring this creation to its completion through humans' stewardship. This foundational truth undergirds the whole Bible and puts every message therein in its place. Like the two ends of a pulled string, Gen 1–2 and Rev 21–22 together determine the character of the sound that can be made in between. The Apostle John also harps on this in his pivotal gospel (1:3). So the next logical step after dealing with the havoc arising from humans corrupting themselves and creation (seals) is to show the perversions creation suffers as a result. These constitute the first four trumpets. But how do all these corruptions come about? Since the first four trumpets do not name culprits, but just announce the outcome, the agents of these destructions may not be totally attributed to humans. It may be that nature without its stewards doing their job according to the original design cannot function properly on its own. Later on in the fifth trumpet, another force seems to be at work. It is that of Satan (the fallen star from heaven) from the bottomless pit who makes his formal debut here (earlier references to Satan in the seven churches are mere metaphors). He has also been implicated in sweeping "away a third of the stars of heaven and threw them to the earth" (12:3). On the surface, Satan seems to be twisting nature (mutated locusts) physically to torment humans and God limits the extent of Satan's destruction. Yet in the hindsight of Satan's circumscribed role only to cheat and accuse (12:10, 20:1-2), the locusts are but lies that torment after events reveal the painful reality of Satan's deception. Satan's lies translate into bloody intra-human strive which deploys all means (horses) at human's disposal. Such is sadly self-perpetuating (front-tail headed destructive horses). In his mercy, God prevents further destruction of his creation and torment of its custodian, and through Jesus' death and resurrection (third episode of the sixth trumpet) eventually brings about the triumph of his reign over the world (seventh trumpet). Unlike that in the seal series, the seventh in the trumpet series is an unequivocal and unqualified triumph. With God's creation being the center of the narrative, the trumpet series encompasses the full scope of God's concern, within which humankind is to find his place and his destiny, and indeed his salvation.

Though the seventh trumpet conveys a sense of finality, it is also seminal: "The kingdom of the world *has become the kingdom of our Lord and of His Christ*; and He will reign forever and ever." . . . "O Lord God, the Almighty, who are and who were, because You have taken Your great power and *have begun to reign*. And the nations were enraged, and Your wrath came" (11:15-18). The final outcome is certain, but it has not yet fully arrived. Only in the last series of seven, i.e., the bowls of God's wrath, is the retributive aspect of God's victory finally dealt with, prompting the "in them the wrath of God is finished" and "It is done" announcements (15:1, 16:17). The seven thunders that were not written down are transformed (3.3 of this reading) and manifested in the bowls. All forms of injustices, sins, perversities are not nothing that can be wished away, even by the almighty and loving God. These have to be tackled and are dealt with in the seven-bowl series which is the retributive counterpart to the seven trumpets.

*While God protects his creation and people in the midst of destruction in the seven trumpets, the seven bowls have no such restraints.* Contrasting with each of God's protections of his creation—limiting destruction to a minority (one third) in each of the first four trumpets, is the unrestrained punishment of God's opponents through his creation in the first four bowls. The created order is the conduit of the creator's wrath to destroy those who destroy his earth. Further, when God gives people fully to Satan's lies, the kingdom of the beast is totally darkened (fifth) with no time limit of five months; when the violence-busting message of Jesus' death and resurrection is not heeded, the conflict involving 2×10,000×10,000 horsemen in the sixth trumpet turns into Armageddon (sixth). God's opponents' predictable response—blaspheming—is finally brought to an end with Babylon destroyed which is also seen as God's triumph (seventh).

Succinctly, the seven seals introduce humankind, the wayward steward, and how God deals with them; the seven trumpets announce God's *full intent and design* on his creation and how he protects and brings his creation to a fitting conclusion in Jesus Christ; the seven bowls complement the trumpets with the full realization of God's focused wrath on the unrepentant. In other words, the seven seals narrate humans' role and its perversion; the seven trumpets show *God's love for all his creation*, and the seven bowls the consequence of rejecting God's love, which is wrath. Together with the heavenly worship chapters (4–5) and the grand finale (21–22), they form a *complete skeleton* to be fleshed out by other chapters.

The enigmatic silent seventh seal now makes complete sense. Voice from heaven conveys a meaningful message. Silence is a void in meaningful communication. Seventh in the Bible means completion. Hour is the shortest time unit in Revelation and one hour can mean one moment. Half a moment conveys extreme rapidity or impatience. The seventh seal stands at the very end of the "human" series of seals and introduces the "all creation" series of trumpets and the negative consequence in the series of bowls. Joining these dots within the context, the seventh seal tells us that heaven *cannot wait to remind fallen humankind that God's created order is waiting eagerly for their full and meaningful participation through the resurrected Jesus to bring about its redemption.* The incompleteness of the seventh seal is only completed by the seventh trumpet's proclamation of God's victory and the seventh bowl's closure of God's wrath in the destruction of Babylon. Completing the trumpets and bowls each involves a human choice—for God and his creation, or the opposite.

In the seventh seal, John is echoing creation's impatience in Rom 8:19–22 ("For the *anxious longing* of the creation *waits eagerly* for the revealing of the sons of God. For the creation was subjected to futility, not willingly, but because of Him who subjected it, *in hope* that the creation itself also will be set free from its slavery to corruption into the freedom of the glory of the children of God. For we know that the whole creation groans and suffers the pains of childbirth together *until now*").

Based on this synopsis, the three series of sevens together, encapsulated as "777," can be taken as an indictment on the "666" reached by self-centered humans in collusion with the beasts under Satan. Through Jesus Christ, humans (seals), creation (trumpets), and God himself (bowls) will enter into the consummate rest while those following Satan are barred from this final Sabbath (see section 7.1 of the second reading).

## 4.2 Some Peculiarities of the Three Series of Sevens: An Interlude and others

The descriptions of the sixth seal and trumpet according to the present reading are significantly longer than that of their counterparts in the series, thus bringing into question whether *an interlude* exists between the sixth and seventh seals and between the sixth and seventh trumpets. According to this view, the sixth seal and sixth trumpet consist only of the first of the three episodes identified here. Our second and third episodes would be interludes which describe God's work to avert that warned-of bitter end. This reading suggests that all the seals, trumpets, and bowls are of one type—*judgments*.

In this view, judgment is negative and destructive. Yet we have seen in the previous analyzes that: 1. the seals are first explanatory narratives for the negative phenomena; moreover they are not uniformly negative, e.g., the saints under the altar in the fifth seal are the indomitable spirit of some who follow God wholeheartedly, this is anything but judgment; 2. God's mercy, and indeed love, rather than destructive and retributive wrath, run through the entire series of trumpets; mercy is the very anti-thesis of judgment; 3. only the bowls have been explained as judgments (16:5, 7) and the absence of such label in the seals and trumpets should lead us to conclude that they are different in kind.

Doom and gloom would be the picture of Revelation if one misses the strident theological description of how humans were well constituted (in the seals) and God's unrelenting mercy and protection (in the trumpets) to *retell God's merciful dealings with humans*. Indeed, reading a "merciful" interlude (i.e., an exception among the rest which is not based on the flow of the narration) into the series of seals and trumpets (before the seventh) would poison our exegesis even before objective analysis is done.

On the other hand, the practical implication of our *no-interlude* understanding is that God has *always* been calling humankind to himself—a merciful overture from the God of love, just as the opening statement of the Epistle to the Hebrews emphasizes ("God, after He spoke long ago to the fathers in the prophets in many portions and in many ways, in these last days has spoken to us in His Son"), but that Jesus is the apex and very center of God's work. The appropriate time is always now and God is always speaking purposefully to all humans through Revelation.

Given our successful tracing of the coherent development of the three series of sevens, we must conclude that the seals and trumpets are emphatically not judgments and that the first two series of sevens are not broken by "interludes." Instead, they are plainly what they show editorially: cogent unbroken narration.

Another obvious editorial peculiarity is that the first four items in each series, unlike the remaining items, show no strong logical connection and are in general shorter. Why? In Revelation, "four" usually conveys entirety, as "four corners of the earth" (7:1, 20:8) means everywhere and "four winds/ four destructive angels" (7:1–2, 9:14) all the ills. Thus "hour and day and month and year" (9:15) covers every moment throughout the entire span of time; "every tribe and tongue and people and nation" (5:9, 7:9, 11:9, 13:7, 14:6) refers to all people. All creatures everywhere are described as "in heaven, on the earth and under the earth and on the sea" (5:13). People are killed by all sorts of ways: with sword, famine, pestilence and wild beasts (6:8). Similarly, "heaven and the earth and sea and springs of waters" (14:7) means all creation and these are the same aspects that are catalogued in the first four trumpets and bowls (with celestial objects replacing heaven to avoid confusion). Humans are thus to love all of creation because the eternal gospel calls us to worship the maker of these four aspects. Similarly four living creatures would represent the entire make-up of humans. All these "fours" are the givens and each of the first four items in the three series show how they can be perverted or attacked to wreak havoc on humankind and the rest of creation. Note that the order and constituent of some of these "fours," e.g., symbolizing all people, differ. The point here is to convey comprehensiveness rather than exact details.

After introducing the general phenomena in the first four, the fifth in each series speaks of a triggering event (seal: saints praying for a reversal of the deterioration enumerated in the first four seals; trumpet: entrance of sins into the world through humans believing the lies of Satan, resulting in the tug of war in the preceding four trumpets; bowl: complete surrender to falsehood within Satan's kingdom, setting them on a course of no return, despite the warning signs in the preceding four bowls).

The sixth in each series details the general development triggered by the fifth. For the seals and trumpets, these developments are in three parts: 1. lowest point reached, 2. actions taken to bounce back from this lowest point, and 3. outlook made possible by these actions. People severely disfiguring God's creation and people cannibalizing each other are the lowest points reached in the seals and trumpets, respectively. God reacts by putting a halt to and reversing these intolerable downward spirals: in the seals by mobilizing the 144,000-turned multitude to protect creation; in the trumpets by cancelling the seven thunders and re-commissioning a new round of preaching. Finally, the people called and sealed can look forward to an eternal life of blissful satisfaction at the end of the sixth seal, whereas Jesus resurrects to shatter, seminally, the opposition's power at the end of the sixth trumpet.

Given that God's wrath proceeds to the bitterest end in the bowls once the threshold (trigger) has been crossed, there is no reversal for the opposition once they reach their lowest point (fully led by the spirits of the dragon and the beasts). Their fate is foregone.

The seventh develops logically (seal: Humankind's fate is bound up with creation's glorification (trumpet) and God's wrath (bowl), hence the end is not announced yet; trumpet: God begins to reign leading up to rewarding his people and destroying the destroyers of the earth; bowl: Babylon's final and total destruction in the completion of God's wrath). Here, the seventh seal may seem to be editorially shortest with only one verse (8:1), but it calls forth, thus subsumes the seven trumpets and seven bowls, making it, in meaning, the most elaborated item in all the three series.

Such an understanding means that the order of the first four items in each series of sevens may be interchanged (with the exception of the first and fourth seals) without great loss of meaning while the order of the last three items must be preserved given their consequential effects. The first four must precede the last three. This also means that the "events/items" in Revelation cannot be read a priori as sequential or consequential. The contents determine how they should be understood. An itemized comparison of the nature of the three series is given in table 6.

The first four in each series are editorially shorter and less action-packed than most of the rest because they present straightforwardly the perversion of a set of givens while the remaining three narrate the actions taken in response to these corruptions.

Another peculiarity is: With the appearance of the ashen horse in the opening of the fourth seal, one fourth of the earth is given over to destruction and death, whereas in the first episode of the sixth trumpet, one third of humankind is killed. Why the difference? Simple fractions (expressed as

1/n with "n" being a whole number) in descending order are 1/2, 1/3, 1/4 ... with 1/2 being the threshold of a majority. In the trumpets, God protects humans and his creation and would not allow a majority to be destroyed, but destruction is indeed serious, hence the next largest simple fraction (1/3) less than 1/2 is used. Yet even without Satan's instigation (recall that only people are dealt with in the seals), humans themselves are still prone to distorting the image of God in them, eventually bringing death to many. The next largest fraction of 1/4 then describes this damage. Though the intent is not to quantify the damage with mathematical precision, the point is nonetheless made that Satan's contribution is *not great* (difference in damage with and without Satan is only 1/12), reinforcing a central message in Revelation (locusts not allowed to kill in the fifth trumpet versus humans' mutual slaughtering in the first episode of the sixth trumpet; Satan's unceremonious judgment in chapter 20) that humans are largely responsible for their own woes.

Since simple fractions are mainly used to describe how destruction is averted, their frequency of use also shows God's relative concern: 1/4 used once in the seals, for humans; 1/3 used thirteen times in the trumpets, twelve times for non-human creation and only once for people.

## 4.3 What do the Seals, Trumpets, and Bowls Symbolize?

On the scroll in the hand of the one sitting on the throne are seven seals. No one is found qualified to open these seals until the Lamb that was slaughtered comes along. This scroll is written on double-sided.

Apart from being the stamp of authority on a document, a seal on a double-sided scroll prevents one side of the scroll from being read. God has fashioned his creation in a way pleasing to him, thus setting his seal on it. This side is open for all to see. Yet the deeper aspect of this creation—its ultimate destiny—is sealed up and hidden from his creatures, until the Lamb takes the scroll from the throne and breaks its seals. Henceforth, a hidden dimension, the inside of the scroll, is revealed to God's creatures. The outside of the scroll, the obvious aspect of creation, is now informed and guided by this hitherto hidden dimension, the dimension of how God works to bring his creation to a fitting conclusion.

Aspects of human nature are fixed in creation as if sealed in the first four seals, but expressing these depends on human freedom. When Jesus breaks each of the first four seals, he not only reveals them as they are now—perverted by humans—but would guide them forward and restore them to accomplish his goals, hence the fifth (humans, by nature, long for justice and restoration of their God-intended role; and now with the seal

Table 6. Structural comparison between the three series of "Sevens"

| Series of seven | 1st four Phenomena | 5th Trigger for further works | 6th Further developments: Struggle for Creation's Future | 7th Logical Finale |
|---|---|---|---|---|
| Seals | Human nature and how it is perverted to harm God's creation | A remnant initiates a counter move by crying out to God for justice | *Lowest point*: People warping God's created order<br><br>*Reversal*: God calls and seals his saints for a counter offensive<br><br>*Outlook*: Promise of reward for standing with God | Not complete without the trumpets and seals |
| Trumpets | Attack on God's creation and how God protects his creation | Satan starts his attacks on God's creation through deceiving humans | *Lowest point*: People—the lynch pin of creation—killing each other<br><br>*Reversal*: God halts judgment with a new message in Jesus<br><br>*Outlook*: People were terrified and give glory to God | Final victory seminally secured and proclaimed |
| Bowls (transformed thunders) | Opponents of God suffer revenge from God's creation | Way of no return is reached when Satan's kingdom is darkened | *Lowest point*: People selling their souls completely to Satan and the beasts<br><br>*Reversal*: none<br><br>*Outlook*: mutual cannibalizing in Armageddon | Babylon destroyed: "It is done" |

opened, the end is within sight) and the sixth (judgment and reward are certain—sealed—but as yet incomplete, hence people's choice to reject or follow God remains open) seal. The seventh seal is only completed by the trumpets and bowls.

In gist, opening the seals *reveals* the *past* of free *humans* created in God's image and *the two possible futures* according to how they relate to God's creation through the work of the Lamb.

Trumpets announce to those who can hear. Unlike the seals which are opened by the Lamb himself, the trumpets are sounded by messengers (angels). Initiating the sounding of the trumpets is the angel adding to the incense (fragrance of creation which is pleasing to God) the prayers of the saints, thus combining the actions of God with those who desire his work.

When the first four trumpets are sounded, one aspect of nature after another is struck by forces whose origin is not specified. Repeated in each is that one third of the target is destroyed, leaving two thirds intact. Announced on the one hand is the destruction through some unspecified forces, possibly a combination of factors, yet on the other hand, simultaneously the limiting of the damage to a non-overwhelming, non-irreversible extent. This limiting of damage and misery is extended to humans (fifth trumpet) and to all creation (sixth trumpet with the cancellation of the seven thunders) resulting in the cosmic triumph in the seventh trumpet. The first six trumpets are thus an announcement of disasters brought about by various forces, human perversion being one and possibly the most prominent, but the focus is on God and the saints who would restrain this destructiveness, climaxing in Jesus' seminal and epochal reversal of the tide of destruction. This last act heralds the end when God would eventually reward his followers and judge those who destroy his earth in the final triumph. God's goodness and justice would fully prevail. Emphasis is on God's triumphal love and mercy rather than on the destructions. Even in the midst of some such destructions, God's protection wins the day. Doom is not inevitable and is indeed conquered by the hope in the Lamb.

In gist, sounding the trumpets *announces* what God is *presently* doing through Jesus to *his creation* to bring it to his victorious and certain end.

Thunders are beyond human control. The same is true for the wrath of God poured down without restraint. But the onset of this wrath of God is introduced by a very human scene—of victorious people singing a song of praise that transcends epochs, a two-in-one song that weaves together the Old and New Testaments (symbolized by Moses and the Lamb). God deals consistently wrathfully with his enemies regardless of dispensations. Such wrath is not abolished even in the Lamb. Out of the designated place where people are supposed to meet God (temple) come seven angels preparing to pour out the wrath. The four living creatures reappear, with one of them handing each of the seven angels a golden bowl. Tracing back to Ezekiel's first encounter with the four living creatures, the first four seals reveal these creatures to be aspects of human nature that emanate from God himself. For sure, this wrath cannot proceed from perverted, bloodthirsty humans eager to pursue a vendetta. Rather, the four living creatures are constantly in the presence of God. They are the human nature that God has initially and always intended. Though corrupted before, they are now restored in the saints through the Lamb. A reasonable guess is that this living creature is the lion-faced one, representing the majestic and dignified (hence also righteous) side of God's image in humans, supported by the other three creatures, since all four creatures move in space-defying unison according to Ezek 1. God is bringing about his wrath through his restored agent—the saints. The mess created by humans is being forcefully mopped up in God's wrath by none other than humans. They are former Babylonians who have now shared in divine nature (14:1) after re-aligning themselves with God's original intention. They triumph over the beast and his paraphernalia.

Unlike the magnanimity and protection of God in the trumpets that are designed to call humans to repent for the good of creation and their own good, God's bowls of wrath brook no such liberality. Even the temple in which humans can meet God is barred entry to those at the receiving end of God's wrath. On these people and their works, the patience of God has expired. Yet there is no indication where the point of no return lies; only God knows. The bowls symbolize the fearful end that awaits those willfully persisting in their opposition to the creator.

Without the mitigating mercy of God when creation takes its revenge on its attackers and destroyers, the resulting wrath is total.

In gist, pouring the bowls *warns people* how God *is judging and will judge* the unrepentant *through the saints and mediated by God's creation* to complete his ejection of corruption from the wholesome creation.

Various aspects of the three series are summarized in table 7.

## 5. THE MORPHING SYMBOLS OF THE BEASTS, WOMEN, WOES AND HOLY CITY

Finding out what Babylon and the beast(s) symbolize and how they interact offers a good illustration on how to interpret other symbols.

### 5.1 Beasts

Chapter 13 dissects the kingdom of the beast as having *three components*: 1. coercive politico-military power, 2. deceptive religious establishment, and 3. conniving or deceived subjects. These three form a complete human trinity string-pulled by Satan. The first two components are both called beasts ("Then I saw *a beast* coming up out of the sea, having ten horns and seven heads . . . " (13:1); "Then I saw *another beast* coming up out of the earth; and he had two horns like a lamb and he spoke as a dragon" (13:11)) and their collusion holds together until its kingdom (now of the beast in singular) is darkened in the fifth bowl. Then they mount an all-out suicidal offensive against each other in the sixth bowl.

Table 7. General comparison of the three series of "Sevens" in Revelation

| Series of | Focus on | To illustrate how God will | What does God's work involve? | Outcome |
|---|---|---|---|---|
| Seals | Custodian of God's creation—Humans | Deal with the stewards of his creation—punish the rebels and vindicate his followers | Created humans in his image, listens to man's cries for justice, separates the people and will guide one group to serve his purpose | People being separated for God's purpose; the chosen is called to work with the Lamb to protect the earth; closure still awaits the 7th trumpet and 7th bowl |
| Trumpets | God's creation in its entirety | Protect and restore creation through the death and resurrection of Jesus | Protected his creation despite contrary forces, stops his total wrath, will bring his creation to victory in Jesus' resurrection | Transformation of the kingdom of the world into the kingdom of the Lord; God's reign begins with people recompensed accordingly |
| Bowls (transformed thunders) | God's enemies bent on destroying creation | Destroy Babylon and the beasts which pervert and destroy his creation | Lifted his protection from his opponents, allows perversion to fester unchecked, the opposition will self-destruct | Destruction of Babylon through the retaliation of God's creation, inevitable internal conflicts and strife; God's wrath completed: It is done |

True to the progressive nature of Revelation, the animosity between the beast(s) and Babylon is first hinted at in the violent and deceptive tactics in controlling the populace in chapter 13 and later expanded on when Babylon was split into *three parts* in 16:19. God's response to the blasphemies from the kingdom of the beast is not to destroy it directly, but to bring about a split, presumably along the fissures between the three components that constitute the kingdom of the beast and possibly within each component, in what is *collectively called Babylon* until then (section 5.3 discusses the three parts in greater detail). Naturally, a divided kingdom will not stand, but self-destruct.

Yet after this three-way split in the last bowl of wrath in chapter 16, only two characters are mentioned in the magnified view in chapter 17: Babylon and the beast. Either the two former beasts are now considered as one or that only one of the two former beasts remains. The description of this one beast fits that of the political establishment, the first beast in chapter 13. But when final judgment comes for the anti-god alliance, three individualized entities are again presented: Babylon in chapter 18, the political beast and explicitly the false prophet (beast rising out of the earth) in 19:20 ("And the *beast* was seized, and with him the *false prophet* who performed the signs in his presence, by which he deceived those who had received the mark of the beast and those who worshiped his image; *these two* were thrown alive into the lake of fire which burns with brimstone").

Two questions need to be answered: First, does Babylon include the two beasts? The answer is "yes" and "no." Before the judgment of God, the two beasts are part of Babylon, but when God judges by splitting her three-way in chapter 16, Babylon represents only the populace distinct from the two beasts. Subsequent zooming in reveals the innate fault lines and the symbols are refined. Such ambivalence is indeed realistic since there is no absolute distinction between the three forces—political, religious and economic—as demonstrated throughout history. Described here are not three distinct entities that are warring against each other, but the conflicting and irreconcilable self-interests that are tearing communities, societies and nations apart when only humans self(ish) interests—666—and not the harmony demanded in God's Sabbath are their target.

Second, where is the religious beast in the struggle between the beast and Babylon? Given the specific mention of three entities reinforced by three sixes in chapter 13 and Babylon's three-way fracturing in chapter 16, the most logical guess is that the beast on which Babylon, the great prostitute, sits is a composite of the two former beasts—political-cum-religious. These two are viewed as one because they supported each other and they both exert influence on the populace as if from above. Amazingly, the collusion of political and religious forces to usurp power is not shaken off even in modern "secular" states with an "educated" population after twenty centuries since Revelation! This description is poignantly accurate: *religious forces are often used to deceive,* as in the denial of the scientific fact of climate change. Now in chapter 17 they are being controlled by their former subjects, the populace, which has arrogated to themselves the name "Babylon" because of the amazing consensus among the masses, a unanimity of purpose that has not been seen since Gen 11 when the people tried building the Tower of Babel.

Regardless of whether the two beasts in chapter 13 are described as one in chapter 17 or only one is intended, the above highlights the plasticity of the symbols in Revelation: Babylon includes the beast(s) when the beast's kingdom is mentioned in chapter 16, but only the populace in chapters 17–18 when it comes into conflict with its own political (and religious) authority; the beast can refer to one or both entities mentioned elsewhere depending on the context. What remains unchanged is that these all belong to the same camp opposing God. All of them will be vanquished. The same plasticity is needed in understanding the beast that comes out of the abyss to kill the two witnesses—Jesus (11:7). History tells us that Jesus was sent to the cross when the religious and political forces colluded. The exact identity of the dominant force—political or religious—is not the issue, rather it comes out of the abyss.

Diviners have been trying to decipher the identity of the beast from extant political establishments based on its depiction of having roots from five previous heads and will gain the power of ten horns. But none of the numbers we have identified so far is open to such one-to-one matching in history. If this were intended, God would have said so as he has revealed here each of the churches, seals, trumpets, woes, and bowls. Revelation being what it says it is, what God has not identified or revealed is not meant to prompt readers to pass their time in speculation. It conveys significant moral messages, rather than lessons in secular history. Otherwise, our biggest challenge is not to identify each of the ten horns that will arise, but each of the 144,000 that stand with the Lamb on Mount Zion since this number is not generic like 10 or 1,000 or myriads of myriads but has the most significant digits (3) of all numbers in Revelation. So far, no one has the logical temerity to rise to that challenge!

Both the Books of Daniel and Revelation describe beasts arising from the sea with multiple heads and ten horns. Is it then not reasonable to bundle the beasts from the two books for interpretation, especially when they share other distinct features—like a lion, bear, leopard; strong and terrifying . . . etc. (compare Dan 7:4–7 and Rev 13:2–4). After all, when the enigmatic four living creatures in Ezekiel are interpreted together with those in Revelation, they cross-illuminate each other.

Yet there are many differences between Daniel's and Revelation's beasts. In Daniel, there are four separate beasts purposely ordered (first, second . . . ), *coming one after another.* Yet there is just one beast of this kind (politico-military) in Revelation which brings together some features of each Daniel's beast in different order—leopard (appearance), bear (feet), lion (mouth). This beast in Revelation is *one undivided animal not only in time, but in authority* (representing Satan). It has ten horns and *seven* heads, but in Daniel, only the *third beast* (leopard) has *four* (not seven) heads; only Daniel's fourth beast has ten horns. More so, Revelation has a second beast arising from the land, a faith-based one, not found in Daniel.

While all the above would certainly demand caution in bundling Daniel's beasts with Revelation's for interpretation, the clincher is the overall contextual consideration. Consider the four living creatures in Ezekiel and Revelation: they both emanate directly from God (in fact, that encounter is straightforwardly called "visions of God" in Ezek 1:1 and the descriptions in Rev 4 *neatly fit this title*; there is only one God) and hence unencumbered by particular history, giving a consistent setting. But such is not the case for the beasts. In the second half of the book of Daniel (chapters 7–12), he received a series of visions over some years with the later ones shedding light on the earlier. All these pertain specifically to his people (the exiled Jews) within his time and geopolitical surroundings, hence contemporary powers are mentioned by name—Media and Persia, Greece . . . etc. Specific outcomes in the power struggle between these local and transient kingdoms were also foretold. Yet when Revelation mentions the beast, not a whiff of such particular history and geography is evident. So can Daniel's multiple beasts be the key to unlocking the mystery of Revelation's first and singular beast?

If Revelation's context is nothing less than universal, then the Holy Spirit is not bound by the meaning of the symbols of the Old Testament when he uses the broadly similar symbols to convey the beast's power and character (which are familiar to the readers of the Old Testament), but would point to a different reality appropriate to the cosmic context of Revelation. So the politico-military might of the former *four local transient* beasts are now symbolically amalgamated into *one beast which transcends but also subsumes local history and geography*, i.e., universally applicable. That being the case, interpreting Revelation in light of *any other* biblical "prophecies" (Dan 7, 12; Matt 24 . . . etc.) without rigorously putting the symbols in the proper context flies in the face of common prudence. The same applies to equating awkwardly the 1,290 days of Daniel with the 1,260 days of Revelation. It is like demanding a grownup to re-fit into her former baby clothes.

There is only one way to do this, Procrustes's way—mutilate the object! And unfortunately this is not far from the ugliness in how some treat Revelation. Jesus' milder wording is putting new wine into old wineskins.

It is reasonable to demand that Revelation, being the Bible's conclusion, will not contradict the truths taught consistently throughout the Bible. Nevertheless, it is a different matter and altogether wrong to demand that Revelation's scope, convey by its symbols, be constrained by or consistent with that of earlier local and time-limited symbols. God's communication to us overflows its previous banks repeatedly, starting from Genesis, until we come to Revelation when God places a no-tampering warning over it.

## 5.2 Two Women, Two Cities: Is there a Role for Israel?

Thus primed by the plasticity of the symbols of the beasts, we are poised to track the development of two women and two cities.

The first apocalyptic woman in the letter proper (chapters 4–22; the woman Jezebel in 2:20 falls outside this general letter) is *described in creation's terms*: clothed with the sun while stepping on the moon and crowned with twelve stars. She appears in chapter 12 immediately after the seven trumpets. This woman bears a male child who is to rule the nations with a rod of iron, an unmistakable allusion to Jesus and the authority given to him (e.g., Isa 9:6) based on his resurrection and ascension. This woman and her offspring are persecuted by the dragon, but helped by the earth in drinking up the dragon's flood water, while she is taken care of by humans for 1,260 days as well as by God for a time, times and half a time. These timescales form a symmetry with the Sabbatical timescales used before the two witnesses' resurrection.

This woman on God's side is matched by her opposite in chapters 17–18, also in the form of a woman, but luxuriously adorned and holding a gold cup full of abominations and of the unclean things of her immorality, sitting on a beast. Nothing suggests that God's created order is allied with her. Instead, she is the great harlot who has *corrupted the earth* through her trading with the merchants of the world who become rich through such activities. Further on, this woman has morphed into *a city called Babylon* which we have seen was initially controlled and exploited by the beasts in chapter 13, but has now reversed her subservient position to make the beast(s) her workhorse by sitting on it. Her destruction through the actions of the beast(s) is orchestrated by God.

As if to counter-balance the harlot-Babylon description, the godly woman is further symbolized by *a city*, completing the symmetry between the two camps. In chapter 19 she is portrayed as the pure bride of the Lamb (in deliberate contrast to the great abominable whore) who appears as the *New Jerusalem* in the last two chapters of the Bible. The rejection of the harlot is ultimately consummated by the marriage of the Lamb; the destruction of the city Babylon is ultimately consummated by the advent of the holy city, the New Jerusalem. Revelation is both a tale of two cities as well as a tale of two women.

Of all the possible symbols, why have two women and two cities been chosen to symbolize the players in the great struggle? Appropriate for any logical writer, the Holy Spirit has taken up the beginning of the Bible to conclude God's message to his creation. When Adam and Eve fell from grace, God pronounced on the serpent that he would "put enmity between you and *the woman*, and between your seed and her seed; He shall bruise you on the head, And you shall bruise him on the heel." And on *the woman*: "I will greatly multiply your pain in childbirth, in pain you will bring forth children . . . " (Gen 3:15–16). And such are what happened: the woman (representing also her godly offspring) and the serpent (also representing all those who follow him) have been in conflict ever since, but the male child (the woman's seed in the narrow sense) born (Jesus' resurrection) through great pain (Jesus' excruciating death) has dealt a lethal blow (on the head) to Satan. What was prophesied in the opening account is now fully fulfilled in the conclusion.

A city is where humans concentrate their activities to achieve security and live for a *common purpose*. The first city in the Bible was built by the son of Cain, the first murderer in human history. After the flood, the tower and city representing all human activities to exclude God were built on the plain of Shinar. There God confused the tongue of the builders resulting in their babbling to each other. This foiled project is Babylon.

Such babbling has been reversed for God's chosen when the Holy Spirit enables different people who have hitherto been babbling past each other to speak God's truth to each other intelligibly despite their different inherited (or mother) tongues. The project of building a city, frustrated in Gen 11 with Babylon, can now resume, but with a diametrically opposite goal: to welcome God in. This city that shows itself clearly on the Day of Pentecost when God started uniting his people from all the nations (Acts 2:1–12) is seen in chapter 21 to be opening its gates to all nations through the twelve tribes of Israel. It is a fulfillment of God's promise to bless all the families of the earth through Abraham, and is founded on Jesus Christ (a descendent of Abraham in both the biological and spiritual sense) who is simultaneously historical (twelve Apostles) and transcendental (having resurrected and ascended to heaven). Unison in singing and praising God is the signature of this city.

Those not part of God's city remain committed to building Babylon, thus wallowing in the natural fruits of their confused tongues—coercion, deception, and mutual animosity leading to their own undoing.

Founding a city on Jesus' work makes all the difference in the world, factually. In Babylon is found the blood of all the saints throughout history while in the New Jerusalem the saints volunteer their service of glory and honor for its beautification and up-building (21:24–26). Human ego submitted to the Lord of the Sabbath is not only rendered harmless, but unleashes godly creativity to bless creation. The contrasts between the two women are summarized in table 8.

But who exactly is the godly woman? Tracing developments since Gen 3, the woman represents all those who have followed God since Adam and Eve fell (Abel, Seth . . . Noah . . . Abraham . . . , not to mention the many others whose names are written in God's book of life but do not appear in our Bible). From this godly humanity eventually comes Jesus, the male child, the promised seed. This humanity is Jesus' brethren (Heb 2:11). This woman is pregnant, longing for the birth of the savior in hope. Seen this way, the woman and her offspring mentioned in chapter 12 are one and the same, sharing a symbol as plastic as that for the dragon. Yet 12:17 ("So the dragon was enraged with the woman, and went off to make war with the rest of her children, who keep the commandments of God and hold to the testimony of Jesus") gives a contrary impression—the woman is somewhat distinct from her offspring. The possibility is then raised that the woman, instead of being the entire godly humanity throughout history, is just the nation of Israel.

In one dream of Joseph (Gen 37:9–11), sun, moon, and eleven stars together with the dreamer himself (the twelfth star) represent the entire makeup of Jacob's family, thus suggesting that this woman "clothed with the sun, and *the moon under her feet*, and on her head a crown of twelve stars" may be Israel. Yet such angle would necessitate taking Israel as condemnably and inexplicably transgressing the fifth commandment by stepping on his own mother! But if we set aside this very unfilial suggestion for now and note that Revelation's symbols are somewhat plastic, then perhaps the "woman as Israel" angle can be entertained. Can the woman being persecuted by the dragon indeed be taken narrowly as the nation of Israel or the ethnic community of the Jews distinct from the god-fearing humanity throughout the ages? Let us now consider this possibility by trying to fit it into the overall context of Revelation.

As far as we can make out, Revelation *has always adopted a universal scope* encompassing all humanity in God's entire creation. The seven

Table 8. Contrasting the two women in Revelation

| | God's woman | Satan's woman |
|---|---|---|
| Origin in the Bible | • Traced to Eve and God's verdict on her seed (Gen 3). | • Traced to Babel when humans wanted to replace God (Gen 11). |
| Appearance | • Clothed with the sun, feet on the moon, crown of twelve stars on her head | • Clothed in scarlet and purple; luxuriously adorned and with blasphemous names |
| History and behavior according to Revelation | • Gave birth, through much pang, to a son and some other offspring;<br>• Being persecuted by the dragon;<br>• Doubly cared for—for 1,260 days and time, times and half a time<br>• Kings bring her honor and glory | • Lives luxuriously;<br>• Makes rich the kings of the earth through trading;<br>• Boasts that she is not a widow and will never see misery;<br>• Blood of all the saints found in her |
| Relation with creation | • Helped by the earth which swallows up the flood water from the dragon | • Corrupting the earth through her immorality |
| Relation with her partner | • Follows the Lamb wherever he goes<br>• God gives her a name and she sings an exclusive song to God | • Subjugated by the beasts through coercion and lies (inferred from ch.13);<br>• From being controlled by the beast to commanding the beast |
| Reactions to her end | • All the saints rejoice at her marriage to the Lamb | • Kings of the earth startled and mourn at her speedy destruction |
| Eventual relation with God | • Accepted by the Lamb to be his bride;<br>• God is in her midst perpetually | • Destroyed by her partners whom she wants to control;<br>• God completes his wrath in her |

churches, while rooted in history, can represent any group of believers finding themselves being challenged in their own situation. They are neither ethnic nor Jewish. The two heavenly worship scenes include all without the slightest hint of ethnicity (The Lamb is rooted in Judah, but the praise of his redemption is universal; Judah stands for God's promise rather than ethnicity). Nothing can be more universal than the rainbow around God's throne. Though the sixth seal mentions the twelve tribes of Israel, they are symbolic (each idealized as exactly 1,200) of God's choice within a humanity that has corrupted its way in God's creation, a fact abundantly clear when all the seals are taken together, with the first four as portraying human nature (and not ethnic trait) and its universal consequences when misdirected, and the fifth describing all the saints. The trumpets are no different. The first five trumpets and first two episodes of the sixth trumpet are all universal. Clearly in the middle episode of the sixth trumpet, any allusion to Israel is absent—John is commanded to "prophesy again concerning many peoples and nations and tongues and kings" after the seven thunders are averted. Even in the last episode of the sixth trumpet, the two witnesses, nations, temple, outer court, holy city ... etc. are all generic, devoid of allusion to Israel. The holy city is not the geographic Jerusalem, but the entity that eventually comes down from God in 21:2. All these must be taken as symbolizing the players and prize in a cosmic struggle for them to make sense, not to mention the oft-repeated Sabbatical timescales which come directly from God's original creation *before ethnicity has any meaning*. Any attempt to read the seventh trumpet as less than universal is shameless heresy since it diminishes Jesus' triumph. What follow the trumpets—analyzes and comparison of the two opposing camps, the destruction of Babylon in the seven bowls which is explained further with the individualized downfall of Babylon, the beast and Satan—are all universal.

Within this overall flow, allusions to the twelve tribes of Israel are finally explained to be twelve gates that welcome nations into the city which is founded on Jesus' twelve apostles. As if to exorcise any residual doubt on Revelation's exclusively universal trans-historical scope, these 12+12, which are earlier depicted as twenty four elders, have been worshipping God in a timeless manner until their identities are revealed in the city. The nation of Israel is not timeless. Also in this light, the ethnicity of the 144,000 simply evaporates since this does not result from the twelve tribes self-multiplying, but from twelve tribes multiplied by twelve apostles, then again by 1,000.

Taking the godly woman in chapter 12 as the nation of Israel would completely destroy the integrity of Revelation's universal description and the beauty and symmetry (e.g., between woman-bride-Jerusalem and woman-harlot-Babylon) therein, unless we can identify an extant nation called

Babylon. The common purpose for all the saints (uncountable multitude) rallying behind the Lamb would also be segregated along ethnic lines (with 144,000 standing out) with much confusion. Dismembering Revelation that way would leave the resulting body parts ripe for cannibalizing by hungry and filthy scavengers.

History also rules out the godly woman as Israel. It cannot be the nation of Israel that gave birth to Jesus since Israel as a nation ceased to exist after its two exiles in 722 and 586 BC. Whatever was left of a Jewish political entity in Jesus' time was the partial self-rule granted by its Roman overlord, prompting the many tragic Jewish revolts against the Romans which eventually ended in 70 AD when the highly circumscribed autonomy that was granted was finally taken away in the sacking of Jerusalem. John wrote Revelation more than two decades afterward. More so, whatever "Jewish nation" there was at the time of Jesus was opposed to him, bringing about his death rather than giving him birth! More practically, being Israel (or Jewish) can have many contradictory meanings—ethnic, religious, national, genealogical (through the female line), by faith as demanded by Paul, symbolically by John right in Revelation (2:9, 3:9) . . . etc.—that such interpretation is as useless as it is impossible.

No doubt, God has chosen Israel to carry his blessings to all nations as he promised Abraham and that has come to pass in Jesus Christ, the Lamb at the center of history. *Though there may be a continual significant role for Israel as a nation in the world, just as there are roles for each nation on earth, this is not at all the concern of Revelation.* Around the manifested cosmic center, *all nations* are called to the Lamb. If one demands that ethnic or political Israel be read into Revelation because of current events (e.g. restoration of a Jewish state), then this would violate the most basic principle of any communication, let alone biblical interpretation, in finding meaning first within its own context. Such readings would enter into the running annals of ignorant babbling.

A nation defines citizenship through tangible externalities. God accepts the heart which is beyond human scrutiny. Revelation concludes with God's city, not an ethnic city.

With Jesus' ultimate claim to be the way, the truth, and the life (John 14:6), the entire God-fearing humanity is now taken up by Jesus and has access to God through him. This community of God-fearers is the offspring of the godly woman, but paradoxically also the woman herself since she has not ceased to exist, but is nourished to the very end (1,260 days). Employed here is not an *either-or, but a both-together* symbol. This kind of paradox is not alien to biblical description, as seen in Jesus responding to challenges on the reality of eternal life. In Matt 22:42–46, he poses a counter riddle based on the popular belief at the time that the Messiah is David's son: "'What do you think about the Christ, whose son is He?" They said to Him, "of David." He said to them, "Then how does David in the Spirit call Him "Lord," saying, "The Lord said to my Lord, "Sit at My right hand, Until I put Your enemies beneath Your feet"? If David then calls Him "Lord," how is He his son?" No one was able to answer Him a word, nor did anyone dare from that day on to ask Him another question." Interestingly, Jesus did not find fault with the popular belief, but neither did he straighten out the human logic after dumbfounding his opponents. Rigid human categories are not up to the task of dissecting trans-temporal divine work. Jesus was content to leave loose ends in our human logic. Quantum physics has also done the same with the natural world. Perhaps we should also.

As Revelation goes, Israel, in whatever way she is understood, has a role in God's scheme only to the extent that she was chosen to show forth God's goodness to the nations and this hinges on her response to God. To the extent that she lives up to this calling to bring the world closer to God, she has already played her role. Revelation is *silent on any further developments on national or ethnic Israel*. The godly woman's offspring in 12:17 is now focused on Jesus because of the fact of his bodily resurrection. Yet, this offspring form a continuum with all the other God-fearers throughout history, Israel included. The dragon has not left the woman alone and the woman has not been separated from her children, as it might seem, but *she has taken on an additional identity in her offspring* to become the target of the dragon's persecution.

## 5.3 The Enigma of "Threes"—Woes, Split in the Great City

"Three" (*treis* in Greek) is an enigmatic number in Revelation and is used specifically (i.e., for distinct items) four times: 1. the number of woes (each brought out by one of three angels sounding the last three of the seven trumpets, 8:13), 2. three plagues—fire, smoke, and sulphur—which are instrumental in killing one third of humankind at the beginning of the sixth trumpet, 3. three evil spirits coming out of the mouths of the main characters in Satan's camp—Satan, beast, and false prophet, and finally, 4. the great city is split into three in God's final judgment in the seventh bowl. What constitute the woes and the three fragments of Babylon, namely the first and last "three," need to be identified.

All the explicit uses of "three" are linked to God's wrath visited upon his opposition. Such is clearly seen by contrasting these with the description of the "eternal gospel" in chapter 14. There, three angels proclaimed three messages successively. Naturally one would expect these to be introduced by something like: I saw three angels and the first angel... Instead, for the first angel: "And I saw *another* angel flying in midheaven, having an eternal gospel to preach..." as if there is continuity with some previous angels in a series, but there is no such series. Then "And another angel, a second one, followed, saying, "Fallen, fallen is Babylon the great..." and finally "Then another angel, a third one, followed them, saying with a loud voice, "If anyone worships the beast..." Altogether these three proclamations give the distinct impression that it is done deliberately to avoid using the number "three," which indeed is reserved for God's wrath in Revelation. Perhaps another reason why there is such an awkward avoidance of the number "three" is to emphasize that there is only one eternal gospel, namely to fear and give glory to the creator of everything, and that the proclamations of the other two angels are simply the implications of not choosing the one and only eternal gospel on the cosmic and personal levels. Such implications are not to be confused with the only good news per se.

Three (first specific use in Revelation) woes are announced before the final three (fifth to seventh) trumpets are sounded: "Woe, woe, woe to those who dwell on the earth, because of the remaining blasts of the trumpet of the three angels who are about to sound!" (8:13b). The passing (away) of the first woe comes at the end of the fifth trumpet (9:12), suggesting that being taken in by Satan's lies is the first woe. Then the passing of the second woe (11:14) is announced at the end of the very long sixth trumpet which sees rampant violence among humans, God halting punishment, and preaching a new message centered on the resurrection of Jesus. Why would all these constitute the second woe?

Woe is meant for God's opposition. Jesus' victory means that the lifeworks of God's opposition have now been voided and their lifelong illusions are completely shattered by this rude awakening in Jesus' resurrection. Such complete negation of the opposition's belief, labor, and hope makes up the second woe. *Both the first and second woes have passed away* because of what Jesus' resurrection exposes: Satan has been lying all along and the love of the creator God rather than violence will win the day. These are fait accompli.

In the same verse which proclaims the end of the second woe, the coming of the third woe is announced, but *when or where does it end is not found* anywhere in Revelation. The content of this third woe can be taken as all the miseries God's opponents face, as described in subsequent chapters: being thrown down to earth; diabolic torment within Satan's camp; wrathful judgments from God; collapse of Babylon; being excluded from the beautiful city of God; eternal burning in the lake of fire... etc., with all these encapsulated in the seventh trumpet which announces the transformation of the kingdom of the world into that of our Lord and his Christ. But John has not forgotten to announce the passing away of this last woe. Instead his omission tells us that *this last woe would be unending for the opposition* because the force of Jesus' victory on the non-repentant will continue as long they remain defiant.

Following the storyline from chapter 13 on, the three fragments resulting from the fracturing of the great city in the seventh bowl in chapter 16 can point to different things. If chapter 13 is understood to emphasize the active work of Satan after he delegates his work to his puppets, with him pulling strings only from behind, then the three fragments are the first and second beasts and the populace marked with the insignia of 666. On the other hand, if the two beasts here are taken as one (since chapter 13 calls them both as beast and chapter 17 mentions only one beast), then Satan can be understood as the first fragment, to complete this evil trinity.

How the various anti-god parties meet their final fates is elaborated in chapters 17–20 after the great city splits into three in the last bowl. Animosity between the anti-God fragments is made explicit in chapter 17 as a cause of Babylon's destruction. Then reversing the order these parties appear in chapter 13, Babylon—the populace engaging in economic activities—is first destroyed in chapter 18, followed by the unceasing lake-of-fire torment of the beast and false prophet in chapter 19 and finally by Satan's torment in chapter 20. Identifying exactly the "three" in these chapters faces the same difficulty as before: Does the great city fracture into: 1. beast, false prophet, and populace, or 2. Satan, beast-false prophet, and populace?

In themselves, both understandings are possible. But is identifying the three fragments important? Strategically it is, since the answer will guide how or with what weapons the saints should challenge the opposition. Based on the overall emphasis of Revelation, I would have to choose the first interpretation—the fracturing of Babylon follows the *three clearly identifiable and material parts* demarcated in chapter 13. Satan himself is not a fragment from the fracturing because:

1. he is described as delegating his dirty works to his material proxies, thus focusing the saints' attention on the tangible expressions of Satan's lies in politics, religions, and socio-economics;
2. Satan's downfall is painted as happening on an altogether different plane through the out-of-character dry description in chapter 20;
3. the influence of Satan, from whose mouth the first evil spirit comes in the sixth bowl, is already fully embodied in his delegated constituents in chapter 13, hence he has no separate work;

4. Satan cannot be reduced to the level of his puppets and spoken of as a constituent of the great city without him losing his role as the chief deceiver-cum-accuser.

An apparent difficulty in the above take is why does chapter 17 only highlight the enmity between one beast and the populace, now referred to as Babylon. If my choice of the three constituents above is correct, one would expect chapter 17 to detail a tripartite struggle. Yet the same objection can also be raised about the second take since Satan is not mentioned in chapter 17 either. Suffice it to observe that Revelation's emphasis is on calling the deceived (the multitude) out of Babylon rather than saving those who purposely deceive to maintain their own power to serve Satan's destructive purpose (the two beasts), much less to redeem the arch-deceiver himself since Satan is not redeemable. Babylon ends when no one buys her goods while the remaining three parties end in eternal torment in a burning lake. The power structure of Satan's camp in chapter 13 is embodied in the two deceiving beasts and can be described as either one or two seats of power. Here the religious beast is the slavish front for the political beast, hence the ambivalence in describing them. There may be enmity between the two beasts and they may cannibalize each other, as hinted at in chapter 16, but such is not Revelation's concern and hence not elaborated in chapters 17 and 19.

The saints are to expose the *embodiment of the evil powers* and principalities of their age, be they manifested in politics, religions or socio-economics, through the truth of the one eternal gospel: "Fear God, and give Him glory, because the hour of His judgment has come; worship Him who made the heaven and the earth and sea and springs of waters." Then Satan, the *nefarious spirit*, will be judged by God himself, not by humans.

## 5.4 The Destiny of the Holy City—
## from Temple to No Temple, from "Seven" to "Twelve"

The holy city is not only a future to come. In the last episode of the sixth trumpet, the holy city already makes its debut, but the nations trampled on it for 42 months (11:2). In the fullness of time (chapters 21–22), those who formerly trampled on the holy city are either inside it as kings carrying their nations' tribute, after having switched sides, or are excluded from the city (22:15) for remaining with the lost cause. When the holy city is first mentioned, only a small part of it—the temple of God and the altar—was measured with a rod of ex-human origin and no size is given, but when the holy city comes to full maturation, the whole city and its wall, are measured by a rod that works equally on heavenly (angelic) and human scales with no unit conversion needed. Its gigantic size is also given. While the holy city was initially divided according to what was measured and what was not, no such distinction exists in the New Jerusalem where the temple (also the altar) and outer court are no more.

In between the first and the last mention of the holy city are the resurrection of the two witnesses; seminal victory of God's kingdom; battle between the camps of the Lamb and the beast; judgment of Babylon, the beast, and Satan; and the marriage of the Lamb. In the end, sacralization (illuminating the outer court with divine presence of the temple (18:1)) and secularization (enriching God's original domain (temple) with spoils from former rebels (19:17–18) interpenetrate to welcome the presence of God into one undivided holy city, now everywhere suffused with and empowered by the presence of God and the Lamb.

"Seven" stands for completeness. God worked creatively in six days and rested on the seventh. Revelation is thus replete with sevens. Given this background, it is thus very surprising that in the city, the grand finale to which all creation looks, the *number seven plays almost no role*. One of the seven angels who had the seven bowls of God's wrath talks to John in 21:9, but that is just a vestigial usage of seven inconsequential to the main thrust. This last use of seven marks a very significant transition. In chapter 21 before this verse, the sole actor is God who has completed what is humanly impossible—doing away with suffering and death—and has renewed everything. After this verse, the actors are both God and humans, but the emphasis is on the latter. The number "twelve" has completely replaced "seven."

One stark difference between how seven and twelve are used lies in their multipliers. Meaningful multiples of seven are not found in Revelation. Superficially, one may point to two prominent numbers—1,260 and 42 (associated with days and months, respectively)—as counter examples, but they are not. Our analysis in the second reading shows them to have been derived from dividing seven idealized years into two halves and converting each half to days and months to illustrate what each party (God's followers and opponents) goes through. Also, the popular self-multiplier—7×7 used by Jesus to emphasize completeness—never occurs in Revelation. By contrast, the number twelve has been multiplied by two to give the number of elders—24, and by itself to form 144 which first appears as the number of people chosen, after being multiplied by 1,000 to indicate an uncountable multitude. Finally in the last two chapters of the Bible in which the city appears in full glory, twelve appears in: 1. its raw form—as the number of tribes of Israel (also as twelve gates) and of the apostles (also as twelve exquisite foundation stones) that together make up the twenty four elders that appear a number of times before; 2. its enlarged form—12,000 stadia; and 3. its self-multiplied form—144 cubits, being the thickness of the city wall.

While seven stands for completeness and hence cannot be enlarged (no multiplication), twelve stands for God's choice of humans which, from a seminal beginning of one person (Abram), expands into twelve sons, each in turn birthing a tribe. Then Jesus' twelve apostles are multiplied to God's choice of the twelve Israeli tribes and from there, those chosen of God expands almost beyond measure (1,000). God's completion of his work at the end of his week (after 3.5 days + time, times and half a time) ends in those chosen being multiplied countless folds. In Genesis, God wanted humankind to be fruitful and multiply. But after Adam and Eve sinned, much of the multiplication ended in trampling on God's holy city in chapter 11. God wants another multiplication, not biological, but through the convergence of his promise (12 tribes) and the response from his chosen (12 apostles). This mysterious multiplication eventually grew into a city described by twelve and its multiples. Standing on the seven of God, the twelve multiplies creatively and open-endedly.

Revelation is addressed to seven churches—the world-wide community that bears the name of Jesus—but these seven churches are just provisional, soon to be replaced by the ultimate twelve's in the New Jerusalem. The creative acts of God in the first six days have reached its zenith not in God's promise alone, but in the union of God's promise and choice with the multiple responses of the chosen to God's calling. *God has made good on his promise to Abram with the twelve stars crowning the godly woman in 12:1.*

At the end of the saints' work—their seven years of Sabbath symbolized here as 2×1,260 days—is found a most surprising use of "12." Never before in Revelation has "twelve" been applied to time, but now the tree of life bears *twelve kinds of fruit*, yielding its fruits every month, presumably one kind each month, with its leaves for the healing of the nations. Though the number of nations is not mentioned, the twelve fruits suggest symbolically that there are a corresponding number of nations or types of nation. Even the individuality and idiosyncrasies of the saints—the twelve symbolic tribes each with its unique character—are being accommodated by nature's rhythm. In fulfillment of God unchanged intention, the works of the saints in bringing God's rhythm of seven to his creation end in resonance with nature. *Citizens of the New Jerusalem find their destiny in the embrace of God's creation. The divine and natural calendars have merged.*

When God's seventh day arrives for his creation, God is well-pleased to defer to his chosen twelve living by his light. The Lord of God's Sabbath is now the Lord of God's Jubilee. Hallelujah!

## 6. IT IS A MATTER OF TIME

Unlocking the meaning of time is a key to making sense of Revelation. We have dealt with this issue in the first reading where indefinite (generic) timescales (1,000 years, 1 hour) and definite (specific) timescales (1,260 days, 3.5 days, 42 months) are differentiated. The latter is found to correspond to a Sabbatical timeframe in the second reading.

But common understanding of time has another angle: the order in which things happen. The descriptions that come closest to ordering happenings are the series of sevens—the seals, trumpets, and bowls—since unlike the seven churches, these are specifically numbered. Yet, the contents of these series suggest that they cannot be sequential. The first four seals, representing four aspects of human nature cannot be segregated and be operative one after another. They are *concurrent rather than time-sequenced*. The same is true of the fifth seal since saints throughout the ages have not waited until after one single triggering event before they cry out to God for justice and restoration. Whenever there is wickedness, they cry out. In line with the nature of the first five seals, the separation of those fleeing from those welcoming the wrath of God in the sixth seal cannot refer to one specific universal moment or period in time as people have been trying to hide from (of course unsuccessfully) or longing for the wrath of God from time immemorial. As such, the great tribulation the saints have gone through is the numerous episodes played out in the lives of individuals, communities, nations . . . etc. throughout the expanse of time. The only commonality is that they suffer for remaining true to God.

In a similar way, the seven trumpets cannot be understood as sequential either. The destructive forces attacking nature represented by the first four trumpets, regardless of who or what unleashes them, do not follow an order, but come upon the earth and its inhabitants somewhat haphazardly. Through God limiting rather than promoting their destructions, the message of God's *unchanging protection and love* is conveyed. In the fifth trumpet, those who have bought into the deceptions of the angel of the abyss have been tormented by the aftermath of Satan's lies since the time of Adam, and as always, God limits the duration and damage, leaving room for repentance. Concurrent with this miasma are humans turning against each other in an ever downward spiral of mutual destruction at the beginning of the sixth trumpet. Thereafter in the same trumpet, God acts on behalf of his creation to avert the imminent doom that would otherwise overtake his appointed steward of creation by bringing about victory through the resurrection of Jesus. On the surface, the contents or "events" of the sixth trumpet seem to be chronologically ordered though the trumpets making up the series do not follow any time sequence. Yet Jesus comes on the stage *not in response to any particular cataclysmic event* humankind has precipitated, but in God's own time to reverse humankind destructive behavior through his seminal example of dying for sinners. His atonement is effective for all times.

When John narrates the fall of Babylon in chapter 18, he adapted the description from Ezek 26–28 where the collapse of Tyre is prophesied. This illustrates the same paradox—seemingly one-off, but in fact ever-true: it must be granted that Tyre's own downfall is *one of the many downfalls of Babylon* throughout history. As such, each collapse of a god-defying human enterprise throughout history is a Babylon fallen, but the ultimate Babylon would eventually fall.

In the hindsight of Jesus being placed at the center of history (resurrecting at the 3.5-day point) and the description of Christ's trans-temporal existence in chapter 20 (reigning for one thousand years), Jesus' resurrection and the resulting victory in the lives of his disciples, though fully historical, also take on a trans-temporal dimension. This can be likened to the eye-opening of the two disciples walking with the resurrected Jesus on the road to Emmaus (Luke 24:13–35). When the "Eureka" moment arrives, they realize that the Jesus who was their teacher in human form has always been present throughout history since creation, as things have been written about their teacher as if those events were history (e.g., Isa 53).

*This dual yet complementary sense of time—simultaneously historical yet transcending particular history; simultaneously present and ever-present; simultaneously past and future while being anchored to the present—must be our guide to appreciating the real import of Revelation's message.* Through this bridge, one symbolic act in a historic moment is extended throughout the expanse of time (*chronos*) and the many events past, present, and future are subsumed under one decisive appointed time (*kairos*).

Appreciated this way, the rest of Revelation now reveals its true sense. God has reigned on earth since creation through the ministration of his saints under the ever-working Christ, but the decisive victory of the historical Jesus seals this reign for all ages, hence the "kingdom of the world has become the kingdom of our Lord and of His Christ; and He will reign forever and ever" (seventh trumpet). The struggle between the woman and the dragon in chapter 12 has been going on since Eve and Adam ate the forbidden fruit and will continue to the end of history, but it has always been centered on the male child being born of this woman. Since his first lies to

Eve, Satan, and his camp, have always operated through the evil trinity of political oppression, religious deception and economic manipulation, but the battle front in history has always been drawn between those for and those against Jesus leading them to the final Sabbath in chapter 13. Those in God's camp have always enjoyed sweet fellowship with the creator in God's family, and springing from this is the earth harvested (cleansed of evil), but partnership between God and humans has always been through Jesus, the son of man, as shown in chapter 14. God has always demanded justice in Old Testament times, but with Jesus ushering in a new dispensation in history, the song of Moses and the song of the Lamb have melded into one grand new song to bring about God's righteous wrath in chapter 15.

As in the first two series of sevens, the first four of seven bowls of wrath in chapter 16, being destruction through God's creation, are neither ordered in time nor causally related, while the remaining three bowls reinforce each other, with the outcome being the destruction of the human enterprises that arise from people desiring to be God themselves. Starting with the first confusion of tongues in Babylon shortly after the great flood, numerous Babylons have been destroyed by the Lamb in numerous "decisive" moments. Invariably carrying the seeds of their own destruction are the godless political, religious, and economic forces, each bent on total domination and control to "rule as a queen" and to banish seeing misery. Heads (political and religious powers *throughout history*) and horns (political and religious powers that collude together *at any one moment*) in chapter 17 have been the trade-mark of the camp opposing God's rule since creation, but these have not lasted and will not last because each harbors the same evil desire of wanting to be the supreme authority to the exclusion of others. Wherever the light of God has illuminated the earth, a Babylon—kingdoms, enterprises, religions and even individuals bent on self-aggrandizement—has fallen, but there will come a time when the last vestige of challenging God's sovereign rule will be defeated by the light of God's angels, namely humans. Then will the Babylon finally be destroyed. Whenever a Babylon has fallen in history, a beast and a false prophet (also a beast) have been judged and thrown into the lake of fire and the ongoing wedding of the Lamb in chapter 19 has drawn one step closer to consummating his marriage.

Since the pronouncement that the kingdom of the world has been transformed into the kingdom of God at the end of chapter 11, many events great and small in history *have been subsumed under and portrayed as the ultimate, one-off event* leading up to the end of history, e.g., totalitarian "666" control established over humans in chapter 13, double harvesting the earth in God's winepress in chapter 14, three-fold splitting of Babylon in chapter 16, demise of Babylon in chapter 18 . . . etc. Yet Revelation now overlays those events with a universal reference grid in chapter 20 to put the previously colorful descriptions into cosmic perspective. Both representations—the one-off final victory of God over Satan and the many events that lead up to, but also consummate, the final event—are poignantly melded into the *decisive, epochal yet non-specific descriptions* like: "I saw thrones and they sat on them" (thrones point to decisive authority, but who are "they"?); "will reign with Him for a thousand years" (reigning is firm, but one thousand years is indefinite); "... and sealed it over him, so that he should not deceive the nations any longer, until the thousand years were completed; after these things he must be released for a short time" (Satan's deception is for sure, but how short is a short *chronos*?) ... etc., reinforced by purposely taking the vividness and colors out from the whole chapter.

In the backward shinning light of chapter 20, 9:15 in the sixth trumpet now reveals its true meaning. "And the four angels, who had been prepared for *the hour and day and month and year*, were released, so that they would kill a third of mankind" refers *not to a specific cataclysmic event in the past, present or future, but rather the many lethal conflicts between humans throughout the eons.* Such is totally in agreement with the flow of the trumpets which paints a universal picture of God's unrelenting protection of his creation and humans throughout the ages. Similarly, the first five of the seven heads (kings) of the beast in chapter 17 refer generically to *all the political powers before the present* rather than five specific epochs that can be traced by historians. These five kings are just gap fillers to fix every reader in the time of the sixth king, that is *always* at the threshold of the last one—the seventh—to come. Believers should *always* be on alert.

When the life, beauty, and excitement return, after chapter 20, to the last two chapters of Revelation, their portrayal can also be read as an inter-penetration of current events with the ultimate divine goal, mundane history woven into the final prize, or the present shot through with eschatological sparkles. While current history can be taken as starting with the fall of humankind in which evil—death, pain, tears ... etc.—is inevitably and inextricably part of our experience, a sharp break from this history is wrought by God in Jesus' resurrection in which the former things resulting from the corruption by sin is no more. As a consequence, a foretaste of the eternal bliss in the city has been dispensed throughout history to those who have followed the one who claims that he has never stopped working with his Father since creation (John 5:17). This whets their appetite for the unalloyed ultimate. In response, these people have lived according to the image of the creative God to bring forth glory and honor for the beautification of the camp of the saints which, through the super-natural transformation of God, will eventually dovetail with the city in its manifold full-blown beauty.

Even the New Jerusalem to come was sized by John using a human-angelic measure. The ever-present call to forsake Babylon for the camp of the saints has always been complemented by the perpetually open pearly gates of the city. The New Jerusalem is as relevant in the time of Abel as now and as in the future since people participate in the shaping of the city they were, are, and will be looking for (Heb 11).

In chapter 21, the true identity of the twenty four elders in the city of God has been revealed as the twelve foundation stones and twelve gates. This further illustrates Revelation's portrayal of time-bound activities by timeless apocalyptic imagery from another angle: the two pivotal yet historically transient leaders (twelve tribes of Israel and twelve apostles) in the city are at least two thousand years apart, but they (12 + 12 elders) are described as simultaneously unceasingly praising God in the heavenly worship.

Transplanted from the Garden of Eden into the city is the tree of life on both sides of the river of life. The former curse on the ground now belongs to a past dispensation. Humankind was barred from that prized tree, the natural support of all life, since God ruled that fallen humans should be sustained through their hard toil ("Cursed is the ground because of you; In toil you will eat of it all the days of your life. Both thorns and thistles it shall grow for you; and you will eat the plants of the field; By the sweat of your face You will eat bread" Gen 3:17b–19a). Yet relief from this curse did not have to wait until the new heaven and earth. After bringing the Israelites out of Egypt, God institutionalized the Sabbatical year for them. Through this practice, the Israelites are to bring their land into the grand harmony under God. Successive observance of the Sabbatical years would ultimately lead to the Jubilee year. During the Sabbatical year, humans are to forego the dubious security of their own agriculture in exchange for direct nurture through the vast natural creation of God. Eventually, the knowledge, hence also respect, that humans thus gain from nature would bring about the redemption of God's sub-sentient and non-sentient creation, which is the freedom of creation Paul teaches in Rom 8:18–22. It is not by co-incidence that the Sabbatical year cycle, properly centered on Jesus' victory through his resurrection, symbolizes the total "duration" of history with 1,260 days for the two pre-resurrection witnesses in the sixth trumpet and another 1,260 days for God's post-resurrection protection of his people. The message is clear: whenever humans bring God's creation into harmony with themselves, a foretaste of the lost tree of life with its leaves and fruits is available to inspire us forward, and on and on until the consummate tree of life appears for the healing of all the redeemed nations.

If each of the seemingly decisive and final events narrated in Revelation can also be understood as being played out on different timescales in the lives of individuals and communities in between God's curse on the ground in Genesis and the full reappearance of the tree of life in the end, then the narratives in *Revelation will indeed be relevant all the time everywhere*. Even chapters 12 to 22, which seem to narrate the saints' struggle *after Jesus' victory*, can be taken as descriptions of the many conflicts that extend back to *before Jesus*. Nothing would be passé until the final moment, known only to God, arrives. Such is the never-fading worth of the concluding book of God's oracle in Jesus Christ to humankind.

Our modern sense has habituated us into approaching all "time" as the same chronology on one linear scale. Without appreciating John's skilful use of God's timescales—Sabbatical/creational yet cosmic; transient yet ever relevant—and their full implications which make every passing hour, day, month, year, and *importantly week*, meaningful, one can end up with some gargantuan misunderstanding.

Consider the beast which has seven heads and ten horns in chapter 17. An angel clearly explains the seven heads as seven kings *at different times*. In contrast, the Lamb has, by default, only *one head*, but "seven horns and seven eyes, which are the seven Spirits of God, sent out into all the earth" (5:6). God always has his creation and the people therein in mind and hence *the gospel issues from one mind and has unchanging validity* (14:6) since the fall of humankind. Regardless of the changing circumstances, people should always—eternally—"worship Him who made the heaven and the earth and sea and springs of waters." Yet rebelling against God can take many guises throughout history and lies can be told in countless ways, hence the different heads on the beast/dragon. As in simple mathematics, there is only one right answer, but numerous ways to get it wrong.

According to Revelation, segmenting time (e.g., baselessly reading the seven churches as seven periods) into different dispensations is Satan's scheme. God singly honors people from all ages responding to his one eternal gospel.

Based on different meanings of time in Revelation, we can say:

1. Time in Revelation is riveted to an immovable center—Jesus' death and resurrection in chapter 11; from this center, all creation is seen as God working to complete his creation in seven days and humans co-working with God to complete their works in seven years.

2. Also from this absolutely fixed center, both past and present times are re-cast, hence re-interpreted, as open to the future; even the past can be described in future tense (end of section 5.4.3 of the second reading; chapter 11); "which must soon take place" (1:1, 22:6) entails applying Jesus' victory to both past and future.

3. Creation's history is laid out before God in an instant; time to history's prime mover—Jesus—can thus be timeless (chapters 4, 5, 20).

4. To us who are still caught up in the flow of history, time is never passé and every cosmic description in Revelation can be played out in the lives of individuals, communities and nations; thus Revelation never loses its significance on any scale these time-travelers find themselves in (chapters 12–19).

5. Forward flowing time for humans with its vicissitude begins from God's creation. It will be caught up into the eternity of the new creation of God and humans in God's fullness of time (chapters 21–22).

6. Time in Revelation can only be described and its significance appreciated by each person caught in his/her own time, but not measured by any human scale and pocketed as a human chronograph.

7. The Holy Spirit throws open God's Sabbath to the participation of all saints. God's first Sabbath, looking back to his creation, has now burst its old boundaries. A new and fulsome Sabbath can be glimpsed through Jesus from the here and now. *Creation now looks forward rather than backward in time.*

Week and Sabbath are the same word in Greek: *Sabbaton*. Thus *Jesus is Lord of the whole week* given his unfailing presence with his saints in chapter 20. He is the cosmic Lord. Simultaneously, he is *Lord of the Sabbath* which emphasizes the process leading up to the end point—the Omega point itself, the total victory that was irrevocably set in motion by his death and resurrection symbolized in chapter 11. He is the creator who is still working with his chosen. As time (*chronos*) enmeshed in the week grinds on for the saints, their eyes are refreshed by the Alpha (God's beginning) which is completed in the Omega (Sabbath) through understanding God's *kairos*. A schematization of this understanding of time follows in figure 4.

## 7. SYMBOLS AND HOW DO THE PLAYERS FIT IN TO THE OVERALL GAME?

Unlike a long novel with an unmanageable number of characters, Revelation only has a few major players, yet each is portrayed by a variety of symbols appropriate for each scene. A legitimate question is why does the conclusion of the Bible use symbols rather than plain language, or more precisely, why does it use plain language to describe symbols? Here is a common sense explanation.

To start, note that Revelation's symbols are not just symbols, but mostly exotic portrayals *far removed from our daily experience*. Even the two witnesses are no ordinary symbols given the wonders they perform, and their death and resurrection. Such symbols offer a *timeless, borderless flexibility* that direct language cannot match. Take the symbol of the beasts. If a political or religious body is identified using plain language, e.g., the Roman military machine and the cult of emperor worship, then it would leave out the many other entities of different sizes and guises having the same nature—violent, oppressive, and mendacious—reaching back to far antiquity and forward to the indefinite future. The same can be said of the harlot sitting on a beast bent on economic successes for self-glorification. But through symbols, *Revelation's subversive message* is carried to every nook and cranny of creation, potentially effecting a transformation unlike anything direct naming can achieve. People like labelling to achieve their own ends. Calling our community a "church" can be a means of self-sanctification: we have a special relationship to God and are the light of the world . . . etc. But Revelation's exotic symbols would pierce this façade and examine its entrails. Any oppressive action (e.g., imposing nationalism through law enforcement) and denial of the truth (e.g., scientific certainty of man-induce environmental damage) are properly the action of the beasts. A "church" idolizing materialistic success or conniving with injustice is properly Babylon even when it dangles some god-words on its lips. This is another reason why all efforts at shedding light on Revelation through historical and political matching, which can only deal with Procrustean and transient labels, e.g., Israel, US, Russia, Arabic countries, EU, China . . . etc., have failed and will fail. Revelation's symbols do not distinguish between a one-man beast or a national beast, a one-clan Babylon or a conglomerate Babylon. Sanctimonious and protective labels are mercilessly blown apart by Revelation's symbols to expose the cleansing needed. Who then are followers of the Lamb rather than members of a church?

It is highly revealing to note that the main body of Revelation (4:1—22:5), the letter each church has to read, never once uses the word "church." But in the introduction (chapters 1–3) and the closing remark (22:16), when God is addressing concrete communities that are *identified with Jesus in name*, they are called churches. The lesson: whether they are worthy of the label "church" depends on how they follow the Lamb to resist Babylon. Since the symbols are so far away from the familiar, they will not be confused with our well-worn labels, thus retaining their power to subvert for healing and renewal. The same logic applies to most other symbols—the two witnesses (rather than the Law and Prophets), the woman bearing a male child (rather than Israel), the bride (rather than Eden) . . . etc. Labels fortify the status quo, but Revelation's symbols subvert.

With this background, Revelation's *target audience is all humanity rather than the churches in name*, be they a local or worldwide entity. That is why Revelation often seems to be speaking to the so-called non-believers (14:6–12, 18:4, 22:17). The church is just the first recipient and those who call themselves church should reasonably pay closer attention to Revelation's utterance. In the end, every living person must judge which camp—God's or Satan's—he/she belongs to based on symbols, rather than human labels, and face up to the consequence. Welcoming or fearing Jesus' return can be a useful touchstone.

Who then are the major players in this cosmic struggle? They are paired up according to their role as:

1. God (a) versus Satan(b);

2. Jesus (a) versus the beasts (b);

3. The Saints (a) versus people opposing God (b).

Such a limited depiction does not mean that the Holy Spirit is not actively at work throughout history. On the contrary, he is ever-present, constantly revealing from the Father and the Son all things and bringing to our remembrance all that Jesus said (John 14:16, 26). Though the Spirit comes forth at critical moments to reassure and call (14:13, 22:17), he pervades the entire Revelation in a way that defies imaging, hence my description of only God and the Lamb here. Correspondingly, the opposition has evil spirits and demons, but they are also not taken up here. Angel(s) also play an active role throughout Revelation. Yet from what we can make out, many of them are human agents and they can take God's or Satan's side. These are thus grouped under the saints or their opponents. The remaining angels are cast as messengers or workers of an indeterminate type rather than independent actors, hence not included in our list of players. A non-exhaustive trace of the major players, with their salient nature, deeds and/or symbolic representation now follows.

## 7.1 The Major Players

1a **God** (when described, always sitting on the throne)

1. Sitting (faceless) surrounded by a rainbow and worshipping creatures and elders (4:3)

**Figure 4.**   Schematization of the two major timescales used in Revelation

| Son of Man—Lord of the Sabbath, Creational Perspective ||||
|---|---|---|---|
| Beginning of History— Creation | Center of History, Jesus' Resurrection (Raising of the two witnesses) || Completion of History— Holy City |
| In the beginning | Old Testament | New Testament | Come, Lord Jesus |
| God's perspective | Tolerates abuses by his opponents, but resurrected the two witnesses (11:1–12) | Gives wings to the woman to fly to the wilderness and be nourished (12:13–14) | God's wrath on Babylon; Marriage of the Lamb; City, River & God's presence. |
| **God's timescale** | ←——— 3.5 days ———→ | ← time, times & 0.5 time → | |
| | ←——— God's week of seven days ———→ || |
| God's followers' perspective | Two witnesses prophesying wearing sackcloth (11:3–6) | Woman gives birth and flees to the wilderness to be nourished (12:5–6) | No more death, tears; glory, honor into the City (21:1–22:6) |
| Timescale | ←——1,260 days——→ | ←——— 1,260 days ———→ | |
| **Human Timescale** | ←———Human Sabbatical cycle of seven years ———→ || In harmony with God and creation |
| Timescale | ←—— 42 months ——→ | ←—— 42 months ——→ | Judgment of Babylon, beasts, false prophet and Satan |
| God's opponents perspective | Trample over the holy city (11:2) | Beast blaspheming and warring against the saints (13:1–7) | |
| **Christ—Lord of the Week, Cosmic Perspective** ||||
| Past | Present || Future |
| God's verdict on humans and Satan | ←——— 1,000 yrs, God restrains Satan, Saints reign with Christ, Satan let out briefly ———→ || Every person judged before God |
| Fall of Humankind | . . . S/T/B . . . S/T/B . . . S/T/B . . . S/T/B . . . S/T/B . . . * || New Jerusalem |
| | Great Tribulation of All Believers Opposition's 5 months of torment by mutated locusts 1/3 creation (humans) damaged (killed) Many (144,000, uncountable multitude) chosen Three Woes announced for the opposition Eternal Gospel preached to all and sundry All other activities in Creation || |
| 1st to 5th heads (kings) | . . . 6th . . . 6th . . . 6th . . . 6th . . . 6th . . . 6th . . . 6th . . . head (king) || 7th head + 10 horns |

\* S/T/B: Seals, Trumpets, and Bowls

2. Receiving praises because of his holiness, eternity and creation (4:8–11)

3. Holding in his right hand a scroll with seven seals (5:1)

4. Refusing to meet some people (no entry to the temple) in his final wrath (15:8)

5. Sitting on a great white throne judging the living and the dead (20:11)

6. Illuminating the city and guiding the people therein with the Lamb (21:22–24)

7. Providing water of life from his throne to sustain all creation (22:1–2)

1b **Satan** (the supreme opponent to God)

1. Angel of the abyss, having fallen from heaven (9:1)

2. Darkening the sun and the air through the smoke from his abyss (9:1–2)

3. *Abaddōn* and *Apollyōn*—leading his army of mutated locusts to torment humans (9:7–11)

4. Great red dragon with seven heads and ten horns to destroy God's male child (12:3–4)

5. Warring with Michael and lost; thrown down to earth (12:7–9)

6. Delegating his authority to the beast (13:4)

7. Chained for a thousand years (20:2)

8. Must be released from prison to deceive the nations for a short while (20:3)

9. Thrown into the lake of fire to be tormented endlessly (20:10)

2a **Jesus Christ** (most exquisitely described of all major players, working across time)

1. Author of Revelation (1:1)

2. Alpha and Omega, the first and the last (1:8, 17, 21:6, 22:13)

3. Living One who was dead but alive forevermore holding the keys of death and of Hades (1:18)

4. Son of man with many esoteric descriptions speaking to seven churches (1:13–16; chapters 2–3)

5. Lion from the tribe of Judah, root of David, who overcomes (5:5)

6. Lamb that was slain taking the scroll from God's hand (5:6–7)

7. Hailed as worthy to receive power, riches, wisdom, might, honor, glory and blessing (5:11)

8. Opens each of the seven seals (chapters 6–8)

9. Two witnesses testifying for God for 1,260 days (11:3–6)

10. Two witnesses killed but resurrected and taken up to heaven (11:7–12)

## THIRD READING—STRINGING TOGETHER THE GEMS

11. Male child born to rule the nations with a rod of iron, persecuted, but taken up to God (12:5, 19:15b)
12. Michael leading his angels in casting the opposition to earth (12:7–9)
13. Lamb leading 144,000 on Mount Zion (14:1)
14. Son of man harvesting the earth with the saints and treading God's winepress (14:14, 19:15)
15. "Faithful and true, Word of God" sitting on a white horse preparing for the marriage (19:11–18)
16. Throwing the beasts alive into the lake burning with fire and brimstone (19:20)
17. Killing the opposition with the sword from his mouth (19:21)
18. Christ, reigning with those who comes back to life for one thousand years (20:4)
19. Lamb, being the lamp in the city (21:23)
20. Descendent of David, the bright morning star promising a quick return (22:16–20)

**2b Beast** (one or two, political and religious leaders colluding under Satan across time)

1. Comes out of the abyss and kills the two witnesses (11:7)
2. First one arises from the sea and blasphemes God (13:1, 6)
3. Mimicking the Lamb as if being slain and comes back to life (13:3)
4. Delegated authority by Satan to act and receive worship (13:4)
5. Controlling all peoples and even overcoming the saints (13:7)
6. Second one arises from the land and deceives the people through religious means (13:11–15)
7. Orchestrates normal human transactions with a mark of 666 (13:16–18)
8. Scarlet, with ten horns and seven heads, being sat on by a harlot (13:1, 17:3)
9. Heads are past, present, and future kings, horns are kings in powerful collusion (17:8–13)
10. Hates and wants to destroy Babylon (17:16–18)
11. Thrown as beast and false prophet into the lake of fire (19:20)

3a **Saints** (despite their separation in time and locale and their different roles, they are seen as one camp in chapter 20)

1. Seven churches to receive the entire message of Revelation from Jesus (1:11; chapters 2–3)
2. Represented by the twenty four elders leading worship of God (5:9–13)
3. Original nature emanating from God as four living creatures, prompting worship of God (4:6b–7)
4. Killed for God and crying out under the altar for speedy justice in the fifth seal (6:9–11)
5. 144,000 sealed from the twelve tribes of Israel, chosen to protect God's creation (7:2–8)
6. Uncountable multitude being cleansed by God and come through the tribulation (7:9–17)
7. People giving glory to God after one tenth of the city fell after Jesus' resurrection (11:13b)
8. Woman with sun, moon, and twelve stars giving birth to a male child (12:1–5)
9. Woman and her offspring persecuted by the dragon but helped by the earth (12:13, 16, 17)
10. Woman protected for 1,260 days and time, times and half a time (12:6, 13)
11. Blameless and given the name of the Father and singing an exclusive song with the Lamb (14:1–5)
12. Those dying blessed in the Lord because they can rest and their deeds follow them (14:13)
13. Three angels flying in mid-heaven proclaiming one three-part message (14:6–11)
14. Two angels coming out of the temple and altar harvesting the earth with the son of man (14:15, 18)
15. Those victorious over the beast and his image, singing a unified song (15:2–4)
16. Great multitude in heaven leading the praise of God for his righteous judgment (19:1–7)
17. Birds flying in mid-heaven feasting on spoils during the wedding of the Lamb (19:17–18)

18. Resurrected and sitting on thrones reigning with Christ throughout history (20:4)

19. Names of whom are found in the Book of Life, immune to the second death (20:6)

20. First twelve elders; ever-open twelve gates (tribes of Israel) inviting all into the city (20:12)

21. Last twelve elders: foundation stones of the city—twelve apostles' teachings (20:14)

22. Kings of the earth and of nations bringing their glory and honor into the city (21:24–25)

3b **People opposing God** (despite separation in time, they are seen as one opposition in chapter 20)

1. Four horsemen materializing the twisted image of God in humans (6:1–8)

2. From all walks of life making a mess of God's creation (6:12–14)

3. Fleeing the wrath of God knowing the mess they have made (6:15–17)

4. Those without the seal of God, hence tormented by the mutated locusts (9:4, 6)

5. Troops of cavalry, twice the number of the saints, destroying each other through violence (9:16–19)

6. Unrepentant survivors of their own violence (9:20–21)

7. Nations which tread underfoot the holy city for forty two months (11:2)

8. Destroyers of the earth being destroyed by God (11:18)

9. Worshippers (and makers) of an image of the political beast (13:4, 12, 14)

10. Receivers of the mark of the beast (666) and are thus controlled (13:16–17)

11. No rest day and night because of their identification with the beast (14:11)

12. Unrepentant, and blaspheme God when struck by God's wrath in his bowl (16:8)

13. Deceived by demons from the Euphrates for the battle of the great day of God (16:13–14)

14. Babylon (Satan's entire human camp) splitting into three mutually-hostile parts (16:19)

15. Babylon (woman riding on the beast) trying to subdue the beasts (17:16–17)

16. Trapped in Babylon with every unclean and hateful birds, demons, and unclean spirit (18:2–3)

17. Saying in their hearts: "I sit as a queen, I am not a widow and will never see mourning" (18:7)

18. Corruptor of the earth and deceiver of the nation through her sensuality (18:1, 19:2)

19. Great and small men, free men and slaves being devoured by birds in mid-heaven (19:18)

20. Nations coming up from the broad plains of the earth besieging the camp of the saints (20:8–9)

21. Anyone whose name is not found in the book of life, hence thrown into the lake of fire (20:15)

22. Outsiders to the city: sorcerers, immoral persons, murderers, idolaters, . . . liars (21:8, 22:15)

Pairing up the major players as done here is prompted by the actions in the final judgments of the characters in Satan's camp. God sitting on the throne dumps Satan the deceiver into the lake of fire. God establishes his creation through the truth which undergirds the harmonious workings of his creation. Satan tries to destroy God's creation by distorting God's truth at every turn of event. It is only fitting that the *chief liar (Father of lies—John 8:44) meets his fate at the hand of the source of all truth.*

Though the dragon (Satan) is portrayed as going after the woman with the male child who is to rule the nations with a rod of iron in chapter 12, its context indicates that the dragon there represents the entire camp of Satan (with seven heads and ten horns (3) which are the signature of the beast; referred to as dragon and his angels in (7)) rather than the deceiver per se. A more focused passage shows that the two witnesses—Law and Prophets— who are to be understood as the trans-temporal Jesus, was actually *killed by the beast that comes out of the abyss* (11:7). Here, the arena of operation of Christ and the beast is clear. Throughout the Old Testament, the Law and Prophets have been addressing concrete political and religious issues concerning God's people. Pure "spiritual" issues are far from their minds. This tradition is taken up by Jesus when he confronts his opponents. These two aspects converge in the Sabbath when this seemingly religious issue that Jesus challenged was taken up by the political authorities (the Herodians, the Jewish Council and finally the Roman powers) to bring about Jesus' crucifixion. Revelation simply restates these historical events using the apocalyptic symbol of beast. *The beast is also revealed to be two-in-one* in chapter 13, political and religious machines colluding under Satan's delegated authority, in a direct correspondence to the *two-in-one witness* killed in chapter 11. After the two-in-one existence of both the Lamb and the beast has been described once, they both are portrayed as single beings again.

The lies of Satan are concretized by the two beasts which later on at their downfall are called the beast (singular) and the false prophet (19:20). Fittingly, Jesus, symbolized by the two witnesses, was killed by the two-in-one beast, but it is also an utmost fitting ending that it was the *Jesus Christ who is alive forever and ever (1:18) to throw the two beasts alive into the lake burning with fire and brimstone for unending torment (20:10).*

Babylon is a human enterprise. All the people stamped 666 constitute Babylon. The lies of Satan are expressed politically and religiously by the beasts which are also humans. These lies find a ready host among those who knowingly want to lie and be lied to. They, sitting on the two-in-one beast, desire to control their rulers and invent their own religion. This inevitably brings about a mortal struggle with the beasts (17:3, 16). Babylon eventually falls when the restraint God places on people killing each other in the sixth trumpet is lifted in the sixth bowl of his wrath. Unashamed, hence unrestrained, violence on each other within Babylon eventually does Babylon in. Following this logic, "the war of the great day of God, the Almighty" (16:14b) is not the multitude against God, but people with the mark of the beast fighting each other to death! Common folks—the multitude on both sides—marvel and rejoice at the downfall of Babylon which represents all the people from all walks of life participating in corrupting God's good creation.

But does Revelation not say that the one sitting on a white horse kills his opponents after they gang up against him (19:19–21)? Also, before the devil, Satan himself, is thrown into the lake of fire and brimstone, the multitude besieging the saints' camp is devoured by fire from heaven (20:9). Do these not indicate that the Lamb and God on the throne intervening directly and physically to bring about the downfall of the human populace opposition one and two levels down, respectively?

Note that in chapter 19, the Lamb kills his opponents by the sword which comes from his mouth: the word of truth finally vanquishes falsehood. But this word is proclaimed not with a loudspeaker from heaven, but by an angel flying in mid-heaven (14:6–11). Mid-heaven creatures always fly between God in heaven and the opposition on earth and are the saints—humans. In the trans-temporal and universal description of chapter 20, the initiator of the "fire from heaven" is not revealed, but given that the victorious saints are symbolized as reigning throughout history in 20:4–9, the natural inference is that the opposition throughout history has been cleansed or *vanquished by the works of the saints*. These saints, following God and the Lamb, brandish God's truth in the eternal gospel to defy the beasts and Babylon with their lives. Babylon falls when no one buys her cargoes.

Also, in chapter 12, Michael (Jesus himself) leading his angels is not fighting against Satan in person since Satan is explained to have delegated his power to the beasts in chapter 13.

God delegates his power to the Lamb (opening the seven seals) because of Jesus' resurrection. The Lamb leads his saints to battle. The saints overcome Babylon, destroying the foundational support of Satan's camp. In this grand conclusion of the Bible, *victory is won level by corresponding level, and player by corresponding player, without confusion*. The roles and responsibilities of each player are clearly laid out for actions to avoid undue expectations.

## 7.2 The Ultimate Prize—God's Creation in Revelation

What then is the nub of the struggle? Is God fighting to reclaim his lost glory, to regain his lost sovereignty over humans, to snatch humans lovingly from perishing, to defeat the Serpent and the beasts, to complete his wrath on the unrepentant, or to heal his wounded pride? All, even the last one (jealousy), are true. Yet if any one or a combination of these is taken as the ultimate, it would be totally missing the point.

Running through Revelation is the unmistakable theme of God as creator who will consummate the creation that he called into existence in the beginning:

1. A rainbow surrounds the throne of God without anything (creatures, humans or objects) intervening between them. God is *reminding himself first and foremost* of his unchanging commitment to his own creation (Gen 9:12–17; Rev 4:3). A transient phenomenon after the Noachian flood is now elevated to the presence of the eternal God.

2. Concluding the first worship scene is the assertion that God is worthy to receive glory, honor and power *because he creates all things, rather than he has made humans* who are not even directly mentioned (4:11). Humans are only a part of this creation.

3. When redemption is effected by the Lamb taking the scroll from God (the Father), praises are first initiated by the twenty four elders and four living creatures, but then spread to every nook and cranny of God's creation (5:13-14). *Extending redemption to all creation is the goal. Praise from all creation is the rightful response.*

4. Humans made in the image of God are intended to rule majestically over creation, leading to its continual renewal (first four seals, 6:1-8). *The role of humans to care for creation is clearly spelled out.*

5. Nature is cast as a victim of human perversion—blackened sun, bloody moon, stars falling to earth, a split sky, displaced mountains and islands (6:12-17; section 3.2 of this reading)—which prompts *God to choose the multitudinous 144,000 in the sixth seal to reverse the abuses.*

6. God's work with only humans (seals) is not complete until all creation is brought into his redemption (trumpets) and evil eliminated from his creation (bowls), hence the half-hour deafening silence in heaven in the seventh seal (8:1).

7. The natural world is the object of God's protective love, with damage to each aspect limited to a minority of one third in the trumpets (8:7—9:20). Mutual destruction of humans is similarly circumscribed.

8. *God's opposition is not cast as sinners or rebels . . . etc., but summarized poignantly as the destroyer* (unusually given in both Greek and Hebrew) whom God's opposition follows. Deceiving is Satan's tactics, but his ultimate purpose is to destroy (9:11). God is beyond destruction, hence Satan's prize is to destroy God's good creation. This is where the battle line is drawn.

9. God cannot tolerate his creation to be destroyed through human waywardness. He confers his self-reminding rainbow on a strong angel and starts a series of actions leading to the great reversal: God's wrath stopped (forbidden thunders), a new message preached to many peoples, nations, tongues, and kings (chapter 10) which culminates in Jesus' work and the final triumph in chapter 11.

10. God avers to destroy those who destroy his earth, proclaims through his angel an *eternal gospel* which demands singular worship of him who made the heaven and earth and sea and springs of waters, rather than of a personal savior of some human "spirit" (11:18, 14:7).

11. The earth partners with the saints by drinking up the flood water pouring from the dragon's mouth to sweep away God's woman (12:15-16). Such is God's intention. In sharp contrast, the natural world: a. is

never a protection of anyone who destroys the earth, as is mistakenly believed (6:16, 20:11); and b. is a vehicle for God's wrath on his opponents (first four bowls (16:2–9)).

12. Harvesting the earth, which elaborates on "destroy those who destroy the earth," is to rid the earth, i.e., creation, of the damage inflicted by human sins (14:15–20). *The earth is not destroyed, but cleansed to reveal its intended glory.*

In the end, the picture of all pictures is: Fed by the river flowing directly from God's throne, the tree of life spontaneously brings out leaves to heal the nations (22:1–3). In this grand harmony within all God's creation, its very material attributes cannot be spiritualized away since the Holy Spirit immediately parenthesizes this with "There will no longer be any curse." To the extent that the curse on the ground in Genesis was material, the ultimate healing of creation is, and will also be. Inclination to short-change this very material message is to take away from Revelation and is anathematized (22:19).

Jesus, once again the Alpha and Omega, Son of Man, Lord of the Sabbath, has now realized God's ultimate Sabbath in materializing the Jubilee year that was never observed in full before. Hallelujah!

## 7.3 The Grand Game

When all the players have been assembled, their roles clearly assigned, and the battle line marked out, how does the war proceed? When did it start and how will it end? These are what Revelation answers for us.

Truth manifesting itself in order, creativity, goodness, lawfulness, wisdom, and beauty emanates from God through Jesus Christ and the Holy Spirit to creation. The custodianship of this creation has been given to humankind who occupies a position between the creator and creation itself, as if flying in mid-heaven. To prove their loyalty, hence also their worthiness to steward God's wonderful and awesome creation, they have to be tested by the untruth.

Of unknown origin is Satan, but his intention is known: to destroy God's wonderful creation and return it to the void and formless state before creation. If truth and wisdom build up creation, undoing creation means introducing falsehood and folly into creation through its stewards. Such is the specialization of the father of lies and accusations, the chief destroyer.

Representing all the stewards of creation to come, Adam and Eve went through the test by Satan and failed. Untruth has temporarily succeeded and its consequences reverberated throughout creation. Yet this is just the first round. God would henceforth protect his creation from irreversible harm.

Jesus appears on the scene in human bodily form to deal the consummate liar the fatal blow. Because of Jesus' bodily resurrection, all of creation, not the least is the material part, has been, is, and will be snatched from the jaws of death—the ultimate void, formlessness and meaninglessness. Creation will be renewed and transformed through the same power that resurrected Jesus in bodily form. Ultimate triumph is secured and proclaimed.

Yet mopping up the mess left behind by Satan's lies is a journey and is complicated by the ferocity of Satan making his last-ditch effort to collect as many formless trophies as possible before he is rendered totally toothless and is eternally tormented. Matching Jesus' bodily appearance on earth is Satan's bodily delegates—his beast(s) who coerce and deceive a host of otherwise fitting stewards of God's creation.

The Lamb's blood, their testimony for the truth (word), and their own lives are the weapons of the saints. The holy city will eventually overcome the city of lies—Babylon—which is so fittingly self-deceived to believe in her deity and total self-sufficiency. The siren blares out to the citizens of Babylon to forsake the fallen and falling city lest they go down to eternal torment with it.

Satan's and the Lamb's camps already show irreconcilable differences in the here and now: violence, lies, manipulation, and ceaseless strife in Satan's camp versus harmony, truth, spontaneity, and rest in God's camp.

From the seminal beginning in God's choice of Abram (renewed in Israel) and the Apostles, the New Jerusalem will emerge strong and beautiful to assimilate all the creative efforts that God's original steward has to offer it, while being founded on the powerful super-natural transformation that is pregnant in the bodily resurrection of Jesus. Hallelujah!

The roles and positions of the players and center of the conflict are schematized in figure 5.

# Figure 5. The Cosmic Struggle

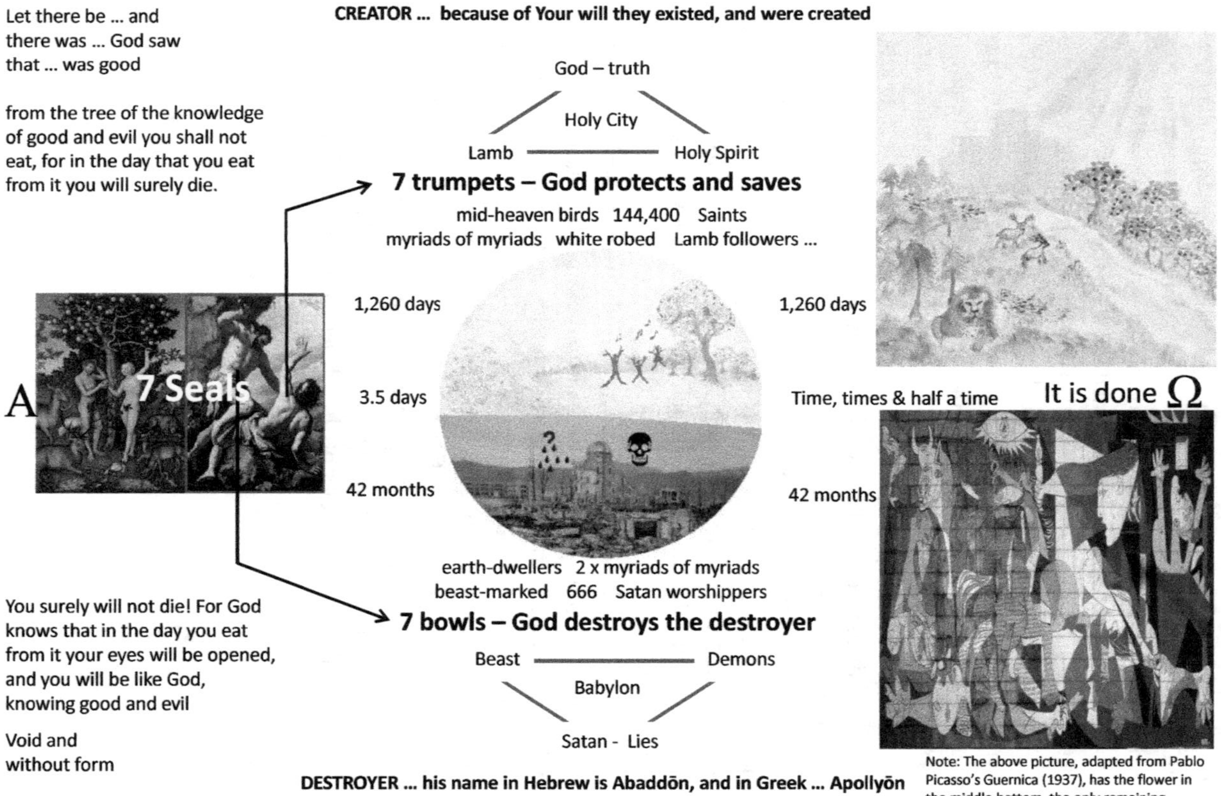

CREATOR ... because of Your will they existed, and were created

God – truth

Holy City  Holy Spirit

Lamb ——— Lamb followers ...

mid-heaven birds  144,400  Saints
myriads of myriads  white robed

**7 trumpets – God protects and saves**

1,260 days

Time, times & half a time    It is done Ω

42 months

1,260 days

3.5 days

42 months

earth-dwellers  2 x myriads of myriads
beast-marked  666  Satan worshippers

Beast ——— Demons

Babylon

Satan - Lies

**7 bowls – God destroys the destroyer**

DESTROYER ... his name in Hebrew is Abaddōn, and in Greek. ... Apollyōn

A ... 7 Seals

Let there be ... and there was ... God saw that ... was good

from the tree of the knowledge of good and evil you shall not eat, for in the day that you eat from it you will surely die.

You surely will not die! For God knows that in the day you eat from it your eyes will be opened, and you will be like God, knowing good and evil

Void and without form

Note: The above picture, adapted from Pablo Picasso's Guernica (1937), has the flower in the middle bottom, the only remaining vestige of hope, taken out.

# 4

# Fourth Reading— Hear God Speak Plainly through Revelation

IN THE PREVIOUS THREE readings, I highlighted some outstanding features of Revelation which give an indication of how the book should be read, then we tried to understand it based on an utterly common-sense guiding principle—within an expanding context until sense can be made of each passage (and we almost never have to go beyond the Bible to make sense of the whole book!). In the third reading, we tried to join the dots identified in the second reading to understand the progressing narration of Revelation. Here, in the fourth and final reading, we are poised to grasp the important lessons the Holy Spirit is teaching us.

## 1. INTERPRETING REVELATION THROUGH ITS POSITION IN THE BIBLE

No one can miss the sense of finality in Revelation. This comes not only internally from its narration, but also from the testimony of the Christian community who decided to put Revelation at the end of the collection of writings which they considered as God-inspired and has a special status in instructing believers on the truth of God. This collection starts with what the Jewish community has already considered authoritative for their faith and identity, but goes beyond that with another "testament" which narrates and interprets what Jesus has done. Specifically, the former collection of the Israelites starts with God's creation—Genesis. The Christian addition to this collection ends with Revelation. Poignantly, *the Christian community sees Revelation as the fitting conclusion to the introduction which is Genesis*. Such also corroborates the internal testimony demanded by Revelation—the message is complete and final that no one is to take away from or add to the message therein without incurring divine wrath!

The majestic pronouncement "It is done" in Revelation now reverberates with the explosive announcement of "In the beginning God created" in Genesis. A conclusion must respond to the introduction in any thoughtful and meaningful writing, and in this case, a collection of writings, which Christians ascribe to one Author, despite the many people who indeed took up the pen to put the messages therein in readable form. With the understandings of the two books—Genesis and Revelation—so inextricably tied together, one obvious question arises: Given that Revelation is highly symbolic in conveying its message, how are we to read Genesis?

To avoid confusion, a categorical clarification must first be made. Symbols (both objects, e.g., the beasts, locusts, city . . . etc. and actions, e.g., harvesting the earth, pouring from a bowl . . . etc.) are to convey a reality. Rather than side-stepping reality, a symbol affirms the very reality it represents. The only question is what that reality is. The very letters and words on this page are pure symbols, but the reader can make sense of these strings of symbols to relate to a message or a reality. A higher level of symbolic representation is the metaphor in which the symbol-to-reality correspondence is shifted, making it less direct, using information within the context. The more direct the symbol bears to reality, the easier it is to interpret. When the person who died and rose from the dead is called Jesus (a name which symbolizes), we can easily relate the symbol to the historical person. However, when he is described as the Lamb with seven horns and seven eyes, a few more mental steps have to be taken to relate this somewhat indirect symbol to the same historical person. But in the mental process, other aspects come into view. Such increases the difficulty in coming to grips with symbols, but the reality symbolized is never ever dismissed. In the end, all communication through language is symbolic and every symbol points to and affirms a reality. Symbols differ only in how directly they correspond to the realities they represent.

So to what reality do the symbols in Revelation point? Answering this will shed light on understanding Genesis. But the reverse is also true: how we understand the symbol-to-reality correspondence in Genesis also sets the tone for our understanding of Revelation. From the angle of logical flow and indeed common expectation, one should be reading from beginning to end, namely to understand Revelation based on Genesis. How do we then read Genesis, especially the first three chapters? What are the realities these chapters describe? There can be many interpretations of what these three chapters of Genesis convey, but some salient assertions cannot be denied without calling the entire book pure fantasy unworthy of reading. These realities must be accepted:

1. God created the physical/material universe—the cosmos—and made humans in his image;
2. Every aspect of this material creation is good and together represents the very good totality God has intended for all his creatures;
3. God commissioned the humans that he made, among all the other creatures, to rule over his creation;
4. God planted a garden (Eden) in his creation and placed the first human couple—Adam and Eve—in it;
5. God commanded the first human couple not to eat from a tree named the Knowledge of Good and Evil;
6. The first human couple bought into the lies of a character in the form of a serpent and acted out their disobedience towards God;
7. God's verdict handed down in response to human rebellion is that the seed of the woman would bruise the serpent on the head while the serpent's seed would bruise him on the heel;
8. Cursed was the land because of humans' rejection of God's injunction in favor of the serpent's lies;
9. The first couple was sent out of the Garden of Eden and the tree of life was barred from them.

The chapters that follow record that a number of other miseries also came upon humans and creation because of human sins, but here, the symbol-to-reality correspondence becomes much closer, with a whole string of sexual intercourses, births, sibling and peer rivalries, murders, flouting of punishments, artistic and technological developments . . . etc. which are all too familiar to us, hence less factually controversial. Yet, the first three chapters of Genesis flow naturally without a break through to the chapters that follow, demanding that if the rest of Genesis, and indeed the rest of the Old Testament, is to be taken as materially "real," the first three chapters must also be. Such is corroborated by the very strong dose of present materiality found right in the middle of the first three chapters (2:10–14)—four rivers in geographically identifiable places with precious minerals . . . etc. So one must at least assert that Genesis' language (which is nonetheless a set of symbols) does point to a very physical/material reality that we can all relate to in the here and now. On this very real physical and material foundation of Genesis we still stand. Such will continue into the future.

And what better place to start by recognizing the last book in the Bible responds fittingly, forcefully, and intelligently to its introduction? And what is more assuring to know that what Revelation points to will become fully real in God's choice time, a reality that we are at least partly familiar with in the here and now? Given such, the warning at its end becomes meaningful: one cannot tamper with the reality God has established with impunity.

Having thus established the material reality behind Revelation's symbols, one can still be at a loss on how these symbols are used. Let me illustrate from the last two chapters of Revelation. Does the description point to the obliteration of the sun, moon, and sea (21:1, 23, 22:5), and by implication, the advent of a totally other-worldly existence that bears no relationship to the present created order? This seems to be corroborated in the earlier scene of the judgment before the great white throne where "earth and heaven fled away, and no place was found for them" (20:11). Yet in chapters 21–22, Revelation also talks about this new heaven and earth, represented by a city. In it, there is the tree of life and no more curse. Kings of the earth will bring into it glory and honor of the nations. All these would only make sense if the present earth persists since it was the ground of this earth that was cursed (but will be no more) and humans were barred from the tree of life (but will be re-endeared to and sustained by it). Taken together, these descriptions can be confusing.

But contextual symbols have often been used in Revelation. A prominent example is the "angel" (messenger) who can be from the abyss or from God or simply representing humans, depending on the context. In the same way, "earth" can literally mean the good creation over which God jealously guards against destruction (e.g., in the seventh trumpet). Sea and earth also point to the very physical creation in the trumpets and bowls, but in chapter 13 these are also used as metaphors for the unpredictable political arena (sea) and the more lasting religious arena (earth) from which the two beasts arose. Further on, "earth" finds its meaning in contrast to "heaven" as the abode of God's opposition from chapter 12 on. So following the sensible rule of seeking the real meaning of a symbol first from its immediate context, one can say that the group of "symbols of absence" in chapter 21, namely sun, moon, temple, and night, is to be understood by contrasting them with their substitute which in this context is God himself, rather than the objects they actually are. People have been using the sun and moon as guidance for their living. Some have even turned to the stars to find their fates. Now in the city, God is guiding them directly while they live in his material creation, hence they will not have to seek other guidance except from God. As such, the Bible only says that there is *no need of the sun and the moon for guidance rather than there is no objects called sun and moon* in the machinery of the new heaven and earth. Willingly submitting to this administration of God will do away with fumbling and stumbling in darkness, hence no night. If so, the temple is also a distraction since God is already among humans all the time. In other words, these are aspects of a God-and-Christ-centered living which do not entail doing away with the physical world, but require the recognition of the ultimate source of all guidance in ruling over creation, as intended. Also, humans' fickle political arena represented by the tossing sea is finally replaced by the direct administration of God and the Lamb which happens right here on earth, hence the otherwise out-of-place remark of *"there is no longer any sea"* right before the arrival of the holy city. By contrast, God's eternal and placid rule has never been abrogated since "before the throne there was something like a *sea of glass* (without the vicissitude brought about by storms and waves), like crystal" (4:6a). The prerequisite of the New Jerusalem is clearly stated.

After some of the symbols are sorted out (naturally within the immediate context), the stark material reality the remaining symbols represent cannot be dismissed. The heaven and earth created in Genesis, after being cleansed of the corruption of Babylon under the influence of the beasts who live out the lies of the evil puppet master will be fit to accommodate a new reality where "there will no longer be any death; there will no longer be any mourning, or crying, or pain" in an existence without curse. This original creation, heaven and earth, will *definitely not be obliterated, but restored to what it is originally intended for.*

Revelation as the Bible's conclusion also arrogates to itself the right not to be restricted by previous biblical symbols. On the contrary, the meaning Revelation gives to its symbols stands on their own as final. We have encountered how the four living creatures in Ezekiel are fully revealed in Revelation, and how the historical timescales in Daniel are taken fully liberally to convey something that is only appropriate on the cosmic level. In the last chapter of Revelation, the river of life, obviously adapted from Ezek 47, is given a totally new dimension within the new heaven and earth—Ezekiel has his whole vision pegged to the temple's restoration while John emphatically says that there will no more be a temple! Endlessly confusing it is for those who do not accord Revelation the status it announces—to be the Bible's ultimate conclusion. Without recognizing Revelation's pre-eminence, its exegesis falls victim to human's whim.

Even if Genesis sets the foundation for Revelation that is not to be violated, does not the difference in their literary type open Revelation up to other interpretations? It has often been pointed out that Revelation belongs to the apocalyptic genre which is usually produced during times of great uncertainty and distress to comfort the readers. This type of literature makes heavy use of exotic symbols and views history as if it is directed by divine forces from above. Commonly taught is that writings belonging to this genre have to be interpreted by the rules of this genre. By implication, common sense is not sufficient.

Bluntly, such assertion is cart-before-the-horse tautology. If some commonality defines a group, that definition only serves to inform for easy identification, in this case for the readers to pick reading material, but not to constrain or guide the understanding of each member. Otherwise, it is just re-stating a definition. For example, a group of students who go through a male high school famous for science during a certain decade would probably all be boys speaking and writing the same languages and like exploration . . . etc. But to claim further that each of them must be a successful career scientist would be absurd as one may end up being a drunkard sleeping on the street while another winning the Nobel Prize for physics. A biblical illustration is Jesus' parables. After carefully studying the context and content, the reader determines that certain utterances of Jesus are meant for conveying certain truths through story-telling and the story is just made up rather than historical. Then and only then can one classify the passage as a parable. The reader can then compare parables. But one is back to square one if one imposes the definition of parable on what one has identified as parable to understand its meaning further. *Nothing more is gained through this.* As such, classifying Revelation as apocalyptic serves to group writings together for comparison, but to hope for deciphering Revelation's true meaning through this grouping is as good as learning to behave as humans towards life's end after discovering that one is human for the first time!

In summary, without going through the hard but exciting exegesis, genre labeling suppresses individual thinking. But once the rigorous analysis is done, genre is no more than a dispensable label.

If we take Revelation as coming from the Holy Spirit through the Apostle John, any intra-genre interpretation using other "apocalyptic" writings would be even more frivolous. Good writers do not consciously write to conform to the characteristics of a genre, but express their ideas as they see fit. As such, an intra-genre analysis within the Bible serves very little purpose. Because parts of the Book of Daniel, Matt 24 (or even 1 Thess 4) have been identified as having apocalyptic content (or of the same genre), common is the practice to bundle these together for interpretation. The beasts, 1,290 days, "time, times and half a time" in Daniel and "the desolating sacrilege" in Matthew have been yanked out of their proper context to be pasted on the closest symbols in Revelation to spin fanciful, but untenable "predictions" that have been disproved consistently throughout history. Great is the energy wasted, but greater is the damage done to the credibility of Christians who do not condemn, as God demands, those mutilating the Bible to gain a following. Soothsayers and astrologers masquerading as prophets should have no place among believers.

It is true that the Bible comprises works written in different genres to speak appropriately to different situations, yet the key to understanding Revelation has nothing to do with genre, but is to respect the common sense guidance of the Holy Spirit who inspires both the writers to write and the early Christian community to arrange the writings into the book that we call the Bible.

Often different views in interpreting Revelation argue over whether the book should be taken literally or symbolically. Yet as we have seen before, every word and string of words in any writing is symbolic. A large patch of salty water is usually symbolized by the three characters "sea," but the ceaseless waves on the sea can be borrowed to point to the turbulent political scene. Both are symbols and the difference between these is in the "distance" between the symbols and the reality they represent. In effect, the literalists are demanding that the symbol-to-reality distance be always kept to a minimum, but *often according to the literalist's own whim*. This means that Jesus would be sitting on a white horse having a sword coming out of his mouth smiting the nations when the nations have now progressed to much more sophisticated weaponry, guns, bombs, nuclear devices . . . etc., since Jesus' time. Many other exotic descriptions—of Satan, the beasts, angels . . . etc.—will then have to be taken "literally." But if we make exceptions to a "literal" understanding of many passages, then where is the ground for not allowing some sensible distance between reality and symbols in other passages, e.g., the one thousand years, first resurrection and reigning with Christ in chapter 20, based on the context, style, and the flow of the whole book?

Sufficient it is that Revelation does not negate the reality of Genesis which gives a more "literal" description. Since Revelation has to generalize for the semi-open future, its symbols have to be sufficiently broad and general. That every follower of Christ from all ethnicity and geographical locations throughout the vast expanse of time would be using whatever means available to them to preach repentance to the opposition without compromising their position is succinctly symbolized by an angel flying in mid-heaven preaching an eternal gospel testifies to the power of "less literal" symbols. Such symbols are appropriate for a future which is sealed by Jesus, yet open to all to participate in. Another example is the son of man sitting on a cloud harvesting the earth: the flesh and blood yet transcendental

Jesus who has ascended to the throne of God is taking the lead in cleansing the earth of abominable corruption induced by the opposition to God and he will complete the work duly (chapter 14). Many other such examples of powerful symbols abound.

In the end, let us see how the *consummate interpreter—Jesus—*might read Revelation.

Since Jesus has now been singled out as the divine Son of God in Christianity, much about how he came into consciousness as that divine figure is no longer widely discussed among his general followers. It is just assumed that he is special from birth and it is beyond us to comprehend how he knew he is the Son of God. He just knew it. Yet if one reads the Bible carefully, it is only reasonable to assume that Jesus had a normal, though sinless, childhood and he gradually came into that consciousness through his reading of the Hebrew scriptures and the relationship he developed with his Father (Luke 2:41–52). On the outside, what distinguishes him from the many lunatics who claim to be hearing voices or seeing visions is probably the open and public affirmation that he received from the Father at his baptism and during the Transfiguration and finally in the Garden of Gethsemane. Yet for him personally as a full human, how Jesus interpreted the Old Testament "prophecies" as being fulfilled in him would form the basis of his consciousness.

If the foregoing is correct, then Jesus' human conviction has to be so strong that he was convinced without a doubt that he would rise again on the third day after being killed by his opponents in Jerusalem. This is no joke as one's life, the only thing that a person has, is at stake. Certainty is called for and Jesus had that certainty when he spoke of his future resurrection (Matt 16:21; Mark 8:31; Luke 9:22).

What concerns us here is how Jesus interprets the Old Testament "prophecies" which he thought would apply to him. The most prominent of these prophecies centers on the "Servant" passages in Isa 42–53 where the Servant can sometimes be understood as an individual and yet also as the nation of Israel which is sometimes slightly remonstrated by God. The original mission that the "nation" of Israel was intended to, but did not, fulfill because of its waywardness, is fulfilled in the individual Servant which Jesus interprets as himself. As such, Jesus has also identified himself as Israel which though punished by God in the exile, would one day be re-constituted as prophesied in Ezek 37 using the dry bones turning into a living hoard as symbol. But given the symbolic and sometimes poetic language these passages use, there can be much leeway in interpretation. For example, Ezek 37 can *hardly be taken as a bodily resurrection of an individual* and Isa 53 can be taken as the faithful Servant continuing to exist in his spiritual progeny while he himself resides "spiritually" in the outer reaches of heaven enjoying the fruits of his labor *without a bodily resurrection. But this is not how Jesus reads it.* As opposed to skimping on the thrust of the "prophecies," he takes the force of these sayings to the full and *indeed reads more liberally into these passages than is allowed by an analytical reading.* How he reads the Bible would fail our modern scholarly standard! More so, he bet his life on such reading! In the end, his liberal reading is more than fulfilled. No spiritualization is needed. God does not need us to save his face.

If Jesus were to read Revelation now, how would he interpret the prophecies of the fall of Babylon and the advent of the holy city . . . etc.? In his eyes, will evil come to an end in this real world that God loves and will real harmony and mutuality be established between God, humans and God's creation?

In the end, while most of the Bible between Genesis and Revelation can best be interpreted against their respective backgrounds—historical, cultural . . . etc., demonstrated in the second and third readings is that *such background is not essential for this concluding book to make sense,* making Revelation a timeless theological masterpiece that those *who respect Revelation's unique position* and are conversant only with the main themes (not some obscured reference) of the Bible *would grasp fully.* If Revelation makes sense of some historical situations, that does not mean it was written initially with that situation in mind (e.g., Christians in the early church within the Roman empire . . . etc.), any more than a master key is designed for the first lock it opens! Able to open any lock must be its touchstone. As such, *the Bible's concluding book is among the most democratic books in the Bible.*

## 2. WHAT LESSONS CAN THE SEVEN CHURCHES DRAW FROM REVELATION?

### 2.1 A Meta-Narrative

In our second reading through Revelation, I skip over Jesus' specific messages to the seven churches in chapters 2–3 on the understanding that the subsequent chapters which contain a more comprehensive message would speak to these churches better than the brief introductions in these two chapters. Chapters 2–3 only highlight the peculiar situation, challenges, weaknesses and opportunities of each representative church, but the complete picture is painted in chapters 4–22. From this grand mosaic are the theologies, encouragements and corrections to be distilled. Such is clear when the true Author said at the end (22:16): "I, Jesus, have sent My angel to testify to you *these things for the churches . . .* "

Despite this understanding, I still harbored a secret wish. Following the prevalent ethos of targeting solutions to solve specific problems, I was hoping to find verses, passages or teachings that would speak directly to and resonate with each church in their unique circumstance. Such a targeted approach has great advantage as we as-yet-mortals have limited knowledge and resources to address inter-linked issues, hence we isolate problems (identify the main factors or forces and assume the others are relatively unimportant, at least for the task at hand) and solve the main ones first. Great progress in science and medicine has been made through these reductionist simplifications.

Naturally I looked for the tonic that would illuminate the situation of each of the seven churches, lift each out of its predicament and strengthen it for the journey ahead. But by and large, I failed. It then dawned on me that despite the many specific teachings the rest of the Bible is offering its readers, e.g., the Ten Commandments in addressing very specific, though comprehensive, real-life issues; Paul's teaching on justification by faith, idolatry, immorality, false teachings, love . . . etc., *Revelation has zoomed in on one perspective. It calls each church to put itself squarely on the grand foundation of Jesus' irrevocable victory to take up the fight to realize more fully this victory that has already been secured.* Needless to say, such a teaching is the basic premise (often unstated) of all the epistles in the New Testament, hence would undergird all the other more specific theological and ethical teachings therein, but Revelation makes this fully explicit as the dominant theme and expands on this with highly informative theological nuances to paint a grand mosaic of full cosmic proportion.

Why has the Holy Spirit, at the very conclusion of his written message to humankind, chosen this theme rather than the more specific messages like what he does through other New Testament writers? Common sense tells us that the last word is the most important.

For God, there is no question on whether the final victory is firm. It is beyond doubt, demonstrated through Jesus' bodily resurrection, guaranteed by the creator himself (Gen 3:15) and conceded by Satan (Matt 8:29). But for each party having to make a choice, one's fate is bound up with the side one chooses. One's actions for or against Babylon would authenticate that choice. All would be lost for those making the wrong choice.

Does Revelation's message then boil down to personal salvation based on this choice? The word "salvation" in many Christian circles has taken on a narrow and narcissistic meaning which Revelation, and indeed the Bible, does not teach. The unmistakable message of Revelation is that God is first and foremost interested in glorifying his whole creation, the same creation described in Genesis. Ensuing from this intention, God has placed humans in his creation to look after it. But when humankind was deceived and failed to discharge their responsibility, God tried to restore humankind through blessing Abram so that "all the families of the earth (i.e., all the different aspects of creation—humans, other creatures . . . etc.) shall be blessed" (Gen 12:3). Revelation teaches the blessedness of all creation is God's ultimate goal. After people have brought glory and honor into the city, in the middle of this city appears a tree of life directly nourished by the river coming from the throne of God. The unchanging goal of God is now clearly articulated. It is within this "salvation" or "redemption" of creation that humankind finds his destiny, through personal engagement.

If God's consistent purpose is to glorify his creation through his followers to reverse the destruction from Satan and his cohorts, then are humans not just pawns in his chessboard, and somewhat disposable? Unfortunately for us, we are indeed disposable since God does not coerce us to change our ways and our willful failure to leave Babylon would trap and crush us in its collapse. But fortunately for us, God is constantly calling wayward humans to become holy turncoats to join him in bringing down Babylon, in fulfillment of "to destroy those who destroy the earth" pronounced at the very end of the final (seventh) trumpet. And most satisfying to us as his creatures is that God loves both his creation and the stewards of his creation. No one party is a disposable stepping stone to the other because creation was designed for inter-dependence and mutuality. God demanding us to take care of his creation in proportion to the love he has for it (Jonah 4:10–11) neither excludes him from loving us nor us loving him. On the contrary, such demand can only be fulfilled through our response to God's all-embracing love in Jesus. This mutually constructive and creative love is inclusive and pervades God's camp. By contrast, mutual ill will prevails between Satan and his followers and among his followers to the detriment of God's creation.

For those who have received God's eternal gospel with joy, they can look forward to more than mutual love. From Jesus' victory in the harmonious holy city ensues forgiveness of sins so that the laborers' expected reward is not robbed of them through the sting of the second death brought about by sins. In fulfillment of the final Sabbath, the believers' labor will follow them (14:13) just like God is enamored of his creation in his Sabbath.

With this background, the eternal gospel preached by the angel flying in mid-heaven, the *only gospel in concluding the Bible*, no longer jars at those of us who have been introduced to Christianity through a "personal" savior. In concluding God's message to humankind, the Holy Spirit is demanding that God's good news, however one is introduced to it, must encompass all of God's creation. This also corrects two major aberrations that have crept into the Christian hope in the last few centuries with very practical consequences.

Faith, hope, and love are the unchanging virtues flowing from the Christian faith and every human intention and action will be judged through these lenses. From these virtues come guidance on how creation is to be cared for, communities are to be organized, laws are to be enacted, science is to be pursued and technologies are to be applied, people are to interact with each other . . . etc. Not only so, if Jesus' victory is real and as John claims in his first epistle (2:8) that "the darkness is passing away and the true Light is already shining," then humanity must be making progress in the expression of these virtues. And two thousand years since Jesus' historic victory should be a long-enough time to judge the materiality of Jesus' victory. So what do we see? The scale of faith shows that though humankind has not all turned to the true God yet in the last two millennia, significant progress has been made, under the influence of biblical faith, with a sizeable and increasing portion of humanity forsaking idol worship and turning to one God. The progress of love is even more significant when even most non-Christians would forsake "an eye for an eye, a tooth for a tooth" to embrace non-violent means to resolve conflicts. But hope has been sadly distorted in the last few centuries by: 1. personalizing our future to the exclusion of the rest of creation, and simultaneously 2. discounting our destiny through denying our bodily resurrection. The practical upshot of these two aberrations is to see all "material" efforts as ultimately meaningless since the material world is irrelevant to our "spiritual" future. Many are these soothsayers who are singing their sickening dirge for this material world. But thankfully, an increasing number has heeded Paul's teaching that "the anxious longing of the creation waits eagerly for the revealing of the sons of God . . . creation itself also will be set free from its slavery to corruption into the freedom of the glory of the children of God" and lived up to that godly calling as creation's liberators, thus correctly re-pointing hope towards the creator God.

None of the three virtues can progress in isolation. Obviously, how can we love our materially poor sisters and brothers as living souls now when all we care is to send them on their way to a spiritual heaven where the material plays no part? How can we have faith in the power of God through us *when we have faith only in a God who has failed to save his very good creation and seeks a climb-down in saving us only spiritually?* But responding to the only eternal gospel, people worldwide are coming to the realization that our personal future is bound up with the future of the whole creation. Their own redemption and subsequent healing serve a larger purpose. This awakening might have been prompted by the series of global crises rather than solely through the biblical message. Nevertheless, true to the eternal gospel, the inevitable collapse of Babylon can be, and often is, a motivation to return to God the creator. The Holy Spirit has clearly laid out the scope of our hope in the eternal gospel to warn us against becoming a Babylon in Christian garb. True believers must capitalize on this aspect of the gospel to further God's kingdom. Then faith, hope, and love can progress in tandem for us to realize our sought-for destiny in God.

Starting from the God of Truth, the Lamb has called and worked together with the saints throughout history to re-establish the truth, distorted by the beast(s) immersed in the lies of Satan, in every aspect of God's administration—political, religious, and economic. Within this final portrait and the struggle that would eventually realize this glorious city, every constituent member of humankind will have to make a decision for or against God.

God is now calling you and me to join in a struggle with determined outcome. With this perspective, every effort would take on cosmic significance. With this lens, every nook and cranny of fallen creation is an object of our labor before the victorious God. With this scope, every disappointment may be ironed out to smooth the way to the city. With this direction, every move is saved from the aimless drift of evolution to become purposeful progress. With this frame of mind, every saint can rise from egoism to the Shalom in God. With the throb of this grand meta-narrative every worthy soul should resonate.

With this wholesome and fulsome foundation, each of the seven churches is now in a position to ask "How should we then live?"

## 2.2 Four Encounters that Register

Revelation is not God's one-way communication of cold truths to the churches through a recording machine named John. There are telltale interactions between the revealer and the receiver. At the most basic level are John's questions in his perplexity and the angel or elder at the scene would explain certain visions to satisfy John's curiosity. Those interactive elaborations form part of the revelation.

At a more personal level, John simply responds emotionally to what he sees. There are four of these records which are unnecessary to the flow of the narrative, but are still recorded for a purpose: to illustrate how a God-fearing person would or should react to the message. As such, these are paradigmatic for the reader's edification and are given below.

Right in the first chapter when John first encounters Jesus, and after seeing the very unusual and exotic features of the Jesus whom he is supposed to know quite intimately (remember John leaned on Jesus' chest during the last supper and claims to have fellowship with this "word of life," (John 13:25; 1 John 1:1–3)), John falls down at the feet of this Jesus like a dead man (1:17). What shocks John into such a spontaneous yet somewhat uncontrollable reaction? Could it be the totally unexpected image presented to him? Yes, the same Jesus he now sees before him is totally unfamiliar. What is it about this Jesus that causes him to be like a dead man? In comparison with the Jesus who is so full of life in many dimensions, John, the biologically and spiritually alive person, seems like a dead man. The life that he knew and preached about (1 John 1) has now manifested oneself as the life in all its multiplicity of dimensions and cast our human lives in a pale light. Then John is assured that he needs not be afraid of this life and in fact this full life of Jesus is the guarantee that John and his listeners would not be shoved aside as "dead," but would participate in this full life because Jesus has tasted death, but now is alive in all the dimensions including the dimension of time: "*Do not be afraid*; I am the first and the last, and the living One; and I was dead, and behold, *I am alive forevermore*, and I have the keys of death and of Hades" (1:17b–18).

The creator God has allowed himself to be restricted by the space-time that he himself created through the person of Jesus. But once freed from these self-permitted constraints in his resurrection, Jesus' other dimensions shine forth to confront the John still trapped in his mortality. He was overwhelmed by the enormity of Jesus' life.

Through this encounter, John has graduated from an already intimate relationship with the historical Jesus before to encountering Christ, the creator, the one who has resurrected to appropriate the fullness of life eternal. This shatters old boundaries that were formed through knowing only the historical Jesus and prepares John to accept the work of Christ described in the rest of Revelation.

After the unfamiliar and incomprehensible dimensions of Christ (a name known only to himself, 19:12) have sunk in, the second encounter left John weeping bitterly (5:4). After Jesus has addressed each of the seven churches, John was shown an eternal scene where earthly beings and all of creation are praising God unceasingly. Contrary to popular imagination, no angel was present! Such surreal scene contrasts sharply with what John, despite his being transported to heaven, is accustomed to seeing in his very abode on earth. Being human, he cannot lose and has not lost his touch with the very "real" world. This contrast between the heavenly worship and what happens on earth elicits in him excruciating disappointment upon hearing that no one in creation ("in heaven, on earth and under the earth" 5:3) is worthy to move creation forward to realize the previous scene of unceasing worship (to open the sealed scrolls). The heavenly, the harmonious, the absolutely satisfying, the totally blissful will be forever a dream—unreachable. The perfect and the present reality will never meet. The hope of all creation is forever dashed. The God who promises will forever be unable to keep his promise. The creator has lost. God has lost. John has allied himself with the losing side. Nihilism has won eternity.

But such is not to be. The wrenching disappointment at what creation is unable to do on its own is now accomplished by the Lamb who has previously manifested his full-of-life dimensionality to John. Henceforth, the Lamb would take creation by its horn and bring it forward until what is now deemed totally unreal and unrealizable will be brought to a fitting fulfillment. God has answered John in his deepest disappointment through what the Lamb would do in redeeming all of creation.

Without taking creation upon his heart as God's appointed steward should; without the deep disappointment in seeing the present fallen reality in which so much ugliness—injustice, wastage, degradation, senseless sufferings—and death are running rampant; without the total hopelessness with corrupted creation in saving itself from self-destruction; without throwing overboard the wishful thinking that fallen humanity without Christ could transcend the aimless drift of chance and the survival of the fittest, John would not have come to know more fully the one and only effective mover of creation: the Lamb that was slain.

This paradigm-setting encounter dismisses escapism. God would not allow this world to be destroyed nor would destroy this world though it sometimes seems to us irreparable because of the abuses of the wayward steward. God has not settled for the face-saving "spiritual" redemption. If that were the case, John would not have wept bitterly but would praise God for receiving his spirit after his mortal body expires. Absolutely barred from fleeing into a non-material existence by the first worship scene, John could not be otherwise, but be deadly bitter in tears. Yet precisely from this seemingly hopeless vantage point is he introduced to where the only hope of all creation lies. Every person's hope for personal salvation is bound up with this universal hope where all of creation will praise God for his redemption.

The ensuing works of the Lamb—starting with recounting the havoc wrought by twisted human nature in the seals, through to God's continuous protection climaxing in the death and resurrection of the two witnesses in the trumpets, and on to the concerted effort of the Lamb and his chosen to destroy Babylon in the bowls—have finally cleared the way for the marriage of the Lamb. After a series of praises from layers of God's creation, another revelation (re-asserted by "These are true words of God") is made: "Blessed are those who are invited to the marriage supper of the Lamb." At this, John seizes the closest living being—the angel who announces to him—and starts worshipping. He is gently corrected but not rebuked (19:9–10).

Another clear milestone is reached and this momentarily overwhelmed John: The righteous acts of the saints are the ticket to the marriage supper of the Lamb! The slain Lamb is not moving creation forward all by himself, but with the saints, not as dispensable tools, but as the guests in his long-awaited banquet where they will meet the bride and the Lamb to share in their eternal happiness.

What was humanly impossible before is not only possible now, but *only made possible precisely with those who have previously lost hope in creation and in humanity*. Babylon, the evil city, built and maintained by people, that seemed ineradicable, has collapsed almost unexpectedly because of the deeds of the saints redeemed by the Lamb. The transformation of being a bystander watching history to a *servant-saint* fully immersed in the righteous torrent headed by the Lamb is so game-changing that John's blunder is condoned rather than condemned. The subsequent rich pickings when the enemy is finally vanquished bear out John's excitement.

But the end of the destruction and the defeat of the unholy trinity—Babylon, the beasts, and Satan—are not the end of the story. Goodness and beauty do not spring up without a reason. Their origin is traced to God's creation, which has since been corrupted by pervading sins. God's narrative is only completed when humans, leading all of creation which has been put under his care, build on this foundation to bring out *additional glory and honor unendingly*, more so than found in God's first creation. The New Jerusalem has enveloped Eden with more beauty and goodness than before, hence the tree of life is found in the middle of the city nourished by water from the river of life. This journey from Eden to the New Jerusalem is propelled by the creativity in every person that God has made, now set free and rekindled in the *servant-saint-kings* by the Lamb to bring forth glory and honor for the beautification of the city. Recognizing that lowly humans led by the Lamb not only can defeat evil, but can also be the source of so much goodness and beauty under the illuminating light of God and the Lamb opens another floodgate to action. This revelation stuns John into another blunder to worship the messenger.

John's similarly misdirected worship in the fourth and last emotional encounter (22:8) is also fitting for the person who has seen it all. Offspring of Adam and Eve with only about one hundred billion brain cells making on average a thousand connections with each and normally less than a century to make use of these will naturally be swamped by the enormity and dimensionality of the creator God, the sweep and breadth of creation's movement, the absolutely intractable evil that pervades the nook and cranny of creation and finally the emergence and victory of goodness and beauty. Rationality only sets out the parameters for mundane understanding, but is of no help in reconciling and internalizing all these overwhelming revelations. In the end, John's attention is turned twice away from human expectation to God in the last two emotional responses. Another dimension has entered the equation—faith. Faith is our only channel to God and makes God and his word real to us.

But who then is this God that the conclusion of the Bible reveals to us?

## 2.3 The Leader—Lord of the Sabbath

Jesus first appeared to John in Revelation as the "son of man" (1:13) who is then described as displaying some otherworldly features. Son of man is a familiar title in both the Old and New Testaments. Foundationally, it means Son of *Adamah*, or more literally son of one hewn from the earth because God made Adam from the soil of the ground. Ezekiel the prophet was repeatedly addressed as son of man, or simply a human. It then takes on apocalyptic dimension in the book of Daniel (7:13) when he saw a son of man coming and who was presented before God within the vision involving exotic beasts and dominion of God. In the New Testament, Jesus has consistently used this title on himself, perhaps to convey his duality to an uninformed audience. To his listeners, the son of man is simply a human person as this son of man comes eating and drinking and has nowhere to lay his head, but on other occasions, the son of man will suffer death, yet will come again to judge the world (Matt 16:13–27, 17:22; Mark 8:31–38, 13:26; Luke 9:22–26).

Outside the Gospels, apart from Stephen seeing "heavens opened up and the son of man standing at the right hand of God" at his martyrdom (Acts 7:55), this self-designation of Jesus is not used again until here in Revelation where, appropriately, the apocalyptic aspect of this title is given full expression. Yet in all these, *a crucial link has to be filled in so that the mundane and the apocalyptic aspects of this son of man can together make sense in one title.* This link is found in Jesus' early use of "son of man" to designate himself.

Shortly after the start of Jesus' public ministry, he was challenged on his disciples' breaking the Sabbath regulation set by the Jews when they gleaned wheat on a Sabbath day. Jesus, after quoting from Old Testament examples, makes a game-changing epochal declaration: "The Sabbath was made for man, and not man for the Sabbath. So *the Son of Man is Lord even of the Sabbath*" (Mark 2:27b–28). The highlighted declaration is consistently recorded *in all three synoptic Gospels except John's*. To make good on such provocative declaration, Jesus initiates a series of very public, highly charged and emotional actions to drive the message into his opponents and followers alike, making these Sabbath challenges the most prominent, and also the most numerous, conflicts Jesus has with his opponents. The first and trend-setting incident happens when Jesus calls a man with a withered hand among the synagogue attendees gathered during one Sabbath day, openly challenges the others on the legality of healing on the Sabbath day, then without waiting for any answer, looks with extreme grief and anger at the people and heals the man. All three synoptic Gospels record this as happening immediately after Jesus' Sabbath declaration, and unifies Jesus' opposition across the political divide (Pharisees versus Herodians) to precipitate the first and running plot to kill Jesus (Matt 12:1–14; Mark 2:23—3:6; Luke 6:1–11). Luke further records two more Sabbath conflicts (13:10–16, 14:1–6) while John adds three more highly detailed and nuanced debates on the Sabbath issue (5:1–18, 7:19–24, 9:13–16). These debates reveal the bedrock belief of the Jews which Jesus challenges and the foundational reason for murdering Jesus.

*Historically and fundamentally, Jesus' opponents murdered him because of his repeated provocative stand on the Sabbath issue.*

*John's missing declaration of Jesus—the Son of Man is the Lord of the Sabbath—is amply made up* when in Revelation, he places Jesus' (the two witnesses') resurrection at the center of God's week of seven days (3.5 days) and at the center of humans' Sabbatical cycle of seven years for both camps (1,260 days for the saints; 42 months for the opposition). Jesus is the undisputed center of God's and humans' work. *History revolves around the Lord of the Sabbath.* From this vantage point, all four Gospel writers record the same declaration of Jesus which reverberates powerfully in unison. John's account of this proclamation is couched in apocalyptic language and given in Revelation to complement and elaborate on the other more mundane declarations in the synoptic Gospels. Could this have come about from four authors uninspired by the same Holy Spirit?

What then do we know about God through this declaration? In God's creation process, his handiwork proceeds from the "good" to the "very good" which signals the completion of his work. Thereafter, God enters into his rest—Sabbath. Such "rest" is characterized by the deepest satisfaction a worker can derive from his handiwork and links the creator to his creation through the most intimate relationship possible—satisfaction, wonderment, pride, appreciation, endearment, delight, love, joy . . . etc. Mutuality between subject and object prevails to the fullest extent possible. God fully embraces his works and his works respond back in unqualified ceaseless praise. Nothing short of perfection enters this reverberating two-way enjoyment.

But as history unfolds, the freedom in humans wreaks havoc on this otherwise perfect relationship. So *God instituted the Sabbath to restore the original relationship.* After choosing Abram with the promise that through him all the families of the earth would be blessed, God foretold that Abram's descendents would go into slavery, but would be delivered. Tasting slavery in which the handiwork of the slave is robbed by the slave master contrasts diametrically painfully with endearment to the fruit of one's labor which God enjoys. The latter is what the Israelites can enjoy upon their deliverance by God. God then instituted a set of Sabbath observances that points to a grand harmony in the Jubilee year. Embedded in and right at the heart of the Ten Commandments is the call for Sabbath day observance. In the way God rested after his meaningful work on six days, humans are also to work purposefully to enter into their own rests. The fruits of their labor are theirs to appropriate and enjoy with no one to rob them of this rightful share. "They will build houses and inhabit them; They will also plant vineyards and eat their fruit. They will not build and another inhabit. They will not plant and another eat" (Isa 65:21–22a). Justice would then be the rule extending to every nook and cranny without exception. But before that finality, the Sabbath for humans is repeated over and over in one's life time until their last days on earth and points to a future beyond their first short sojourn on earth for completion.

Importantly, this personal Sabbath also points beyond the person for fulfillment.

Elaborating on the Ten Commandments, God instituted the Sabbatical year (Lev 25) which humans are *to observe for the land on which they reside.* This Sabbatical year is not for furloughing the land to satisfy human needs, i.e., for his profit, since it demands complete cessation of farming throughout all the land for one full year. Instead, the purpose is to bring creation, represented by the land, into harmony with humans through humans learning more fully how God can and is indeed providing for their needs directly through nature during the Sabbatical year. This gradual learning would inevitably increase humans' respect for nature and eventually end in the Jubilee year (after seven—a complete number of—Sabbatical year cycles) where peace, harmony, and beauty prevail between each person and himself, between each person and nature and also between humans. God accepts this grand and ultimate harmony in his creation and calls it the year of his favor. Jesus proclaims this Jubilee when he inaugurates his public ministry (Isa 61:1–2; Luke 4:16–18).

Thus viewed in the pivots of the Old Testament—creation and the Law—humans' Sabbath day and Sabbatical year institutions rest squarely on the foundation of God's creation and are designed to reverse the curse that came upon the land after Adam and Eve fell. These institutions together look forward to God's final acceptance of his creation into his own Sabbath. In this day of all days, harmony of all harmonies, goal of all goals, humans would be guided by the light that is God himself to bring the fruits of their creative labor into the city where the lost tree of life would reappear.

This rich background then gives full meaning to Jesus' declaration that the "Son of Man is thus the Lord of the Sabbath" and explains the Holy Spirit's usage of the otherwise incomprehensible timescales of 3.5 days, 1,260 days, and 42 months to locate Jesus in God's creation.

Importantly, the Lord of the Sabbath reveals to us a God that humans long for, but not of human construction. In approaching our mediator Jesus Christ, the divide between the human and divine is impossible for us mortals to handle. Taking Jesus as fully a human person, we risk losing his divinity in his humanity. Taking Christ as fully God, we risk losing his humanity in his divinity. The tension therein has troubled Christians down the ages and led to bitter acrimony among schools calling each other heretics! Yet, in the midst of all these, the son of man straddles the human and the divine, and holds both together by his very actions on earth—how he challenged the establishment on the point of the Sabbath. To Jesus' opponents, the Sabbath is just a tradition to be kept at all cost. To Jesus, it is the cosmic cause of *taking creation to its final rest through healing humankind to re-commission their stewardship. Jesus very mundane actions of challenging his Sabbath opponents repeatedly are now invested with the cosmic cause of God for his creation.*

When God resurrected Jesus bodily from the death he suffered at the hands of his Sabbath opponents (Jesus' Sabbath challenges is biblically the primal reason supporting his murder by his opponents), God's cause is fully announced to his creation. What Jesus proclaims at the beginning of his ministry—son of man is the Lord of the Sabbath—is now given God's seal of acceptance in his resurrection. This approval of God means Jesus now stands, first and foremost, at the center of God's Sabbath, for the saints and even for his opponents. John has fully grasped this significance. Jesus' mundane proclamation is now validated for and extended to the whole creation. Fittingly, the Lamb, this Lord of the Sabbath, opens each of seven seals in the scroll in God's hands. With that, the debate on the nature of Jesus—God-human—is given a dynamic and sublimating conclusion by Jesus Christ himself: I am not going to debate my nature which is beyond your feeble mind and logic to grasp; instead, let me take you with my creation on a journey to the final Sabbath that my Father designates as our final rest because the son of man will transform this incomprehensible yet invigorating mystery into practical actions for you creatures under the Lord of the Sabbath.

Who could have invented a God who by healing a few sick persons on some Sabbath days while making a few provocative Sabbath statements would turn himself into the pivot of creation's destiny?

Proclaiming the "son of man is thus the Lord of the Sabbath" is very practical. The Lamb is present with his 144,000 on Mount Zion who sing a song privy only to those whom the Lord of the Sabbath knows. This 144,000-turned-countless multitude all join in, not in idle praises, but in harvesting the earth or ridding the earth of Babylon's corruption and beautifying the New Jerusalem. When the marriage supper of the Lamb comes, those led by the triumphant white horse rider would feast on the fruits of the opposition camp's creative labor which the original laborers would not be able to enjoy because they have reached their limits in 666 and hence cannot enter the seventh day of rest with the Lord of the Sabbath. But "blessed are the dead who die in the Lord from now on! . . . they may *rest from their labors,* for their deeds follow with them" (14:13).

The Lord of the Sabbath challenges us not only to know him through intellectual assent since many intellectual issues are ultimately irresolvable; not only through experience as these vary between persons, but ultimately, by partnering with him through our deeds in realizing the Sabbath that has already been secured on the cross. Sifting through the historical reasons for people putting Jesus to death in the four Gospels reveals Jesus' Sabbath challenge as the bedrock of all other reasons. This historical fact has to be foundational as the Lord of the Sabbath cannot bypass or shortchange history, but *takes up God's cosmic Sabbath within real history as his cause against a real opposition and paid his life for it.* He now calls us as historical figures through the same Sabbath cause that he paid his life for, so that creation would enter God's Sabbath through our laboring 1,260 days under God's nourishment.

Eliminating evil and restoring what has been damaged is just the first part of our task. Such are redemptive actions, but falls short of the call of constructive creativity that is the uniquely human mission. This city goes beyond mere restoration of Eden, but collates the creative fruits of all Sabbath-aspirers under the master builder to become a structure that surpasses the original garden in beauty, goodness, and functionality. Humans' creativity is neither obliterated nor restricted under some strict laws, but let loose on God's creation through the guidance of an even more creative leader, the Lord of the Sabbath. The deep satisfaction with one's labor in the Sabbath is for all to appropriate during the journey. More importantly, goodness in creation is not conserved, but is increased with every step the servant-saint-kings take with the Lord of the Sabbath. What many now see as a preventive (against degradation) and preservative (of what is left) battle for creation is transformed by the Lord of the Sabbath to be a continual creative "let there be . . . " (Gen 1) in the footsteps of the creative God who started it all. Nothing can be more meaningful than this.

If the Lord of the Sabbath has always been calling us through the Bible, why then have we not heeded his call throughout history? Many good thinkers from St. Augustine to Jürgen Moltmann have considered the Sabbath as the grand finale of history and placed great emphasis on it. However, none has linked it to Jesus' self-claim of being its Lord. Omitting the obvious can be very detrimental. In our "theology," there seems to be a compartmentalization of the main foci of the Bible, taking Jesus as the savior of humankind (and for some enlightened, also creation) and the Sabbath as creation's end point, while the Lord of the Sabbath stands on the side, looking helplessly on! The obvious dots have not been connected to form a self-evident awesome picture. Attempts have been made to read Jesus into every biblical passage which at times are done through stretching the meaning way beyond what can be accommodated by common sense. By contrast, the "son of man is thus the Lord of the Sabbath" leaps right out of the pages of the Gospels and yet is inexplicably classified as Jesus' challenge of some obscure Jewish tradition and summarily dismissed. *The hard facts of the Bible do not always get a fair reading.* It is no wonder then that Revelation has been read by some to serve narcissistic and even nihilistic ends.

If the stone which the builders rejected has now become the chief cornerstone, how then are we to build around this cornerstone to avoid being crushed, but to realize our part in God's house?

In the recent trend to put God's creation back where it belongs—as the foundation of the Christian faith—after the pre-occupation with personal salvation has blindsided many believers, there has been a search for a proper title to encapsulate Jesus as the savior of all creation, hence the Lord of All Creation is coined. Without a doubt, Jesus is the Lord of All Creation and such has probably been used, quite intuitively, throughout the centuries. Yet, my question is: if this is indeed Jesus' intended title, why has it not been used anywhere in the Bible? Revelation and Paul come close and call Jesus King of kings and Lord of lords (17:14, 19:16; 1 Tim 6:15), but such similarity is not nuanced. If Jesus had considered saying "I am the Lord of All Creation" too pompous for his listeners to swallow, he could have said: the son of man is Lord of All Creation. But he opted for the "Lord of the Sabbath" declaration instead. What is indeed wanting in the ex-biblical title we concoct for Jesus?

But what is it in a name? In sharp contrast with Jesus' Lord-of-the-Sabbath claim, the Lord of All Creation lacks the dynamism of a continuous forward movement since this creator could have forsaken his creation after his first act and allows it to run on its own, just like the god in our philosophical debate has. He just created and stopped. He is also detached from his creation without the close week-by-week, year-by-year involvement in creation's progress toward the final Sabbath, as the real Jesus shows himself to be in the Gospels and Revelation. Importantly, this Lord of All Creation never recognizes that sins have tainted his creation. He has never cured the sick on Sabbath days so that the healed can resume their Sabbath journeys with God. He has never challenged the people to cast away the wrong backward-looking ideas on the Sabbath so that they can be released into a new freedom. Strikingly, he has also not sacrificed his life or anything of his for the redemption of his people and his creation, hence no resurrection and no victory have followed his first creation. *If redemption is necessary, it is to be accomplished by another Lord. But the Lord of the Sabbath was killed because of his stand on the Sabbath, thus rolling up the creator and the savior into one son of man.* Ironically, inverting the errors of some Christians who ignore the first and last two chapters of the Bible, this Lord of All Creation never progresses beyond Gen 1–2. He has not taken up any cosmic cause through his life. Perhaps he wants humankind to respect and love his creation because he is Lord, despite the fact that he has shown neither sacrificial love nor exemplary work throughout the long history of his autonomous creation. The Lord of All Creation motivates solely through authority; the Lord of the Sabbath motivates through incarnational partnership. In being the apocalyptic son of man, the Lord of the Sabbath stays aloof to judge the world, but bearing the same epithet, the mundane son of man is fit to judge because the Lord of the Sabbath walks with his followers to realize God's ultimate goal (John 5:27). The Lord of All Creation can only judge with second-hand knowledge.

Needless to say, the Lord of the Sabbath is jealous of other titles that lay incomplete claim to his relationship with his creation, as much as the good is the enemy of the best.

## 2.4 Focus of Revelation—The Key that No One Should Miss

After going through Revelation in three readings, we now ask a fundamental question: *Is Revelation telling us something new or is it opening up the full implications of what has already been accomplished?* While a knee-jerk response would take the first stand (who needs to be told of something which is already known?), a proper appreciation of the Bible would suggest that Revelation simply unfolds the ramifications of a fait accompli.

On the cross, Jesus proclaimed "It is done." The finality of this proclamation by the Lord of the Sabbath may suggest that history is completed and time would come to a standstill. No further development would be necessary. However, the Bible does not end with Jesus historical resurrection in the four Gospels; further history is recorded in the Acts of the Apostles and there are further teachings in the form of letters (epistles) to different groups of people in their peculiar situations. History is still being made in this world and creation is still moving in some direction, for better or worse. We now take it for granted that Jesus in his death and resurrection has not closed history to further developments. Yet this is paralleled by the just-as-sure assertions that Jesus' work on the cross is final: "Beloved, while I was making every effort to write you about our common salvation, I felt the necessity to write to you appealing that you contend earnestly for the faith which was *once for all handed down to the saints*" (Jude 3).

How then do we reconcile these aspects? Jesus' death and resurrection are seminal accomplishments that form the foundation of all further historical development. With Satan knowing his defeat and the full judgment of the beasts just a matter of time, history's end is certain. For believers, further development would take the form of claiming enemy territories from the already-vanquished. What is then revealed in the last book of the Bible is the extent of Jesus' victory, if it is not already apparent, and how those in the Lamb's camp can proclaim the fait accompli to realize what has already been conceded.

The "It is done" on Jesus' cross will be fully realized in the "It is done" of the seventh and last bowl of God's wrath on his human opposition and in the "It is done" of the glorification of God's creation in the New Jerusalem.

So will there be any novelty in post-resurrection developments? Of course! Humans made in God's image are insatiably creative and the future is open to scientific, technological, cultural, social, economic, political . . . developments, but the salient fact is that these will move towards the finality already procured by Jesus on the cross. All these are within the elaborations in Revelation, but Revelation focuses on the final consummation on the foundation of Jesus' seminal victory and how Jesus' followers—those who want to partake in Jesus' full victory—should take their stand now.

What then does this perspective say about some popular "Christian" teachings about the future? To highlight Revelation's main points through concrete contrary examples, let us take the popular rapture-tribulation-millennium teaching, a form of which is called Dispensationalism, as a study case. The salient features of this school of thought, being an invention in the last two centuries, is that creation's history—starting from Adam and Eve and ending in the New Jerusalem—is divided into different periods (dispensations) during each of which God deals with his people differently. What concerns this school is how the future is going to unfold *chronologically*. This school believes, based mainly on Revelation and some other isolated Bible passages, that at some point in the future, all true believers would be materially transported out of this world (called the rapture) into an unknown realm to be with God and those who remain on earth would go through seven years of unprecedented misery—great tribulation—after which Jesus would physically come to set up his earthly administration for one thousand years. Thereafter comes a final battle at Armegaddon, then the final judgment. This "timetable" is supposed to have come from the narration of Revelation. Within this scheme Israel as a nation would have a special irreplaceable role.

While one can enter into endless debate on the hermeneutical approach of this school, let us just focus on the broad features of their teachings (excluding the Israel issue which has already been taken up in section 5.2 of the third reading, and Armegaddon) to draw out the basic message of Revelation by contrast. Suffice it here to add that this school mainly uses ex-biblical events (historical, current and projected) to interpret Revelation without first seeking thoroughly the meaning of each passage within its immediate context. At such blatant violation of common sense, not to mention exegetical premise, John would be rolling his eyes in the city!

When asked by the populace to show them a sign (an extraordinary event that portends a greater event to come), Jesus, who has worked so many miracles (healings, exorcism, raising the dead, turning water into wine . . . etc.) that seem to defy the laws of nature, gives a startlingly anticlimactic reply: "This generation is a wicked generation; it seeks for a sign, and yet *no sign will be given to it but the sign of Jonah*. For just as Jonah became a sign to the Ninevites, so will the son of man be to this generation" (Luke 11:29b–30). The same happened when Herod wanted some miracles from Jesus (Luke 23:8–9). Through Revelation, the Holy Spirit is now conveying the same rebuttal to every person craving for the extraordinary. The *death and resurrection of Jesus, presaged by Jonah's experience, are the only cosmic sign that will ever be given*, not because God is reluctant or unable to grant others, but that one cosmos-shattering "sign" is totally sufficient to guide humankind and creation forward and all the other "signs" that some crave are just unfortunate distractions which would take the believers' eyes away from the only foundational focus in the Bible. *This sign must be the sole reference for God's creation to locate its bearing.* Such is clear from the second heavenly worship scene when the slain Lamb is the *only one* who can break the seals on the scroll in God's hand. This echoes the transfiguration experience which affirms the absolute preeminence of Jesus relative to any other potential rivals (Matt 17:1–6). Such is also undisputed when the seventh trumpet, describing God's final victory, immediately follows the resurrection of the two witnesses at the end of the sixth trumpet. Among the damaging distractions (signs) in the popular imagination are the universal sign of a "rapture" that some hold would come around (before, during or after) the time of a "7-year tribulation" of unprecedented scale, both concocted out of unwarranted exegesis and are against sound biblical teachings.

Following closely this understanding is the division of time. When Jesus Christ stands at the center of history through his death and resurrection, no other time division of history is necessary. Indeed, any further "division" of history displaces the centrality of Jesus Christ and would nullify the message of Revelation. This explains why all the specific timescales in Revelation (3.5 days, "time, times and half a time," 1,260 days, 42 months) are narrowly concentrated around and used almost symmetrically before and after the death and resurrection of the two witnesses—Jesus (between 11:2 and 13:5)—while the other generic timescales (1 hour, 1,000 years, and 5 months) are further away from this center editorially. Without grasping the centrality of Jesus Christ, advocates of "seven years of tribulation" (remember in Revelation "years" are only counted in 1,000 and never by any other number) and a millennium of unprecedented Christ's righteous administration are going off a tangent with disastrous consequences. As noted in section 6 of the third reading, any other "dispensations" in Revelation, e.g., reading the seven churches as stages in Christianity's development, originate from Satan's seven-headed beast, not from the God of Jesus Christ.

As a general rule, any Christian teaching that draws focus away from Jesus Christ completed work is always problematic. The popular rapture-tribulation-millennium teaching, purported to be based on Revelation, does that through an elaborately awkward scheme without Jesus (Since these "events" can come about without Jesus, why is this book called the Revelation of Jesus?). Remember Revelation re-tells, forth-tells, and fore-tells. While Christians are to live in the present under the rubric of the unshakable triumph of Christ, drawing strength from the ever-present Jesus continuously, this popular take reads Revelation as mainly foretelling and focuses the believers' eyes exclusively on future events. It then dismembers the purported foretelling of Revelation according to time. Whatever foretelling that is interpreted as fulfilled (or soon to be fulfilled) is (will be) passé and this pockmarks the ever-living conclusion of the Bible. Though the historical writings in the Bible serve to demonstrate God's unceasing works, reading Revelation's foretelling as history (i.e., if it is fulfilled) contradicts its conclusive intent to be always living (1:18). God's unceasing faithfulness has already been fully and conclusively demonstrated in Jesus' death and resurrection, which indeed is the message of Revelation. In the most urgent last words, the Holy Spirit does not allow the luxury to reveal frivolous things that are or will soon be meaningless. Rather, *the foretelling must always be "things which must soon take place" rather than things which will soon be passé.* These "things" will be played out (take place) in a timeless fashion, making them ever clear, fresh, and loud until God consummates his whole work. The ever-relevant nature of chapter 20 coming out of our analysis here is just such an example.

More problematic than invalidating parts of Revelation through time segmentation of the foretold is the frontal assault on the efficacy and adequacy of Jesus' seminal work. Even with Jesus sacrificing his precious life and his victory, the saints are still impotent to "harvest the earth" with the son of man and must await another out-of-the-blue intervention by God, this time greater than the death and resurrection of Jesus Christ in terms of number and physical power. Such an attack on Jesus and his victory must be rebuffed by anyone faithful to our Lord. One should ask: how can these imbeciles be entrusted with the world to come (Heb 2:5–8) without bringing on a greater disaster than before?

From the angle of further development according to Jesus' completed work on the cross and his empty tomb, a literal millennial rule that stands between a purported "great tribulation" and the final judgment is as purposeful and necessary as flogging a dry corpse to death.

When chapter 20 assures those who have suffered for Christ *throughout history* that they have not done so in vain because their works and life testimonies have left an ineradicable influence on the world as if they have been reigning with Christ all along, the popular take pushes this scenario to a future millennium when they can exercise administrative power over a presently unruly society. Their martyrdom has absolutely no effect on this world and it is up to God to reward them in the future, in a way that can be disconnected from their present deeds. An unfortunate rift has opened up between one's work and its impact on God's creation. A damaging rift has opened up between the present and future, rendering the present largely meaningless. But Revelation sees the Lord of the Sabbath working consistently from beginning to end. With Christ's victory, the rift between labor and proportional reward, between the bodily present and the material future, is healed, prompting Paul to assert that "God is not mocked; for whatever a man sows, this he will also reap. For the one who sows to his own flesh will from the flesh reap corruption, but the one who sows to the Spirit will from the Spirit reap eternal life" (Gal 6:7b–8). Yet the popular teaching conveys the exact opposite of what Paul continues to say: "Let us not lose heart in doing good, for in due time we will reap if we do not grow weary." According to Revelation, what we reap is first in this world, and not through a lucky draw.

Having thus been assured in Revelation (e.g., 14:13) and in other parts of the Bible, believers in Christ Jesus are to look squarely at their present situation to "work out your (their) salvation with fear and trembling" (Phil 2:12) under the rubric of Christ's irrevocable victory. No miraculous deliverance is promised, but only the ultimate union with Christ in the marriage banquet of the Lamb and the appearance of the New Jerusalem. In fact, "it was also given to him (the beast) to make war with the saints and to overcome them, and authority over every tribe and people and tongue and nation was given to him" (13:7). If indeed the two witnesses (Jesus) were killed by "the beast that comes up out of the abyss" (11:7), can Jesus' followers be totally immune? Yet the saints are not left (behind) to fend for themselves helplessly. The Lamb is leading them on high ground (Mount Zion) after giving them the honor of bearing the names of the victor and cheering them on with heavenly music. In response, the servant-saints sing an exclusive new song before the throne of God (14:1–3). All these super-material realities centering on the Lamb sustain the true believers in their material and non-material tribulations throughout history. Escapism is never an option. But taking their eyes off the omni-operative Jesus Christ, the popular teachings provide a "rapture" to bypass the present difficulties, and suicidally also snub the biblical focus. Where have these eunuchs ended up rapturing to?

When we take Revelation's focus, namely Jesus, seriously, another plank of the popular teachings falls. All the popular timescales of seven years and 3.5 years associated with the "great tribulation" are "converted" from the original 1,260 days and 42 months. In these unwarranted conversions to suit their scheme, the original intent *is lost together* with the focus on the death and resurrection of the two witnesses. All these specific timescales mentioned in Revelation, including the 3.5 days which cannot simply and meaningfully fit into their scheme, are *focused on Christ's victory rather than human suffering in some "tribulation."* Clearly, the first half of these Sabbath periods (week or Sabbatical year) ends in Jesus' resurrection and the second half ends in the marriage of the Lamb and the New Jerusalem, *both speaking of unprecedented authority, goodness, glory, and victory.* Perverse and ugly is the distortion that ties these triumphant timescales with unprecedented suffering. Needless to say, when beauty is distorted, what else but ugliness reigns. And what would the King do to those bent on rehearsing their own funeral dirges in his son's wedding banquet?

In this light of Jesus' victory must also be the six mentions of "prophecy" in Revelation (1:3, 19:10, 22:7, 10, 18–19) understood, that is in the way John was commissioned to *"prophesy again concerning many peoples and nations and tongues and kings"* (10:11) because what Jesus Christ has accomplished on the cross can and definitely would avert the disastrous self-destruction that would otherwise await the rebels if they refuse to respond appropriately. In the time-honored tradition of Old Testament prophets, the Holy Spirit forth-tells more than he fore-tells. Indeed, the wisdom called for in deciphering the enigmatic 7-head-10-horn beast is for the readers to place themselves always in the "is" of the sixth king without fear of the future seventh king because he will zoom to his destruction. *These prophecies (foretelling) are not at all predictions of future events, but statements on the implications and impacts of Christ's indisputable victory for the future. Such prophecies—of evil's defeat—hold true from now till all evils are vanquished.*

Within the context of the first six seals, the great tribulation encompasses all the harms and miseries that sinful humanity has inflicted on God's creation and on each other since creation. For some, they have *"come out of the great tribulation, and they have washed their robes and made them white in the blood of the Lamb"* (7:14b) which is further elaborated at the end when "the marriage of the Lamb has come and His bride has made herself ready. It was given to her to clothe herself in fine linen, bright and clean; for the fine linen is the *righteous acts of the saints"* (19:7b–8). Here Revelation does not talk about a miraculous transformation of a sin-prone person to become a saint, defanged of the ability to sin. Rather, the robe washed in the Lamb's blood is casually equated with righteous acts as if no one could have mistaken their selfsame identity. Indeed, no one should.

In our theology that prizes clarity and procedure, being saved from and being saved into can be pigeon-holed with the first not necessarily progressing to the second. According to the Bible, one without the other is impossible. The Holy Spirit also makes this clear in Revelation. Faith works itself out in deeds and deeds validate the unseen faith. It is only when the bride is garbed in righteous deeds is she ready for marriage to the Lamb.

In all these is the real mission of the servant-saints. They are blocked from escaping the great tribulation and no signs or miracles other than Jesus' death and resurrection are promised for their assistance throughout the tribulation. But the Lamb will guide them on and cheer them forward through his exclusive presence to the grand finale in the city. In all these, the Lord of the Sabbath has placed unshakable trust in his feeble creatures who once betrayed him.

Revealed here is not a shortcut where God's people are empowered with supernatural ability or helped by miracles to carry out their tasks. (This does not mean that God will not do extraordinary works in the lives of individuals and communities to further his kingdom. He indeed does. But this is a prerogative God reserves solely to himself and such must not distract us from our unchanging original mission.) Faithful to the first and only commission of God to all humans, *the saints are re-assigned their task to look after God's creation in all its multiple dimensions.* Revealed here is that saints on this very earth doing what they were intended to be doing would nudge creation forward to the final rendezvous with God in the city. The servant-saints participation under Christ is the engine for creation's movement. God has not considered it his victory if he seeks a climb-down from what seems to have been his failure when Adam and Eve disobeyed him. Instead, "through the one man's disobedience the many were made sinners, even so through the *obedience of the One* the many will be made righteous." With that, "creation waits eagerly for the revealing of the sons of God" who are now counted as righteous in the Lamb (Rom 5:19, 8:19).

With God intervening first and foremost extraordinarily, uniquely and decisively through Jesus' death and resurrection, its effect is extended to all his children. This also creates tremendous tension between the seemingly extraordinary and the downright mundane for all his children. The not-yet-realized bodily resurrection of the saints have prompted some across the various schools to re-read this resurrection as non-material (spiritual) just so that they will not have to throw away a central plank of Christianity. God is now thrown a sop to save him from the embarrassing failure to save us bodily as implied by Jesus' resurrection. This interpretation is helped when the resurrections in chapter 20 are taken as the dead saints leaving their beautiful legacies in history (as I have done here) while waiting for the day when their works on this earth will catch up with them in eternity.

But with flaming eyes Jesus calls for our trust in him: "*Do not be afraid; . . . I was dead, and behold, I am alive forevermore, and I have the keys of death and of Hades.*" God would have none of the climb-down that well-intentioned but jittery humans have prepared for him. Revelation is proclaimed based on and around the bodily resurrection of Jesus, loudly declared from the beginning, symbolized by the two witnesses in the center, promised to all the saints when their works will eventually follow them. This last resurrection (of the saints) will be made good in God's own time, given concrete form in the city and is reinforced in Jesus' "Alpha and Omega" assertions. All these form a thread that if broken would leave all the pearls falling like lead beads to the ground.

Spiritualizing our promised resurrection is what the Holy Spirit would want to save us from. The materiality of this present existence is affirmed and our very material actions take on meaning insofar as God wants this material-natural world to last, and indeed be glorified. We will not be disembodied phantoms floating in some spiritual necropolis, but be resurrected, hence glorified, beings in a Christ-transformed world where we will continue to bring our very mundanely creative glory and honor into the city in which harmony with a redeemed material world is the rule without exception. To betray our innate wish of a bodily resurrection, also testified to by the Holy Spirit, is also to betray the promise of the Bible. This will eventually eat away at the foundation of all our pursuits as Christians.

Finally, a good illustration of how central Jesus is to Revelation is our take on Revelation's repeated assertions that it deals with what *must* soon take place (1:1, 4:1, 22:6). Most people, without further questioning, would take it that God, in his sovereignty, has pre-determined events to come and their timing. But such stifling determinism is not the monopoly of a sovereign God. Many other worldviews, particularly biological evolution and scientific materialism, would come to the same "deterministic" conclusion. Remember Karl Marx has cast his communism as a scientific certainty based on materialism! Hence it is important to ask further: *what* makes the future spoken of in Revelation a certainty?

Does Revelation answer this? Yes. So is it the sovereign God? Perhaps, but Revelation has no room for a disembodied philosophical teaching on divine sovereignty, let alone pre-determinism. The straightforward answer is the works of Jesus, namely his death and resurrection, for he said: "I am the first and the last, and the living One; and I was dead, and behold, I am alive forevermore, and I have the keys of death and of Hades. *Therefore write . . .* the things which will take place after these things" (1:18b–19). Because the powers of darkness have been effectively defeated, the powers of destruction vanquished in Jesus' resurrection, *these things must come. Such is the basis of Revelation's certainty.* Following from this, what would Revelation convey? Events pre-determined by some sovereign being or clear implications of Jesus' victory? Here in Revelation, John has demonstrated again his logical mind!

Losing this anchor on Jesus, the words of Revelation can be tossed around on the waves of smart speculations, resulting in much seasickness and foul vomiting. Perhaps this also gives a hint on why the conclusion of the Bible uses symbols so extensively: to make room for the self-smart to go the way of their own choice, but also for those who fix their eyes on the Lord of the Sabbath to reach God's destination. Has Jesus not said that his father has "hidden these things from the wise and intelligent and have revealed them to infants" and immediately elaborated that "*All things have been handed over to Me* by My Father; and no one knows the Son except the Father; nor does anyone know the Father except the Son" (Matt 11:25, 27)?

After fumbling through all these smart speculations on Revelation unsuccessfully, hopefully the errant can stumble upon Jesus who has shouted out to them all along. If Jesus were to return today, who would recognize him if they don't see him in his concluding message now?

Rationality around a common center—Jesus Christ—is the hallmark of Revelation. If on the other hand one takes Revelation as a series of disjoint foretold events, as one would read the "prophecies" of Nostradamus (this is the way things will be, don't ask "why"), our pursuit of *God, who has communicated intelligibly and sensibly to humanity*, suffers a very serious blow. Such takes would disfigure both the believers' faith and practice, hence their very lives. Satan dumbs people down by his incoherent lies; God makes his saints wise through his *Logos*.

On the basic rationality that "Jesus Christ is the same yesterday and today and forever" (Heb 13:8), crucial aspects of our knowledge of God (theology), ourselves (anthropology), Jesus (Christology), salvation (soteriology), our world (ecology), and the world to come (eschatology) are united under the immutable and omnipresent Lord of the Sabbath. Hallelujah!

## 2.5 How are the Saints to Conduct Themselves by the Light of Revelation?

The sense that Revelation gives its readers is quite different from that of the New Testament's historical writings (four Gospels and Acts) and the epistles. The Jesus in Revelation is no longer the human figure that walked with his disciples and died on a cross and appeared alive to his disciples after three days. Absent also are the many detailed teachings on personal and group behavior and their theological undergirding that are commonly found throughout the epistles. By contrast, Jesus in Revelation has become a figure that transcends the "mundane," yet is much more actively engaged than seen in all other writings. He is not remote from our daily experience.

Putting first things first, John sees Jesus' victory as the focal point of everything (1:17–18). This undergirds the entire book of Revelation. Because of this seminal but epochal and cosmic victory, the relationship between God and his creatures is restored, hence the *eternal gospel* (14:6–7) that the mid-heaven angels (humans) are to preach *relates all humans to the God who created them*. Such is only reasonable because the other contender for human worship—Satan through his earthly proxies of the beasts and Babylon—has been defeated and it is a matter of time (*chronos*) that this defeat will be fully realized. So only one object of worship remains. He should be worshipped as he should always have been—eternally, because he made us and everything else that we see. Descending from these overarching perspectives to an utmost personal level is the warning that remaining with the loser would bring unending and unbearable torments.

With this sweep of the cosmic through to the individual, this eternal gospel has bracketed all the other teachings in the New Testament and set them in their proper perspective, thus earning Revelation its rightful place to be the Bible's epilogue. Other detailed teachings are not shortchanged, but the pivot around which these other teachings revolve and their foundation are encapsulated for emphasis, if they have not already been made clear enough before. Legalism—the human tendency to take the traditional and routine as the moral imperative while forgetting the real intention—is beaten by the repeated already-and-not-yet victory proclamations in Revelation. Goodness marches forward through creativity to break the shackles of legalism and ossification that would otherwise result without Jesus' final victory in sight.

Yet the Bible's conclusion does not just paint the grand picture, then leaves the readers to fumble for their place therein. Mindful of the still-ongoing struggle between the victor's and loser's camp, Revelation offers specific guidance for winning. In fact, these guiding principles set the stage for the saints to preach the grand eternal gospel in chapter 14. They are fully in line with the purpose and design of God.

When the struggle between God and Satan is first clearly laid out in chapter 12, right after the proclamation of Jesus' seminal victory in the seventh trumpet, Satan is described as deceiving the nations and accusing the brethren (9–10). Immediately thereafter Revelation says: "And they (the brethren) overcame him because of the blood of the Lamb, and because of the *word of their testimony*, and they did not love their life even to death" (11). This zooms right into the heart of the conflict. God establishes the world through the Word Jesus (*Logos*, John 1:1–2). *This Word not only represents the Truth, he is the Truth.* When Satan's lies were accepted by humans, God's truth was distorted, sin resulted, and creation marred. For a long while (symbolically 3.5 days), falsehood runs rampant with seeming impunity, until it was demonstrated that the Truth has won through his resurrection. Truth will be re-established throughout creation for its original goodness, beauty, creativity and constructiveness to shine through. Purveyors of falsehood will find themselves on the wrong side of the victor who will judge them harshly (falsehood destroys the earth and these destroyers will be destroyed). Living according to that future of truth is the saints' song, sung continually before God's throne.

Yet establishing the truth gives Satan another weapon against the saints. Satan, true to his guts, will continue to accuse the deceived-turned-saints for their past misdeeds and present errors. But following Jesus' victory, the saints know that the supreme judge is not Satan, but Jesus who has paid his life (the blood of the Lamb) for the errors of the formerly deceived. So Satan's accusation would just bounce off the saints. Consequently, in gratitude and freedom from Satan's accusation, the saints testify to the *Logos*, the creator, before the still-deceived world. "In the beginning, God created" (Gen 1:1). Creativity, the first revealed attribute of God, is now rekindled by freedom in the creature made in his image. Creation moves forward under its steward.

So convinced by the truth of their hope and fortified by the freedom in Jesus, these brethren consider their lives as a worthy investment in and for Christ, even to the point of sacrificing themselves.

Not carefully reading through Revelation may leave us with a confused picture. Many are the gory images in Revelation that one can come away with, justifying the use of violence on a grand scale: the river of blood coming out of God's winepress for 1,600 stadia (14:20); Babylon being thrown down violently like a great mill stone (18:21); the mid-heaven birds feasting on bodies of kings and commanders (19:17–21) . . . etc. Such carnage is only to be expected when people, deceived by Satan, turn on each other violently (first episode of the sixth trumpet), but are the saints supposed to use violence and bloodshed in their struggle against Satan's camp? Despite these militant imageries, another thread runs through Revelation *for the saints*.

Eschewing a tit-for-tat mentality is the virtue of the saints in face of the onslaught of the beasts ("if anyone kills with the sword, with the sword he must be killed. Here is the *perseverance and the faith* of the saints" 13:19b). No doubt, the beast attacks are real, even killing the saints. Yet the saints are called to patient suffering in face of tremendous pressures and appearance contrary to Christ's victory. Saints are not to take up violent opposition in preparation for the wrath of God, but sing and rejoice their way to vanquishing Babylon (15:2–4)! Such praises and jubilation also precede the annihilating of the beast and false prophets (19:1–4). Yet this is no above-the-cloud or pussy-footed attempt to vanquish evil. What is most significant is the metaphor used in describing the defeat of the beast (political and military in nature as seen in chapter 13) and his followers. Twice mentioned is the sword (a weapon for violence) of Jesus: 1. in smiting the nations (19:15), and 2. killing the rest of his opponents (19:21). What could that really mean? No, the very formidable and ruthless political and military machines that oppress, the deeply entrenched religious establishments that deceive, and their followers besieging the saints' camp are not wished away, but squarely reckoned with. Such cannot be otherwise as the Prince of Peace died fighting their collusion. But they are also the same entities that are the target of Jesus' sword. Yet *Jesus wields the sword with his mouth rather than his hand. The truth, not violence, vanquishes.* After recognizing their palpable ferocity, the saints are not to play according to the enemy's rule in fueling further violence with violence, leading to an unending downward spiral. Such tactic has been tried before, but proves only effective for Satan's cause and endgame. Winning the war to end all wars can only be done through the peaceable Word.

Right in the center of Revelation (both editorially and in meaning) are the two witnesses living out a message that is supposed to stem and reverse the downward slide to unchecked violence symbolized by the two myriads of myriads of horsemen bent on cannibalizing each other. They were killed by the beast from the abyss, but resurrected by God. Based on this central message must the militant and gory symbols pertaining to the saints' response be understood. It is by testifying to the reality of the triumphal Truth in Jesus Christ—dying to bring reconciliation, but accepted by God for resurrection—that the saints win over those ignorant of it. Incongruous it would be that when God wants his creation to be glorified (built up), violence is used to destroy it.

*Revelation never describes the saints' actions with militaristic symbols.* These symbols are used only for the one who reserves vengeance to himself (Heb 10:30). Yet how he exacts this vengeance is an interesting study in divine tactic. As opposed to bringing his wrath upon his enemies directly, it is intra-camp feud that brings about the judgment of Babylon. Falsehood self-destructs. After the truth of Jesus' resurrection, the chief cornerstone of God's work, has been established, "everyone who falls on that stone will be broken to pieces . . . " (Luke 20:18).

But the saints are not to preach to the opposition what they have not first practiced within their own camp. When the Lamb was leading his 144,000 on Mount Zion, "a voice from heaven, like the sound of many waters and like the sound of loud thunder, and the voice which I heard was like the sound of harpists playing on their harps was heard. And they sang a new song before the throne and before the four living creatures and the elders" (14:2–3a). Despite the myriad components (many waters), all these converge to *one harmonious song*, clearly articulated, evoking a harp recital, coming out under the leadership of the Lamb. Often, it is easier preached than to achieve harmony within the Lamb's camp, but the picture is painted here for the reality that should be and will definitely be.

Overcoming evil with good is the tactic of God in the Bible. Revelation concludes this message.

If the city is adumbrated for us in Revelation, is it not the saints' duty to use whatever means, short of falsehood and violence, to bring that city into existence? Such a response is the logical outcome of our modern goal-oriented society and would be unquestioned by most. Yet, Revelation gives us a more nuanced picture.

Let us first affirm from Revelation that God wants to bring all of his creation, every nook and cranny, into his city where pain, tears, and even death are history non-repeated and his presence is unalloyed. This is to be done *in partnership with his saints*. Yet how the different parts of this creation, from the grandest to the tiniest, work together to shape the present and future are forever beyond human comprehension, despite our advance in science, technology, and administration, and fantasizing through science-fiction. Without this comprehensive grasp, the coordinated mechanism for moving creation forward is forever off limits to us mortals. Also, humans never work in concert even among Jesus' followers. The main driver of such seeming incoherence is, ironically, the creativity that each saint has by virtue of being made in God's image! Each of them also has a limited earthly lifespan, making continuity of purpose impossible. If so, how then are we to move creation forward?

Yet this question, totally legitimate from the modern commercial and political angle, is somewhat alien to Revelation and indeed to the whole Bible. Abraham did not know where he was going, but was led by God to a place where only God knew. The saints overcome the beasts, not because they have studied the beast thoroughly to locate its administrative Achilles' heel, but they testify to the truth of Jesus Christ's resurrection with all its implications. They live and act fearlessly according to the victory already won in Jesus and are not disheartened by the setback when wickedness and falsehood seem to have won temporarily, e.g., in state violence in response to sporadic terrorism, or in democratic elections. The blood of the Lamb, truth, and their lives are their only weapons. Without a comprehensive roadmap, these saints follow the Lamb wherever he goes. In this is their real zeal: Because of their unshakable *faith* in Jesus Christ and his victory, their *hope* for the ultimate victory is even burnished by Satan's desperate last-ditch violence, resulting in a greater *love* for God, other saints, and God's creation than for their own lives.

Under the direct leadership of the Lamb, each saint sings to him a new and exclusive song. Gradually, the symphony for the Lamb's marriage emerges, not through a human composer, but by the Lamb who brings the glorious city down to his earth. During this journey, the saints who should proclaim "nothing but the truth" by deeds and words would defer to the Lamb who alone knows the "whole truth." These will leave their influence in history as if they are reigning from the beginning to the end for one thousand years. Dangerous and destructive are the mortals who seat themselves in the throne of some savior to proclaim the whole truth, the final truth and the ultimate way to creation's, or even personal, salvation. Revelation calls them beasts regardless. History is littered with numerous dead beasts proffering their messianic millennialism, some even in Christian garb.

In the end, both the escapist fatalism of Dispensationalism and the "can-do" messianic heaven-on-earth culture that Dispensationalists react against are missing the key biblical point. True saints neither have the final solution nor dream up a rapture to satisfy their penchant for high drama, but faithfully follow the Lamb, the Lord of the Sabbath, with righteous deeds, even to death.

If bringing down Babylon is the earthly struggle Revelation wants the saints to engage in, then knowing the true nature of Babylon will help the saints do their part. Revelation minces no words in describing Babylon. She is the all-pervading populace without God, drunk with self-aggrandizement through her mercenary success, sometimes conniving and colluding with political and religious authorities. These manifest themselves in very tangible and institutional forms in *every society throughout all ages*. As long as these institutions, propped up by Babylonians, fall short of the biblical picture of Jesus' kingdom, with greed, oppression, and deception still persisting in any form, it is a Babylon that has to be opposed. In this light, every institution and government of this world is flawed, to varying degrees, and replacing or cleansing them continually is the call of Revelation. That is why every saint, right where he or she is, can be and must be fighting his or her Babylon according to the eternal gospel. All these subversions, in the name of the son of man, would together move God's city forward without a grandiose human blueprint.

Destroying Babylon leaves no room for a "non-material, spiritual" fight. Engaging the political, religious, and economic sphere, even with as little as giving a cup of cold water to one of the least in a disciple's name, with a view to subverting evil for God is a must. Jesus himself shows us the supreme example. Among his many political statements (e.g., exorcising "legion"—the dreaded Roman army unit—from a demon possessed man (Luke 8:26–37), or "render to Caesar what is Caesar, and to God what belongs to God" (Luke 20:20–26) . . . etc.), Jesus singly claims himself to be Lord of the Sabbath. By directing humans and nature to God as their model when he enters his Sabbath, Jesus sets out two standards: 1. a person has the right to enjoy what is rightfully his through his labor, and 2. non-human creation must be respected for its position in God's order. The Lord of the Sabbath would thus oppose, through his foot soldiers, every human behavior and resulting institution that fall short of these Sabbatical norms. Nothing is sacrosanct if it stands in the way of the Sabbath. This makes the Bible subversive, hence feared by every "establishment" because each is flawed to some degree and needs frequent rebuilding. Revelation, with the Lord of the Sabbath right in the center, is the most subversive of all.

Hopeful now is God's creation because of the trust the Lord of the Sabbath places in his restored stewards of creation.

## 2.6 The Advent

"The things which must soon take place" is the subject matter of Revelation. When will these things come to pass? Many Christians from all ages turn to Revelation for a glimpse of the apocalyptic—unveiling of the earth shattering, epoch-making—future events that are supposed to have been foretold. Indeed, this is a deeply ingrained belief among the different prophetic religions—Judaism, Christianity, and Islam—which see the current state of affairs as undesirable and that God will soon enter, or re-enter, this world in person to set things right. One example is the Jews looking to the coming of the Messiah in the time of Jesus. Christians maintain that the expected Messiah (Christ) has already come in Jesus, but many Jews fail to recognize him and continue to wait.

According to our reading of Revelation, a similar blindness that Christians see in Jews has also come upon them. *The prophesied apocalyptic event that would set the course of history on the right path to restoring creation has already happened in Jesus Christ.* In technical terms, the "eschaton" (the final event in the divine plan) has arrived and this eschaton is Jesus himself and is in Jesus. Having laid out the one and only foundation, the necessary and sufficient condition, Jesus is now working and continues to work with his saints to realize the full dimensions of this end. But many Christians, following *the common, but unchristian, logic of other religions,* have failed to recognize that their Messiah has already set the world moving towards this finality. What they thought is foretold to happen in the future has already happened and we are living in its unstoppable forward movement. In Jesus Christ, the eschaton is the here and now rather than the future to come. So like the Jews who do not recognize Jesus as their Messiah, these Christians continue to long for the realization of something cataclysmic and press the Bible, particularly Revelation, to cough up predictions to suit their fancy.

By recognizing that epoch-making nature of Jesus' resurrection and riveting the Lord of the Sabbath in the center of creation's history, John has *revolutionized our concept of prophecies.* Unlike other religions, the Christian eschaton—end times—stands *not at the end of history, but in the middle, both theologically and chronologically.* This eschaton, after Jesus' resurrection, corresponds to the "time, times and half a time" in 12:14 which emphasizes God's sovereignty over his appointed time (*kairos*) by repeating the word trice. From that center, creation will move forward to realize what has already been seminally, but firmly, established, namely, in Jesus' resurrection, evil is defeated and goodness has started to reign. If indeed we believe Jesus' Revelation, the struggle today must be seen through the lens of the already-vanquished desperately making their last stand against the inevitable. This is Revelation's central fore-telling (11:17–18).

Aside from those things described in chapter 20 which together constitute a pan-historical snapshot of God's work in time rather than as individual happenings, how then are we to understand the timing of other "events" ensuing from the prophesied conflicts described in chapters 12 to 19? From our forgoing analyzes, these chapters are gradual zoom-ins to prepare the saints for the still-raging fight ahead. In these chapters are the modus operandi and internal cohesion of the two opposing camps contrasted, hence revealing the Achilles' heel of Satan's camp and the saints' most effective weapons. God works unceasingly with his saints to destroy the remnant of the unholy trinity (Babylon, beast and false prophet), restore his creation, and save the deceived.

Yet there can be two ways to interpret the realization of these things: 1. as occurrences of many such events on different levels, and 2. as a one-off event that will be realized in an instant through the supernatural intervention of God. So far, based on textual logic and the clear cosmic scope of Revelation, these descriptions are timelessly relevant portraits of the many struggles between God and Satan throughout history. Yet, such a take does not and cannot exclude the other possibility that these can also refer to one-off events. Since both views point to the same end point—establishment of God's kingdom after Satan's kingdom is annihilated, the first take sees a gradual process of God-human joint effort in its realization while the second is more consistent with an instantaneous transformation through a powerful supernatural intervention. I will call these the gradual and instantaneous view, respectively.

Arguments supporting both views can be summoned. Arrayed for the instantaneous view can be: 1. metaphors like "I come like a thief," "in an hour, Babylon has fallen" or from elsewhere in the Bible like "in the twinkling of an eye ... the dead will be raised" ... etc. (3:3, 16:15, 18:10, 17, 19; 1 Cor 15:52), 2. the humanly impossible ending in Revelation, e.g., no more death: if this comes through a direct intervention of God, then there is no reason why this and other events will not happen simultaneously universally, hence the city from God would also arrive in an instant, and 3. the symmetry between Genesis and Revelation with Genesis suggesting a clear cut starting point ("In the beginning ... " regardless of how we want to interpret what follows this start of the creative process) and hence the end point may likewise be sharp and final.

In support of the gradual view are that: 1. many of the metaphors can apply to individuals and events at different times, e.g., every anti-God political and economic power has disintegrated like Babylon throughout history, 2. judgment is portrayed as having already fallen or is continuing to fall on this world because of its unbelief (John 3:18, 16:11), 3. the call of God rings out in the eternal gospel to all even when Babylon is pronounced to have fallen in chapter 18 which further reinforces the teaching that God is partnering with the saints in a drawn-out process to harvest the earth as described in chapter 14, 4. the city is painted not only in a completed state—death and sufferings are eliminated—but at the same time being continually beautified by humans with glory and honor, even after the city has arrived, then the tree of life appears, 5. undesirable elements remain outside the city rather than are totally banished as would be fitting for a once-for-all total victory (22:15).

By its very nature, the language in Revelation conveys a message through a heightened sense of immediacy and universality. Yet, when we rightly understand Revelation as totally Jesus-centered, the message is immediately relatable to saints and villains alike on a daily basis (section 6 of the third reading). Losing that focus, Revelation becomes totally fancifully out of this world, casting our faith into unreality.

What we can affirm is that the two views are not mutually exclusive. At a minimum is that the judgment of the world and its people therein, destruction of Babylon, and the arrival of the city are already happening in myriad ways ever since Jesus' death and resurrection, but that there may yet be a time when God renews this world to bring in what is humanly impossible—no more tears, pain, and death. Regardless of when and how that happens, Revelation, contrary to popular beliefs, focuses our eyes on the here and now. Our sight must be set on Jesus who leads us moment by moment. What a disaster it would be for those who insist that even humans restored by the Lamb would be unable to stem the deluge of evil and are prayerfully, yet misguidedly, waiting for God's supernatural intervention, but how invigorating it is to those who heed the call of God to stand in the gap to *pray the Lord's prayer with their hands*: Your kingdom come, your will be done, on earth as it is in heaven!

God's favorable year—Jubilee—only arrives after humans have faithfully completed their Sabbatical years.

By acknowledging our creaturely ignorance about the future and doing what is clearly called for (Deut 29:29), creation moves forward towards God. Thankfully, the Bible's conclusion gives us a sure anchor in the resurrected Lord of the Sabbath.

## 3. WHY IS MY TAKE SO IRRECONCILABLY DIFFERENT?

After the above exposition, it is time to place my understanding of Revelation along the spectrum of scholarly views. My literature survey *after* completing my independent writing indicates that my approach is irreconcilably different from that used by most scholars and is unique in its broad understanding of key passages. To present these differences, I have used for comparison here a number of commentaries, from the highly technical, scholarly, to the more pastoral which appeal to lay readers (1–7 in the bibliography list; hereafter m denotes the reference number I use and n the page in m(n)). I hope this sweep would represent the diverse thinking on the Book of Revelation. Yet I was surprised to find that the variations in opinions among these commentaries, and indeed all other commentaries in the longer list, are much smaller than the difference between my view and that of their works taken collectively. Thus it is not difficult to highlight the major differences between my view and the rest. These are summarized below.

As I made clear in my introduction, it is important to start reading Revelation without preconceived ideas, which means trying one's best to read it as is, without being bound by a priori knowledge of its history, culture, purpose of writing, author's disposition . . . etc. As such, I have started my book, very untraditionally, with internal observations of Revelation. This is quite unlike most other works I surveyed. Yet this does not mean that these very knowledgeable scholars have not done good independent internal analyzes of Revelation. They must have, but they have just presented the material as convention dictates.

Nevertheless, the first seminal difference surfaces in the perceived time orientation of the book. "what must soon take place. . . . the words of this prophecy" (1:1–3) have been taken by commentators to limit Revelation's narration to the future though allowance is made to cover the present which, in the most generous opinion, includes the life, death, and resurrection of Jesus (e.g., "blended the near and distant perspective so as to form a single canvas" 3(22); "The apocalyptists characteristically retrace history in the guise of prophecy," however "This revelation is concerned with prediction" 4(24, 45)). On the other hand, I have allowed for prophecy to be *forth-telling* and not just *fore-telling* and have not excluded the possibility of John *re-telling* the whole story of creation—*including the past*—to complete the narration as fitting for a conclusion.

Subsequent investigation shows that the fore-telling and forth-telling are inextricably linked in Revelation: the stranglehold of falsehood and the evil socio-political practices built on such a foundation of deception and ignorance has seminally been defeated in Jesus (forth-told or proclaimed) and the entire enterprise will totally collapse (fore-told or prophesied); such a truth has not changed since the very beginning because the creator has willed it so, it is innate in God's creation; humans made in God's image are also designed to align with this truth (re-told or given as background). Such initial differences in my "allowance" have led to my irreconcilable departure from the views of the mainstream.

Another basic difference is my view that Revelation, as the name implies and the book indeed insists, is to be understood, namely that it *reveals clearly* to the readers. Most commentators, especially the more technical ones, have surveyed the many views from major works, but conclude with something like "There can be no specific answer to the question of exactly who or what is symbolized by . . . " 5(192). Such obfuscation simply admits that Revelation has indeed not achieved its purpose to *reveal* to its readers what God wants to convey! I hold a higher view of this book.

To illustrate further, all scholars have commendably linked the four living creatures in chapter 4 to Ezek 1's first vision for interpretation. At this point, difficulties in grasping the true meaning still arise and is totally understandable. Possibilities given are: a. four Gospels, b. Babylonian mythology, c. Assyrian and Babylonian representation, d. divine attributes, e. four tribes of Israel, f. whole of animate creation (6(233–234)), and often without deciding on which one suits the context or is most likely using other criteria. The divine attributes (d) have been elaborated as "courage and majesty (lion), patience and strength (ox), intelligence and spirituality (man), and sovereignty and swiftness of action (eagle)" which, except for the eagle, are very close to my interpretation.

Then the most baffling twist in exegesis occurs. Immediately after the heavenly worship, the Lamb opens each of the seven seals. In each of the first four seals, one of the four living creatures calls out and then a colored horse comes forward. All commentators at this point take *an inexplicable, and to me totally indefensible, shift to the horses to gain insight*. The fact that the four living creatures are ordered in the first heavenly worship scene and this order is clearly brought up in the four seals (second, third . . . etc.) should have been a strong hint. More so, if Ezekiel's living creatures have waited over six hundred years for them to reappear in the conclusion of the Bible, but still prove a hard nut to crack in Rev 4, should we not wait to read the next page of Revelation to make another attempt? If Ezekiel's four living creatures are too remote in time and have slightly different descriptions to that in Revelation, should not the rule of proximity (in-context interpretation) tell us that perhaps two almost consecutive mention of the living creatures (chapters 4 and 6) could be, and indeed should be, read together first for an explanation? Since they are not mentioned further in the Bible, this is our last chance to have them reveal themselves to us! Whatever comes of that can shed light back on Ezekiel's erstwhile description. Jettisoning this hope too soon, these commentators come up with the famous (or infamous?) four horsemen of the Apocalypse to explain Revelation.

Once the decision to abandon knowing the four living creatures that come directly from God in the storyline, what follows veers off course hopelessly! The horsemen become judgments on humankind and each subsequent series of sevens would be escalating judgments more severe than the previous. God becomes a one-sided deity full of wrath and bent on destroying his own creation and recalcitrant humanity. The highly instructive message with subtle but pivotal delineation between the different series, e.g., seals deal with humans while the trumpets with all of creation, is completely lost. Retelling God's work turns into foretelling diasaters. More disturbing is that trying to identify the *broad themes of the Bible* (e.g., God created, humans made in his image are to rule creation for God, humans sinned . . . etc.) are now replaced by trying to match minutely Revelation's statements with mostly obscure parallels scattered throughout the Old Testament. No one can deny John's familiarity with the Old Testament, but his signature lofty theological perspective is much more obvious, and indeed much more essential, in his other writings than the many purported Old Testament quotes. One would expect Revelation to be even more so, if anything. Also disturbingly, these quotes are strewn all over the Old Testament in a haphazard fashion as opposed to being focused on the Bible's introduction—God's act of creation and its immediate aftermath. Pity the music lovers when the symphony director accepts a cacophony as the highest achievement!

Another surprise, which is still inexplicable to me, is why no commentator has noticed the very cogent logic that runs through the last three trumpets. Perhaps when all the seals and the first four trumpets have been habitually interpreted as somewhat "stand-alone" judgments, each to be pictured on its own, then the momentum continues. It does not quite occur that the trumpets' events have to be compared, e.g., angel from the abyss versus four angels from the Euphrates; sting in the scorpion tails versus front-back headed horses; not allowed to kill humans versus one third humankind killed . . . etc. Again, once the plot of the story is lost, the assumption is that there is no storyline and no call to link things up sensibly is sounded again.

Continuing with this "compartmentalized" exegesis, the debate on the identity of the two witnesses and the timescales associated with the players in chapter 11 focus on some possible *present or future entities* which can at best be extended back to include Jesus' earthly ministry. By a large majority, the scholars have decided that the two witnesses represent the church (a New Testament entity—consistent with their futuristic outlook) and the very exact timescales in chapters 11–13 are vaguely (mostly without explanation) echoing those in the Book of Daniel since Daniel also prophesies about the future. Clarity and rigor befitting Revelation are lacking in all these interpretations.

Below is a sample of the diverse opinions on these timescales (all emphasis mine; note that they are mostly *backward referenced to past writing or ex-biblical events*):

- "This parallel to John's historicization of the expectation of Nero's return is of special interest because, as the apocalyptic time period (11:2–3; cf. 13:5) indicates, chapter 11 tells from a different point of view the same story as chapter 13 tells." 1(449);

- "Why some of the periods in Daniel and Revelation are not stated with precisely the same formula is *not clear*. But the exact number of "forty-two" here in 13:5 is *probably* intended to recall Elijah's ministry of judgment (see 11:6), . . . ," " The three-and-a-half-day period during which the bodies are observed evoke the period Christ was in the tomb (*though that was only three days*)." 2(565,594);

- "The figure "forty-two months" harks back to the prophecy in Daniel 9, where the forecast of time down to the confirming of the covenant is said to be "seventy weeks of years" (Dan. 9:24). This *cannot be interpreted* by anyone's calculation *as an exact prognosis* of time." 3(153);

- "Forty and two months (again in xiii. 5) is the same period as 1,260 days (xi. 3, xii. 6). Or "a time, and times, and half a time" (xii.14, Dn vii. 25, xii. 7; 'a time'=one year, 'times'=two years, 'half a time'=six months). That is to say, the same length of time *as in Daniel* is allowed for the treading down of the holy city by the gentiles, . . . " 4(147);

- "The three and a half days of their public exposure correspond to the 1,260 days of their prophetic activity. In comparison, it is a brief period of time." 5(221);

- "The "three and a half days" corresponds to the "forty two months" (+ three and a half years) of 11:2 and again speaks of a short period under God's control. This *is a microcosm of the time God allows* Satan and the beast for their final act of defiance." 6(428);

- "The *background to all three temporal descriptions* is to be located in Dan 8.9–14, which refers to the period of Jewish suffering under the Syrian despotic ruler Antiochus Epiphanes in 167–164 BC." 7(124).

To me, none of the above interpretations can fulfil the book's explicit intent—to reveal and *to do so with Jesus as the source of these revelations*.

Nevertheless, some commentators have hinted at my understanding, yet never brought it to fruition, e.g., "1:4. Seven. The number is chosen intentionally because it designates completeness, perfection, totality. In Judaism its sacredness was enhanced because the Sabbath is the seventh day, the sabbatical year was the seventh year, and the seventh sabbatical was the Jubilee, the year of release." 31(736).

By being open to any interpretation that can see logical development in the narration while looking for these possible keys in major themes of the Bible, I have found the Sabbath—the indisputably overarching purpose of creation—to *fall snugly into place to paint an exact and meaningful picture.* Indeed, in using the Sabbath timescale, Revelation has transcended all the contingent events in the whole Bible. Jesus has thus escaped all the provincial concerns of limited mortals to become, fittingly, the Alpha and Omega, while also being intimately present with them. Following this logical development, the two witnesses would then be none other than the Lord of the Sabbath with the timescales before the resurrection representing the Old Testament (in chapter 11) and that after the resurrection the present extending to the return of Jesus (in chapters 12–13). *The full story of all creation is re-told in Sabbatical time.* My observation that the different timescales are nuanced for different parties are also absent from many extant scholarly works, somewhat puzzlingly.

What I have also insisted is that Revelation reveals to all who believes in Jesus Christ—gentiles or Jews, educated or otherwise. God would be unfairly elitist when concluding his oracle to humankind to put a strong ethnic or even cultural hurdle in its unlocking. One may have no choice in other situations, e.g., when Paul wrote to the different local churches two thousand years ago, each with their set of local circumstances. But God's last words should rise above all these contingent issues, cultures and even history (time) to become timelessly and universally meaningful. The week, and its ending in the Sabbath day, (i.e., work and consummating rest) are clear motifs in the Bible. Both are described by the same Greek word. This same week in our calendar has since been *universally observed.* Looking to Old Testament passages that bear inconsequential similarity for insights to Revelation's main message would be doing so from the wrong end of the telescope.

Grasping the significance of the Sabbath is essential since it is the *only timescale that shows the creator God breaking into his creation, the natural order.* Such is also the clear purpose of Revelation. Without seeing this divine angle, these other works fumble and stumble within a natural rather than divine calendar. Their inability to fit what is properly *kairos* into *chronos* explains the confusion of many of these scholars' works.

Two illustrations of wrong focus are the "one third" and "five months" in the trumpets. Some scholars peg the one third to Ezek 5:2, 12; Zech 13:8–9 and the five months to the biological lifespan of locusts. But the emphasis of these Old Testament one-thirds is on destruction (at least two thirds annihilated) while in Revelation, the opposite is true. That being the case, John is contrasting with the Old Testament to make a negative statement—God is not unloving, but his repeated use of one third suggests a positive teaching. Also, it cannot be expected that all Revelation's recipients are biologists with an insect specialty (not to mention that scorpions do not have a 5-month lifespan). Being distracted into these dubious hints (overtly ex-biblical information of an insect's lifespan) misses the straightforward point—God preserves the majority (two thirds) because he loves his own creation and his stewards (limiting their torment to less than half a year) therein. In diametric contrast to the message of impending doom and misery (escalating judgment on the world and the seven trumpets are between the seals and bowls in severity) suggested by these interpretations, the love of God shines brilliantly through in the trumpets which in the end (seventh) issues forth in the kingdom of the world becoming the kingdom of our God. Contrary to end-time gloom, the loving God rather than the wrathful God reveals himself centrally. Who dare say Revelation is all wrath and doom if one truly grasps the storyline?

Perhaps what most set my analysis apart from that of the rest are my two observations given in the first reading. Few have bothered to analyze systematically how Revelation's time units are counted, and also importantly, to determine if there are peculiarities in the narration. Yet such broad and straightforward analyzes can have tremendous implications. If my observations on the drabness of chapter 20 stand and the meaning I draw from them is possible (being based on *a major theme* that God is untiringly working in Christ with his saints since creation and will judge the world), then all the debates about different forms of millennialism (pre-, post-, a-) could end up moot, with a lot of brainpower and otherwise productive energy evaporating into nothingness!

An example of the general struggle to interpret Rev 20 meaningfully is (emphasis mine): "Some commentators understand this period as a literal one thousand years, but the majority takes it to indicate a lengthy period of undetermined duration. In support of the latter interpretation are such verses as Ps. 50:10, which speak metaphorically of cattle on a thousand hills, and 2 Pet. 3:8 with its equation of one day and a thousand years. *Nothing in the immediate context favors either interpretation*. It is the larger concern to find a consistent millennial position that leads exegetes to commit themselves on the meaning of the thousand years." 5(362)

My impression after reading these scholarly works is that most commentators follow a time-honored ethos considered to be good scholarship. That ethos is to interpret Revelation from Old Testament passages since John may have used them and it is believed that such approach would *somehow* lead to elucidating Revelation's message. On the contrary, I use both the Old and New Testaments, but try to pick up echoes of major Bible themes, believing they would be retold for consistency.

## 4. AN EPILOGUE

Consistent with my insistence that a good conclusion must respond to the introduction, I want to end my presentation here through elaborating on the seven statements I made at the beginning of this book. These common-sense, but essential, points can be subsumed under three groups—nature, focal point and implications.

### Nature

1. Revelation speaks forth a *coherence and complete message.* Such is demonstrated through the current common sense reading. This book then lives up to its very name—*to reveal clearly* step by step to eager souls the essential points of God's oracle to us mortals. This basic intelligibility is itself a proof of the correctness of our interpretation and also shows how God usually speaks to us. One can thus approach the rest of the Bible with similar confidence.

2. Revelation uses *only natural and biblical symbols* to convey its message. If a message is intended for all *peoples and tribes and tongues and nations* that are from as diverse a background as God has allowed it within his creation, then it has better not be held hostage to any culture, history or theological position accessible only to specialists. Indeed, our reading shows that Revelation can be *fully* grasped through only general knowledge of the Bible and the natural world.

3. Revelation *retells God's consistent work from beginning to end.* God does not appear out of nowhere to drag creation and his people to an unknown destiny, but has been working consistently throughout history to bring them to a fitting consummation. His unfailing and unrelenting love for his creation has always been accompanied by his wrath on the recalcitrance. The call to forsake the loser has rung out down the ages. Details of God's work vary, but the constant motifs remain.

**Fulcrum around which everything moves**

4. Revelation is sharply and critically *focused on Jesus and his resurrection*. Seen through this cosmic victory, Jesus is the center of God's universal work, of the everyday outliving of the saints' life and even of those who oppose him. This focus even extends back before the flesh and blood Jesus physically entered his material creation, since he is the creator and the ever-present Christ. Without this centre, Revelation fragments into disjoint and nonsensical debris.

**Implications**

5. Revelation calls for *decisive response from every person* in every age. Never confused in Revelation are the roles of the different players—God, Satan, Jesus, the beasts, the saints and those marked 666. Their roles also determine their proper conduct. Revelation calls oppression, deception and their connivance acts of the beasts; it demands that love, righteousness, and truth should be the norm in God's camp, thus *leaving no neutral bystanders* in its *continual subversion* for God's kingdom.

6. Revelation proclaims that *God loves his creation and will glorify it*. Appropriately responding to the Bible's beginning, Revelation points to the salvation not only of people, but foundationally of God's good material creation. Creation will be protected, cleansed, and reconciled to God, but not destroyed. God's judgment is based on how the creation he loves is being respected. Such holistic emphasis squeezes out any "spiritualized" ex-biblical teachings as heresy.

7. Revelation effectively *closes God's written oracle to humankind*. The greatest sign, that of Jesus' resurrection, has been given; "*the mystery of God is finished*." Saints are not to look outside of Jesus and his fait accompli for extra signs in the many out-of-context, disjoint, and fanciful readings of Revelation, but to look forward to the daylight to be fully ushered in by the Morning Star. "Unfinishing" the finished mystery of God will invite added plagues, as Jesus warns.

# Bibliography

## COMMENTARIES/BOOKS CONSULTED AS BASIC REFERENCES

Bauckham, Richard *The climax of Prophecy: Studies on the Book of Revelation*, T. & T. Clark, Edinburgh. 550pp, 1992.
Beale, G. K. *The Book of Revelation A Commentary on the Greek Text, The New International Greek Testament Commentary (NIGCT)*, The Paternoster, William B. Eerdmans, Grand Rapids, Michigan. 1245pp, 1999.
Ladd, George Eldon *A Commentary on the Revelation of John*, William B. Eerdmans, Grand Rapids, Michigan. 313pp, 1972.
Morris, Cannon Leon *The Revelation of St. John*, Tyndale New Testament Commentaries. 261pp, 1969.
Mounce, Robert H. *The Book of Revelation, Revised Edition*, William B. Eerdmans, Grand Rapids, Michigan. 439pp, 1998.
Osborne, Grant R. *Revelation, Baker Exegetical Commentary on the New Testament*, Baker Academic, Grand Rapids, Michigan. 869pp, 2002.
Smalley, Stephen S. *The Revelation to John, A Commentary on the Greek Text of the Apocalypse*, Inter-Varsity, Downers Grove, Illinois. 633pp, 2005.

## OTHER COMMENTARIES

Barr, David L. *Reading the Book of Revelation A Resource for Students*, "Conclusion" in *Society of Biblical Literature*, editted by David L. Barr. 213pp, 2003.
Barr, David L. *Beyond Genre, The Expectation of Apocalypse* and *Reading the Apocalypse as Apocalypse: The Limits of Genre* in *The Reality of Apocalypse, Rhetoric and Politics in the Book of Revelation in Society of Biblical Literature*, editted by David L. Barr. 306pp, 2003.
Barr, David L. *Tales of the End A Narrative Commentary on the Book of Revelation*, Polebridge, California. 228pp, 1998.

# BIBLIOGRAPHY

Bauckham, Richard *The Theology of the Book of Revelation New Testament Theology*, Cambridge University. 169pp, 1993.

Beasley-Murray, G. R. *The Book of Revelation, The New Century Bible Commentary*, William B. Eerdmans, Grand Rapids, Michigan. 352pp, 1981.

Blount, Brian K. *Revelation A Commentary, The New Testament Library*, Westminster John Knox, Louisville, Kentucky. 462pp, 2009.

Boring, M. Eugene *Revelation Interpretation A Bible Commentary for Teaching and Preaching*, Westminster John Knox. 236pp, 1989.

Boxall, Ian *The Revelation of St. John New Testament Commentaries*, A & C Black (Publishers) Limited, London , 347pp, 2006.

Brighton, Louis *A Revelation, Concordia Commentary*, Concordia Publishing House. 637pp, 1999.

Carrington, Philip *The meaning of the Revelation* SPCK. 416pp, 1931.

Carter, Warren *What does Revelation Reveal? Unlocking the Mystery*, Abingdon, Nashville) 137pp, 2011.

Collins, Adela Yarbro *The Combat Myth in the Book of Revelation*, The Westminster, Philadelphia. 308pp, 1976.

Collins, Adela Yarbro *Crisis & Catharsis, The Power of the Apocalypse*, The Westminster, Philadelphia. 179pp, 1984.

Collins, Adela Yarbro *The Apocalypse*, Michael Glacier Inc. 155pp, 1983.

Corsini, Eugenio *The Apocalypse, The Perennial Revelation of Jesus Christ, Good News Studies* 5, Michael Glazier Inc. 425pp, 1983.

Court, John M. *Revelation*, Sheffield Academic. 133pp, 1994.

de Silva, David A. *Seeing Things John's Way The Rhetorics of the Book of Revelation*, Westminster John Knox, Louisville, Kentucky. 393pp, 2009.

Harrington, Wilfrid J. *Revelation, Sacra Pagina*, (Harrington, Daniel J. as S.J. Editor), Liturgical, Minnesota. 296pp, 1993.

Keener, Craig S. *Revelation, The NIV Application Commentary*, Zondervan Publishing House, Grand Rapids, Michigan. 576pp, 2000.

Koester, Craig R. *Revelation A New Translation with Introduction and Commentary, Anchor Yale Bible*, Yale University. 879pp, 2014.

Lasseigne, Jeff *Unlocking the Last Days A Guide to the Book of Revelation & the End Times*, Baker. 333pp, 2011.

Lilje, Hanns *The Last Book of the Bible*, Translated by Olive Wyon, Muhlenberg, Philadelphia, 4th Edition. 286pp, 1955.

Little, C.H. *Explanation of the Book of Revelation*, Concordia Publishing House. 232pp, 1950.

Massyngberde Ford, J. *Revelation A New Translation with Introduction and Commentary*, Doubleday. 455pp , 1975.

Mangina, Joseph L. *Revelation Brazos Theological Commentary on the Bible*, Brazos, Grand Rapids, Michigan. 272pp, 2010.

Metzger, Bruce M. *Breaking the Code, Understanding the Book of Revelation*, Abingdon. 111pp, 1993.

McFarland Kincheloe, Raymond *A Personal Adventure in Prophecy, Understanding Revelation*, Tyndale House, Inc. 214pp, 1974.

Michaels, J. Ramsey *Interpreting the Book of Revelation, Guides to New Testament Exegesis*, Baker Book House Company. 150pp, 1992.

Michaels, J. Ramsey *Revelation, The IVP New Testament Commentary Series*. Inter-Varsity, Downers Grove, Illinois, 265pp, 1997.

Mounce, Robert H. *What are We Waiting For? A Commentary on Revelation*, William B. Eerdmans, Grand Rapids, Michigan. 141pp, 1992.

Moyise, Steve *The Old Testament in the Book of Revelation, Journal for the Study of the New Testament, Supplementary Series* 189, Sheffield Academic, Sheffield. 170pp, 1995.

Murphy, Frederick J. *Fallen is Babylon, The New Testament in Context*, Trinity International, Harrisburg, Pennsylvania. 472pp, 1998.

Newport, Kenneth G. C. *Apocalypse & Millennium, Studies in Bible Eisegesis*, Cambridge University. 249pp, 2000.

Pate C. Marvin *Four Views on the Book of Revelation*, General Editor: Pate, C. Marvin, Stanley N. Gundry (Series Editor), Kenneth L. Gentry Jr. (Contributor), Sam Hamstra Jr. (Contributor), Robert L. Thomas (Contributor). 252pp , 1998.

Pender, William C. *Revelation, Interpretation Bible Studies*, Geneva. 110pp, 1999.

Prigent, Pierre *Commentary on the Apocalypse of St. John, An Overview of Current Research*, Mohr Seibeck. 717pp, 2001.

Reddish, Mitchell G. *Revelation*, Smyth & Helwys Bible Commentary, S & H Publishing Inc. 472pp , 2001.

Ressguie, J.L. *Revelation Unsealed, A Narrative Critical Approach to John's Apocalypse*, BRILL. 233pp, 1998.

Ressguie, James L. *The Revelation of John, A Narrative Commentary*, Baker Academic, Grand Rapids, Michigan. 288pp, 2009.

Richard, Pablo *Apocalypse*, Orbis, Maryknoll, New York. 183pp, 1995.

Roloff, Jurgen *Revelation, A Continental Commentary*, Fortress, Minneapolis. 275pp, 1993.

Skaggs, Rebecca and Benham, Priscilla C. *Revelation, Pentacostal Commentary Series*. Dorset, 260pp, 2009.

Tenney, C. Merrill *Interpreting Revelation*, Pickering & Inglis. 211pp, 1958.

Thomas, Robert L. *Revelation 1–7 / Revelation 8–22, An Exegetical Commentary*, Moody, Chicago (524pp/690pp), 1992/1995.

Thompson, Leonard L. *Revelation*, Abingdon New Testament Commentary, Abingdon. 207pp, 1998.

Wall, Robert, W. *Revelation, New International Biblical Commentary*, Paternoster, Hendrickson. 295pp, 1991.

Wiersbe, Warren *Be Victorious*, Victor, Wheaton, Illinois. 155pp, 1986.

Wilcock, Michael *I Saw Heaven Opened, The Message of Revelation*, Inter-Varsity, London. 223pp, 1975.

Witherington III, Ben *Revelation, The New Cambridge Bible Commentary*, Cambridge University. 307pp, 2003.

Woodman, Simon *The Book of Revelation*, SCM, London. 259pp, 2008.

# Subject Index

Abel, 50, 68, 87, 116, 140, 154
abyss, 14, 41, 42, 50, 51, 54, 60, 69, 77, 89, 107, 109, 136, 150, 160, 161, 164, 174, 198, 205, 213
Adam and Eve, 37, 51, 53, 58, 81, 89, 97, 99, 100, 139, 140, 149, 151, 168, 173, 186, 190, 195, 200
advent, 24, 97, 139, 174, 179, 208–10
Alpha and Omega, 22–23, 98, 102, 114, 160, 168, 200, 215
altar, 38, 43, 49, 56, 62, 65, 66, 67, 116, 119, 127, 147, 148, 162
angel (see also messenger), 11, 12, 27, 36, 38, 39, 41, 42, 43, 44, 45, 54, 55, 56, 60, 63, 64, 65, 66, 67, 68, 69, 71, 77, 79, 80, 82, 83, 85, 87, 99, 100, 102, 107, 109, 116, 119, 122, 123, 128, 131, 132, 144, 145, 148, 150, 152, 153, 154, 155, 158, 160, 161, 162, 164, 165, 166, 167, 174, 177, 179, 181, 183, 184, 186, 202, 213
animal, 2, 31, 32, 48, 59, 60, 75, 88, 116, 137
Apocalypse, 213
apostle, xiii, 98, 110, 139, 142, 148, 149, 154, 163, 169, 194
ark, 42, 123
Armageddon (see also Tel Megiddo), 69, 70, 71, 72, 126, 131

author, 4, 5, 6, 12, 15, 20, 21, 118, 119, 160, 172

Babel, 43, 71, 75, 76, 78, 79, 136, 141
Babylon, 14, 42–44, 50, 52, 64, 69–74, 76, 77–79, 80–85, 89, 95–96, 97, 98, 101, 106, 109, 126, 129, 131, 133–35, 136, 138–40, 142, 143–48, 151–52, 154, 157, 159, 161, 164, 165, 166, 169, 175, 179, 180, 181, 183, 185, 186, 191, 202, 204, 205, 207, 209, 210, 212
beast, 11, 16, 50, 51, 59–63, 64, 67, 68, 69, 71, 72, 73–79, 81–82, 83–85, 86, 89, 95, 96, 106, 109, 112, 114, 122, 126, 127, 129, 131, 133–38, 141, 142, 144, 145, 146, 147, 148, 152, 153, 155, 157, 158, 159, 160, 161–64, 165–66, 169, 172, 174, 175, 176, 177, 183, 186, 187, 194, 196, 198, 199, 202, 204, 205, 206, 207, 209, 214, 218
beauty, xi, xiv–xv, 28, 40, 98, 116, 124, 142, 153, 168, 186–87, 189, 191, 198, 203
bible, 1–6, 15, 20, 21, 27, 33, 57, 67, 70, 71, 72, 78, 81, 92, 93, 97, 104, 112, 113, 114, 116, 118, 119, 124, 126, 138, 139, 140, 141 . . .

bible (*continued*), 148, 156, 166, 171, 174, 175, 176, 177, 178, 179, 180, 181, 187, 192, 193, 194, 195, 196, 199, 201, 203, 205, 206, 207, 208, 210, 212, 213, 215, 217, 218
blood, 28, 36, 40, 50, 51, 56, 65, 66, 67, 68, 81, 83, 84, 87, 118, 120, 140, 141, 169, 177, 199, 203, 204, 206, 218
bowl, 37, 66–71, 76, 83, 85, 104, 106, 109, 111, 121–23, 124, 125–27, 128–33, 134, 135, 136, 142, 144, 146, 148, 150, 152, 159, 163, 165, 167, 168, 172, 174, 185, 194, 216
brethren, 56, 140, 203, 204
bride, 81, 83, 84, 100, 110, 139, 141, 142, 158, 186, 199

Cain, 67, 68, 71, 72, 87, 116, 139
calendar (natural, divine), 17, 48, 49, 52, 53, 215
camp (God's, Lamb's, saint's, Michael's), 55, 56, 63, 65, 67, 73, 83, 91, 95, 106, 108, 152, 153, 154, 162, 164, 165, 169, 181, 194, 203, 204, 205, 218
camp (Satan's, beasts', opposition's), 59, 63, 64–65, 69, 73, 76, 77, 78, 82, 84, 85, 86, 89, 106, 108, 109, 110, 119, 136, 144, 145, 147, 152, 164, 166, 169, 203, 204, 209
cardinal direction, 70
center, 12, 26, 34, 48, 49, 52, 53, 65, 85, 86, 96, 98, 107, 111, 113, 114, 115, 125, 128, 143, 151, 155, 159, 169, 188, 190, 196, 200, 202, 205, 208, 209, 218
chapter division, 3, 6
*chronos* (linear time), 12, 13, 19, 23, 49, 58, 59, 91, 92, 151, 153, 156, 202, 215
church, 4, 5, 6, 12, 22, 23, 24, 25, 26, 28, 48, 62, 69, 72, 87, 105, 111–15, 124, 125, 136, 142, 149, 150, 155, 157–58, 160, 162, 179, 180, 183, 184, 196, 213, 215
city (see also holy city and great city), 42, 46, 51, 70, 71, 79, 82, 91, 97, 98–101, 106, 110, 111, 122, 138, 139–40, 143, 145, 160, 161, 164, 169, 172, 174, 181, 183, 186, 190, 191, 199, 200, 201, 205, 206, 207, 209, 210, 214
coherence, 1, 2, 120, 128, 202, 206, 217
color, 7, 8, 9, 11, 31, 33, 44, 86, 95, 97, 153, 212
common sense, xii, xiii, 2, 5, 6, 14, 20, 70, 103, 156, 171, 176, 177, 180, 192, 195, 217
conclusion, xiii, 5, 25, 45, 91, 126, 130, 138, 139, 156, 166, 172, 175, 180, 187, 190, 196, 201, 203, 211, 217
confuse, xiv, 6, 21, 76, 78, 79, 81, 139, 140, 157, 204, 218
conquer, 31–32, 84, 88, 95, 99, 132
consequential, 129
context, 3, 5, 13, 15, 20, 24, 34, 36, 37, 44, 50, 55, 56, 57, 58, 62, 63, 72, 74, 79, 82, 85, 92, 94, 105, 111, 113, 117, 118, 119, 120, 126, 136, 137, 140, 143, 164, 171, 172, 174, 175, 176, 177, 195, 199, 212, 218
cornerstone, 73, 103, 192, 205
cosmic, 4, 5, 20, 23, 63, 70, 72, 87, 89, 90, 91, 92, 93, 96, 104, 114, 115, 132, 137, 142, 143, 145, 153, 155, 156, 158, 159, 175, 180, 183, 190, 191, 193, 195, 202, 203, 209, 218
count(ed), 13–14, 24, 37, 46, 47, 48, 55, 86, 98, 196, 216
creation, too numerous to enumerate by page: see sections 3.1, 3.2, 4.4, 4.5, 5.2, 5.4, 11 of second reading, sections 3, 7.2, 7.3 of third reading and section 2.3 of fourth reading for highlights
creator, 26, 28, 29, 30, 45, 53, 59, 62, 64, 65, 75, 82, 83, 87, 90, 92, 100, 105, 108, 121, 133, 145,

SUBJECT INDEX 225

152, 156, 166, 168, 180, 182, 183, 184, 185, 186, 188, 193, 204, 212, 215, 218
creatures (see also living creatures), 26, 28, 29, 33, 39, 40, 77, 83, 97, 103, 105, 116, 128, 130, 158, 165, 166, 173, 181, 191, 199, 202
crown, 31, 33, 40, 138, 140, 141, 149
curse, 39, 45, 68, 72, 73, 95, 100, 116, 122, 154, 168, 174, 175, 190

Daniel, 57, 58, 82, 102, 136, 137, 175, 176, 187, 214
David, 144, 160, 161
day (see also 3.5 days, 1,260 days, and Lord's day), 13, 14, 15–18, 24, 26, 36, 43, 46, 47, 48, 49, 51, 53, 55, 57, 58, 62, 65, 68, 74, 77, 80, 81, 88, 98, 102, 105, 116, 117, 120, 128, 132, 139, 144, 145, 150, 153, 155, 163, 165, 178, 187, 189, 190, 191, 200, 215, 216
death, 22, 31, 32, 33, 34, 35, 38, 40, 41, 42, 45, 46, 51, 52, 53, 56, 60–61, 66, 68, 87, 88, 91, 92–94, 95–96, 97, 98, 99, 102, 107, 110, 112, 113, 114, 115, 116, 124, 129, 130, 139, 143, 148, 153, 155, 157, 159, 160, 163, 165, 169, 175, 181, 184, 185, 187, 190, 191, 196, 198, 200, 201, 203, 206, 207, 209, 210
deception / deceptive (see also lie), 59–60, 63, 76, 89, 90, 91, 96, 108, 125, 133, 135, 140, 150, 152, 153, 203, 211, 218
defeat (see vanquish)
destroy, 39, 41, 54, 55, 69, 73, 76, 78, 81–82, 83, 84, 89, 90, 96, 98, 106, 107, 108, 109, 110, 116, 121, 122, 123, 126, 129, 130, 131, 132, 134, 135, 141, 146, 152, 160, 161, 163, 164, 166, 167, 168, 181, 185, 203, 205, 207, 209, 213, 218

destroyer, 41, 77, 86, 96, 107, 108, 109, 118, 119, 120, 121, 129, 133, 163, 167, 168, 203
disaster, xi, 8, 31, 37, 38, 42, 132, 197
disjoint, 64, 202, 218
Dispensationalism, 194, 195, 207
drabness (of chapter 20), 11, 12, 86, 216
dragon (see also serpent), 55–56, 75, 79, 86, 89, 97, 104, 106, 129, 133, 138, 140, 141, 144, 151, 155, 160, 162, 164
duration, period, 13, 14, 37, 44, 46, 47, 49, 57, 58, 59, 89, 92, 93, 150, 154, 216

eagle, 27, 31, 32, 33, 36, 57, 64, 67, 85, 99
earth (meaning of), 40, 56–57, 60, 64
earthquake, 35, 46, 51, 69, 70–72, 112, 117, 122
east, 68, 69, 70–72, 75, 100
ecology, 202
economic, 62, 77, 79, 108, 135, 146, 147, 152, 157, 183, 194, 207, 210
Eden, 68, 71, 97, 100, 110, 154, 158, 173, 186, 191
Egypt, 50, 66, 70, 78, 154
elders, 12, 26, 27–28, 30, 33, 34, 53, 83, 98, 99, 100, 142, 148, 149, 154, 158, 162, 163, 167, 183, 205
encounter, 24, 48, 90, 105, 137, 183–87
eschatology / eschaton, 153, 202, 208
ethnic, 36, 99, 140, 142–43, 144, 177, 215
Euphrates, 12, 42, 43, 44, 68, 69–71, 75, 76, 163, 213
ex-biblical, 72, 78, 192, 195, 214, 216, 218

fall (of humans, of Babylon), 41, 52, 58, 64, 76, 82, 100, 101, 107, 126, 145, 151, 152, 153, 154, 155, 159, 169, 179, 185, 209, 210
false prophet, 11, 50, 69, 73, 79, 85, 95, 135, 144, 146, 152, 159, 161, 165, 204

## SUBJECT INDEX

father, 63, 72, 76, 86, 96, 128, 153, 158, 162, 164, 167, 168, 178, 190, 201
fine linen, 83-84, 117, 199
fire, 11, 14, 26, 40, 43, 50, 59, 65, 66, 79, 80, 85, 93, 95, 96, 101, 110, 112, 135, 144, 145, 146, 152, 160, 161, 164, 165, 166
first four seals, trumpets, bowls, 27, 30, 31, 33, 35-36, 37, 39, 40, 54, 64, 67, 84, 104, 107, 109, 119, 120, 124, 125, 126, 128-30, 132, 142, 150, 152, 167, 168, 212, 213
five months (see month)
fore-telling, 23-24, 103-4, 196-97, 199, 209, 211, 213
forth-telling, 23-24, 103, 211
forty two months, xii, 46, 49, 50, 51, 57, 59, 61, 86, 92, 113-14, 147, 150, 159, 163, 188, 190, 198, 214
four (see also 4 living creature, 24 elders, first four seals, trumpets and bowls), 13, 14, 27, 32, 33, 34, 36, 37, 39, 43, 47, 65, 67, 70, 80, 84, 85, 90, 100, 107, 128, 131, 137, 163, 173, 183, 188, 191, 194, 213
four living creatures (see living creature)
fractions, 58, 129-30
fruits, 21, 30, 47, 79, 80, 88, 95, 99, 100, 101, 103, 140, 149, 151, 154, 179, 189, 190, 191
fulfilment, 29, 49, 58, 65, 69, 112, 114, 115, 123, 139, 149, 181, 185, 189

garden, 71, 97, 154, 173, 178, 191
Genesis, 5, 20, 70, 79, 138, 149, 155, 168, 171-74, 175, 177, 179, 180, 209
genre, 176-77
geography / geographical, 4, 10, 69-72, 78, 90, 91, 100, 137, 142, 173, 177
God's love, 101, 103, 104, 126, 127, 128, 132, 150, 167, 181, 188, 216, 217

Gog and Magog, 10, 70, 78, 90-91
gospel, 63, 64-65, 70, 72, 82, 85, 88, 112, 113, 124, 128, 144-45, 147, 155, 159, 166, 167, 177, 181, 182, 183, 188, 202, 203, 207, 210
great city, 46, 50, 52, 71, 82, 144, 146, 147

Hades, 22, 91, 93, 95-96, 160, 184, 200, 201
hail, 40, 41, 70, 72-73, 117-18
half (see also three and a half days and time, times and half a time), 13, 14, 16, 37, 41, 46, 51, 57, 58, 89, 106, 107, 113, 114, 126, 141, 148, 167, 198, 214, 216
harlot (prostitute), 73, 76, 79, 81, 83, 135, 138, 139, 142, 157, 161
harmony, 32, 48, 62, 65, 78, 84, 100-101, 106, 110, 135, 154, 159, 168, 169, 179, 189-90, 201, 205
harvest, 63, 65-67, 83, 87, 106, 108, 116, 121, 152, 161, 162, 168, 172, 177, 191, 197, 210
head, 5, 12, 22, 43-44, 56, 58, 59, 60, 63, 72, 73, 74-76, 78, 79, 84, 123, 125, 133, 136, 137, 139, 140, 152, 153, 155, 159, 160, 161, 164, 173, 196, 199, 213
heaven, 26, 27, 33, 37, 38, 42, 45, 46, 50, 55, 56, 58, 59, 60, 62, 64, 65, 66, 70, 79, 82, 83, 85, 89, 92, 97, 108, 112, 122, 125, 126, 128, 140, 147, 155, 160, 162, 165-66, 167, 174, 175, 178, 182, 184, 205, 207, 210
heaven and earth (new), 97, 154, 174, 175
heresy, 115, 142, 218
history (of creation), 37, 52, 54, 57, 79, 86, 88, 93, 94, 107, 114, 115, 156, 195, 208
historical, 4-5, 6, 25, 49, 75, 78, 82, 93, 104, 114, 139, 142, 151, 154, 157, 165, 172, 175, 176, 179, 184, 188, 191, 194, 195, 196, 202, 209

## SUBJECT INDEX

holy city, 21, 46, 49–50, 51, 52, 54, 59, 71, 99, 104, 113, 114, 133, 139, 142, 147–49, 159, 163, 169, 175, 179, 181
Holy Spirit, xiii, 5, 63, 98, 114, 123, 124, 137, 139, 156, 158, 168, 176, 177, 180, 181, 183, 188, 190, 195, 197, 199, 200, 201
horn(s) of the altar, on the beast, 43, 56, 59, 73–75, 77, 79, 133, 136–37, 152, 155, 159, 160, 161, 164, 172, 185, 199
horse, 3, 9, 30–31, 33, 36, 40, 43, 44, 66, 77, 80, 81, 84, 85, 87, 99, 125, 129, 161, 165, 177, 191, 212, 213
horsemen, 33, 43, 68, 126, 163, 205, 213
hour, 13–14, 15, 16, 37, 43, 45, 46, 47, 49, 58, 74, 76, 79, 80, 82, 89, 106, 107, 112, 113, 122, 126, 128, 147, 150, 153, 155, 167, 196, 209

I am, 22, 26, 28, 29, 50, 81, 111, 184, 192, 200, 201
incense, 39, 67, 80, 116, 131
inspire, xiii, xiv, xv, 5, 171, 177, 188
interlude, 127–28
introduction, xiv, 5, 20, 22, 25, 33, 48, 87, 105, 157, 172, 174, 213, 217
Israel, 21, 23, 36, 90, 98, 122, 123, 138, 140, 142, 143, 144, 157, 158, 169, 178, 195, 212
"It is done", 37, 69, 97, 125, 131, 134, 172, 194

Jerusalem, 10, 23, 70, 71, 92, 142, 143, 178
Jerusalem (new), 14, 36, 70, 98, 100, 104, 110, 123, 139, 140, 148, 149, 154, 159, 169, 175, 186, 191, 194, 195, 198
Jesus (as Christ), 87–88
Jesus (as Jesus Christ), 87
Jesus (death and resurrection), 22, 24, 87, 107, 111, 113, 114, 125, 126, 134, 155, 156, 185, 194, 195, 196, 197, 198, 199, 200, 201, 210, 211
Jesus (as interpreter), 178–79
Jesus Christ (cosmic), 115
Jews / Jewish, 5, 15, 24, 36, 41, 48, 53, 60, 72, 74, 86, 118, 137, 140, 142, 143, 165, 171, 187, 188, 192, 208, 215
Jonah (sign of), 195
Jubilee year, 48, 62, 100, 150, 154, 168, 189, 210, 215
judgment, 6, 10, 12, 13, 44, 45, 49, 50, 53, 54, 64, 65, 73, 75, 76, 77, 79, 82, 83, 88–89, 92, 93–97, 110, 113, 114, 118, 121, 122, 127, 128, 130, 131, 135, 144, 145, 147, 148, 159, 162, 164, 174, 194, 195, 197, 205, 210, 213, 216, 218

*kairos* (appointed time), 12, 13, 19, 23, 24, 49, 58, 91, 92, 151, 156, 209, 215
kill, 31, 41, 42, 50, 60, 96, 113, 130, 136, 153, 188, 213
king, 23, 30, 35, 45, 69, 71–72, 74–79, 80, 81, 82, 84, 99, 141–42, 147, 153, 159, 161, 163, 167, 174, 186, 192, 198, 199, 204
kingdom, 24, 28, 30, 53–54, 56, 68, 69, 72, 73, 74, 77, 78, 79, 87, 89, 98, 106, 107–8, 109, 110, 113, 121, 122, 125, 126, 128, 131, 133, 134, 135, 136, 137, 146, 148, 151, 152, 183, 200, 207, 209, 210, 216, 218

labor, 21, 47, 48, 65, 99, 100, 120, 123, 145, 179, 181, 183, 189, 190, 191, 197, 207
lamb, 3, 11, 27–30, 36, 37, 39, 48, 52, 53, 54, 56, 59, 63–67, 70, 75, 78, 83–87, 98, 99, 100, 101, 105–6, 108, 110, 117, 119, 120, 123, 130, 131, 132, 133, 134, 136, 139, 141, 142, 143, 148, 152, 155, 157, 158, 159, 160, 161, 162, 165, 166, 167, 172 . . .

lamb (*continued*), 175, 183, 185–86, 190, 191, 195, 198–200, 203–7, 210, 212
Law and Prophets, 49–50, 104, 107, 112, 115, 157, 164
lie, 41, 42–44, 56, 63, 68, 76, 81, 89, 92, 96–97, 110, 113, 125–26, 128, 141, 145, 146, 150, 151, 155, 164, 165, 168, 169, 173, 175, 183, 202, 203
lightning, 26, 117–18
lion, 27, 30, 31, 33, 40, 44, 59, 67, 75, 86, 88, 99, 100, 132, 136, 137, 160, 212
literal interpretation, 14, 21, 93, 111, 177, 197, 216
living creatures, 9, 12, 26–27, 28, 30–34, 38, 67, 83, 97, 99, 103, 116, 122, 128, 132, 137, 162, 167, 175, 205, 212–13
locusts, 9, 39–41, 43–44, 46, 68, 113, 125, 130, 159, 160, 163, 172, 216
logic / logical, xiii, xiv, 2, 20, 22, 33, 35, 36, 52, 56, 64, 70, 103, 105, 114, 120, 121, 123, 124–25, 128, 129, 131, 135, 136, 139, 144, 157, 165, 172, 190, 201, 206, 208, 209, 213, 215
Lord of the Sabbath, 65, 114, 140, 156, 159, 168, 187–93, 194, 197, 199, 201, 202, 207, 208, 210, 215
Lord's Day, 17, 24, 105

mark of the beast, 61, 67, 79, 86, 135, 163, 165
messenger (see also angel), 38, 39, 50, 51, 84, 102, 119, 131, 158, 174, 186
Michael, 55–56, 64, 160, 161, 166
mid-heaven, 64, 85, 162, 164, 165, 168, 177, 181, 202, 204
millennium / millennialism, xii, 194, 196–97, 207, 216
month (see also forty two months), 13, 15, 16, 18, 41, 43, 46–47, 49, 55, 58, 86, 100, 114, 126, 128, 148, 149, 153, 155, 159, 196, 214, 216
moon, 9, 40, 46, 55, 70, 99, 118, 138, 140–41, 162, 167, 174–75
morning star, 53, 102, 161, 218
Moses, 32, 33, 50, 67, 86, 115, 132, 152
mouth, 12, 22, 56, 59, 60, 67, 75, 84–85, 144, 146, 161, 165, 167, 177, 205
mutated, 39–41, 43, 46, 68, 113, 125, 159, 160
mystery, 27, 34, 45, 115, 137, 149, 218

name, 6, 9, 10, 26, 29, 42–43, 54, 58, 63, 69–71, 75, 76, 79, 84, 86, 87, 96, 98, 136, 137, 140, 141, 149, 157–58, 162–64, 172, 173, 184, 193, 198, 207, 212, 217
narration / narrative, 1, 2, 4, 20, 25, 50, 52, 86, 103, 104, 120, 127, 128, 171, 195, 211, 215, 216
Nebuchadnezzar, 71, 82
New Testament, 20, 29, 72, 80, 86, 87, 93, 104, 112, 115, 123, 132, 159, 180, 187, 202, 203, 213, 217
Noah, 26, 42, 57, 79, 116–17, 122, 123, 140
Nostradamus, 202
number, 10, 13–15, 21, 43, 47, 57, 58, 61, 62, 66, 74, 79, 98, 112, 114, 124, 130, 136, 144, 148–49, 150, 163, 189, 214, 215
number (definite, specific), 10, 14, 114, 136, 148
number (generic, non-specific), 10, 36, 196

observations (basic), 2, 3, 6, 7–13, 13–15, 32, 70, 73, 105, 211, 215, 216
Old Testament, 4, 15, 23, 26, 29, 47, 48, 50, 56, 57, 70, 72, 82, 86, 87, 90, 98, 103, 104, 115, 123, 132, 137, 152, 159, 164, 173, 178, 187, 190, 199, 213, 215, 216–17
one hundred and forty four thousand (144,000), 35–37, 56, 61, 63–64,

## SUBJECT INDEX 229

66, 70, 84, 99, 117–20, 123, 129, 136, 142, 159, 161, 162, 167, 191, 205
one-third, 39, 41, 42, 44, 52, 67, 119, 122, 126, 129, 130, 132, 144, 159, 167, 213, 216
one thousand two hundred and sixty (1,260) days, xii, 21, 46, 59, 51, 55, 57, 61, 86, 113, 114, 137, 138, 141, 143, 150, 154, 159, 160, 162, 188, 190, 191, 196, 198, 214
order(ed), 11, 20, 31, 67, 83, 86, 94, 96, 114, 128, 129, 130, 137, 146, 150, 151–52, 212
ox, 27, 31–33, 67, 99, 212

peace(ful), 80, 84, 85, 189, 204
player, 9, 10, 39, 59, 75, 79, 104, 107, 139, 142, 156–64, 166, 168, 169
political, 5, 60, 62, 74, 75, 76, 77, 78, 79, 80, 96, 108, 135–36, 143, 147, 152, 153, 157, 161, 163, 164–65, 174, 175, 177, 183, 188, 194, 204, 206, 207, 210, 211
position, in the Bible, 171–79
prayer, 38, 39, 41, 67, 108, 116–17, 131
principles, xiii, 3, 20, 143, 171, 203
prophecy, 23, 24, 58, 69, 78, 82, 102, 103–4, 109, 114, 115, 199, 211

queen, 81, 152, 164

rainbow, 29, 44, 45, 116–17, 123, 142, 158, 166, 167
rapture, xi, 194–98, 207
redemption (see salvation)
reign, 10, 28, 30, 31, 33, 37, 49, 53, 71, 85, 88–89, 93, 108, 125, 129, 134, 151, 153, 159, 209
religious, 60–62, 73–75, 77, 79, 80, 81, 86, 108, 133, 135–36, 143, 147, 152, 157, 161, 164–65, 174, 183, 204, 207
repent, 44, 54, 64, 73, 121–22, 133
rest, 15, 47, 48, 51, 62, 64, 65, 93, 99, 108, 127, 162, 163, 169, 188, 190, 191, 215

resurrection, 1, 2, 22, 24, 42, 46, 48–49, 51–53, 57–61, 71, 72–73, 74, 77, 85–96, 105, 106, 107, 109, 111–15, 121, 122, 125, 126, 134, 138, 139, 144, 145, 148, 151, 153, 154, 155, 156, 157, 159, 166, 169, 177, 178–80, 182, 184, 185, 188, 190, 194, 195, 196–97, 198–201, 203, 205, 206, 208–10, 218
re-tell, 1, 104, 127, 196, 212, 215
reveal / revelation, 1, 6, 21, 24, 27, 30, 34, 41, 44, 84, 100, 102, 113, 132, 183, 185, 186, 212, 214, 217
Rome / Roman, 5, 60, 74, 78, 143, 157, 165, 179, 207
rule, 30–32, 42–43, 48, 54, 55, 56, 65, 70, 84, 86, 87, 90, 99, 101, 110, 112, 113, 152, 164, 167, 173, 175, 189, 197, 205, 213

Sabbath, 15, 24, 48–49, 61–62, 65, 79, 86, 98, 99, 100, 121, 127, 135, 149, 150, 152, 156, 159, 165, 168, 181, 187–93, 198, 207, 215
Sabbatical year, 47–49, 51, 100, 154, 189–90, 198, 210, 215
sacralization, 164
saints, 36–39, 41, 43, 54, 55, 56, 57, 59, 64, 66–68, 83, 87, 88, 91, 95, 96, 97, 106, 108–10, 113, 114, 116–17, 122–23, 128, 131–33, 143, 146–47, 149, 151, 153, 155, 156, 162–63, 166, 169, 186, 197, 198–200, 202–8, 210, 218
salvation, redemption, 36, 56, 71, 72, 83, 123, 125, 180–81, 185, 192, 202, 207, 218
Satan, 11, 12, 41, 44, 55, 56–57, 58, 59–63, 69, 76, 77, 81, 85–97, 108, 111, 118, 119, 121, 125, 130, 133, 139, 144, 145, 146–48, 152–53, 158, 160–61, 164–66, 168–69, 180, 202, 203–4, 209, 218

## SUBJECT INDEX

scope, 4, 6, 36, 63, 66, 70, 78, 93, 114, 121, 125, 138, 140, 142, 183, 203
scorpions, 44, 213
scroll, 27–28, 30, 38, 42, 44–45, 48, 53, 113, 114, 130
sea, 26, 40, 44, 56, 59–60, 67, 80, 82, 93, 95–96, 98, 133, 147, 155, 161, 167, 174–75
seal(s), 27, 30–38, 45, 53, 66, 104, 105–7, 116–22, 124–34, 150–51, 167
secularization, 148
sequential / sequence, 2, 38, 52, 95–96, 105, 119, 129, 150–51
serpent (see also dragon), 43, 55, 58, 89, 139, 166, 173
seven, 1, 15, 25, 37, 40, 44, 45, 47–49, 51, 53, 74–79, 89, 105, 112, 124, 125, 147–49, 155, 164, 188, 189, 195, 196, 215, 217
seven-seven-seven (777), 62, 127
sign, 117, 195–96, 218
silence, 37–39, 45, 54, 66, 116, 126, 167
six-six-six (666), xii, 61–63, 73, 75, 77, 78–79, 127, 135, 146, 152, 161, 163, 165, 191, 218
smoke, 38, 43, 68, 83, 144, 160
Sodom, 43, 50, 70, 78
son of man, 49, 65–66, 67, 87, 108, 121, 152, 159, 160, 161, 162, 168, 177, 187–93, 195, 197, 207
song, 26, 28–30, 63, 67, 78, 86, 122, 132, 141, 152, 162, 191, 198, 203, 205
spiritual, 81, 83, 86, 119, 139, 164, 178, 182, 185, 200–201, 207
split (three-way), 106, 109, 135, 144
stars, 40, 53, 55, 56, 102, 118, 125, 138, 140, 149, 161, 162, 174, 218
sting, 39, 41, 43–44, 95, 181, 213
storyline, 2, 12, 104, 120, 213, 216
structure (of Revelation), 3, 4, 111
struggle, 10, 55–57, 60, 61, 72, 73–79, 101, 104, 108, 109, 115–20, 135, 137, 139, 147, 151, 158, 165, 166–68, 183, 203–4, 207, 209

sun, 40, 46, 55, 68, 70, 87, 100, 118, 119, 138, 140–41, 167, 174–75
sword, 22, 60, 61, 62–63, 85, 100, 128, 161, 165, 177, 204–5
symbols, 20, 29, 57, 70, 140, 143, 157, 172–74, 177, 178
symmetry, 57, 58, 59, 70, 113, 114, 138, 142, 209
synoptic Gospels, 188

tail, 59–60, 79, 125
Tel Megiddo (see also Armageddon), 71–72
temple, 42, 46, 49, 65–66, 68, 70, 118, 132, 133, 147–48, 175
Ten Commandments, 47, 180, 189
thousand years, 14, 18–19, 89, 92–94, 151, 153–54, 195, 206
three, 59, 69, 73, 75, 80, 108, 109, 123, 127, 129, 133–35, 144–47
three and a half (3.5) days, 18, 21, 46, 48, 49, 50, 51, 52, 57–59, 61, 86, 92, 98, 112–15, 149, 150–51, 159, 188, 190, 198, 203, 214
thunders, 26, 42, 44–45, 60, 79, 113, 117–18, 121–23, 124, 125, 129, 131–32, 134, 142
time, 10, 12–13, 14–19, 23, 24, 41, 49, 51, 52, 53, 56, 58, 75, 78, 79, 87, 91, 92, 94, 96, 102, 104, 105, 119–20, 137, 149, 150–56, 162, 184, 194, 196, 197, 209, 211, 214
time, times and half a time, xii, 12, 13, 55, 57, 59, 82, 92, 113, 138, 149, 159, 162, 176, 196, 208
timeless, 27, 142, 157, 179, 197, 209, 215
time units / time-scales, 13–18, 43, 46–47, 49–51, 53, 55, 57, 86–87, 89, 90, 92, 96, 104, 113, 114, 126, 138, 142, 150, 154, 155, 159, 175, 190, 196, 198, 213, 214–16
torment, 39, 41, 42, 44, 46, 64, 68, 81, 107, 109, 110, 113, 125, 145, 146, 147, 150, 160, 163, 165, 169, 203

transfiguration, 50, 115, 178, 196
tree (of life), 32, 71, 77, 100, 149, 154–55, 168, 173–74, 181, 186, 190, 210
tribes of Israel, 21, 35, 98–99, 123, 139, 142, 148–49, 154, 162, 163
tribulation (great), 24, 36–37, 56, 91, 105, 107, 117, 119, 122, 150, 159, 162, 194–99
trinity (unholy, evil), 95, 146, 168, 186, 209
trumpet, 37, 38, 39–54, 55, 56, 57, 63, 64, 66–70, 76, 77, 78, 79, 85, 89, 96, 104, 106–9, 111, 113, 114, 116, 118, 119, 122, 123, 124–38, 142, 144–45, 147, 150–51, 153, 154, 165, 167, 174, 181, 185, 196, 203, 204, 213, 216
truth, 60, 72, 76, 84–85, 100, 109, 124, 138, 139, 143, 147, 157, 164–66, 168–69, 176, 183, 203–5, 207, 212, 218
twelve, 21, 35, 36, 55, 98, 99, 130, 138–40, 142, 147–50, 154, 162, 163
twenty four (24) elders (see elders)
Tyre, 82, 151

ugly / ugliness, 28, 95, 138, 185, 198
universal, 25, 33, 34, 36, 66, 69, 78, 83, 88, 91, 93, 99, 100, 104, 107, 121, 122, 137, 140, 142, 150, 153, 166, 185, 196, 210, 215, 218

vanquish, defeat, 11, 12, 58, 60, 61, 76, 82, 84–85, 88–89, 90, 95, 98, 106, 110, 136, 152, 165, 166, 186, 194, 199, 201–2, 204, 205, 209, 211
victory, triumph, 11, 24, 28, 33, 48, 52, 53–54, 56–57, 59, 61, 63, 67, 72, 77, 90, 93, 95, 96, 106, 108, 113, 115, 119–22, 125, 126, 131, 145–46, 148, 151, 153, 154, 155, 156, 166, 180–82, 187, 194, 197–201, 202–4, 206, 210, 218

violence, 32, 42, 43–44, 59, 63–64, 66, 85, 108, 109, 126, 145, 163, 165, 169, 204–6

week, 15, 24, 43, 47, 48, 49, 51, 53, 73, 105, 113, 149, 155, 156, 159, 188, 198, 214, 215
weight (talent, denarius), 9, 72
wind, 118, 128
winepress, 65, 84, 87, 119, 152, 161, 204
wisdom, 5, 32, 33, 61, 67, 78–79, 160, 168, 199
witnesses, xii, 8, 42, 46, 49–53, 57, 60, 61, 65, 69, 82, 86, 87, 88–89, 96–97, 104, 111–15, 122, 136, 138, 142, 148, 154, 157, 159, 160, 161, 164, 165, 185, 188, 196, 198, 200, 205, 213, 215
woe(s), 64, 85, 130, 144–46, 159
woman, 8, 10, 11, 12, 55–58, 64, 86, 89, 104, 138–44, 149, 151, 159, 162, 164, 167, 173
worship, 12, 26–30, 31, 33, 38, 59, 62–63, 64–66, 67, 72, 83–84, 89, 98, 100, 102, 103, 105, 106, 108, 111, 128, 135, 142, 147, 155, 157, 162, 163, 167, 182, 184, 186, 202
wrath, 35, 45, 53, 54, 66–69, 71, 83, 84, 92, 97, 99, 100, 106, 107, 109, 112, 113, 117–18, 121–23, 125–27, 129, 132–33, 134, 135, 141, 144–45, 150, 152, 159, 163, 165, 166, 167, 168, 172, 194, 204, 205, 213, 216, 217

year, xii, 13–15, 18–19, 21, 37, 41, 43, 46–49, 51, 53, 58, 72, 85–86, 88–89, 92–94, 100, 113, 128, 148, 149, 150, 151, 153–55, 168, 188–90, 196, 198, 206, 210, 214–16
YHWH, 23, 26, 33

Zion, 10, 32, 63, 70, 87, 117, 119, 136, 161, 191, 198, 205

# Scripture Index

## GEN

| | |
|---|---|
| 1 | 30, 192 |
| 1–2 | 124, 193 |
| 1–3 | 172–73 |
| 1:1 | 114, 204 |
| 1:16–18 | 46 |
| 1:28 | 31 |
| 2:10–14 | 173 |
| 2:16–17 | 90 |
| 2:19–20 | 48 |
| 3 | 140 |
| 3:4–5 | 77 |
| 3:4b–5 | 81 |
| 3:11–13 | 97 |
| 3:14 | 89 |
| 3:15 | 58, 180 |
| 3:15–16 | 139 |
| 3:17 | 67 |
| 3:17–18 | 31 |
| 3:17b–19a | 154 |
| 3:19 | 71 |
| 3:22–23 | 71 |
| 3:24 | 71 |
| 4:1a | 71 |
| 4:10–12 | 67, 72 |
| 4:16 | 71 |
| 5:27 | 92 |
| 8–9 | 57 |
| 8:21–22 | 116 |
| 8:21b | 45, 122 |
| 9:2 | 31 |
| 9:12–17 | 166 |
| 11 | 136 |
| 11:4 | 42 |
| 12:1–3 | 36 |
| 12:3 | 181 |
| 19:24–27 | 43 |
| 37:9–11 | 140 |

## EXOD

| | |
|---|---|
| 3:14 | 26 |
| 10:1–20 | 39 |
| 20:8–11 | 47 |
| 31:13 | 15 |

## LEV

| | |
|---|---|
| 10:1–2 | 116 |
| 25 | 189 |
| 25:1–8 | 47 |

## DEUT

| | |
|---|---|
| 5:12–15 | 47 |
| 6:5 | 33 |
| 17:6 | 112 |
| 19:15 | 112 |
| 29:29 | 210 |
| 30:15–19 | 33 |

## 1 KGS

| | |
|---|---|
| 1:50–51 | 43 |
| 2:28 | 43 |
| 18 | 50 |
| 19:18 | 122 |

## PS

| | |
|---|---|
| 19 | 29 |
| 50:10 | 216 |
| 103:5 | 32 |
| 104 | 29 |
| 110:1 | 55 |
| 133:3 | 32 |

## ECCL

| | |
|---|---|
| 1:13 | 4 |
| 1:14 | 4 |
| 12:13 | 4 |

## ISA

| | |
|---|---|
| 5 | 103 |
| 6:8–13 | 23 |
| 9:6 | 138 |
| 42–53 | 178 |
| 53 | 151, 178 |
| 61:1–2 | 189 |
| 65:21–22a | 189 |
| 65:25 | 101 |

## JER

| | |
|---|---|
| 31:33 | 114 |
| 38 | 23 |
| 51:61–63 | 42 |

## EZEK

| | |
|---|---|
| 1 | 27, 33, 34, 38, 212 |
| 1:1 | 137 |
| 1:5 | 27, 34 |
| 1:8 | 34 |
| 1:10 | 34 |
| 1:28b | 34 |
| 2 | 45 |
| 5:2 | 216 |
| 5:12 | 216 |
| 26–28 | 151 |
| 26:1—28:19 | 82 |
| 37 | 178 |
| 38–39 | 90 |
| 46:1 | 99 |
| 47 | 100, 175 |
| 47:1 | 70 |

## DAN

| | |
|---|---|
| 7 | 137 |
| 7–12 | 137 |
| 7:4–7 | 136 |
| 7:13 | 187 |
| 7:25 | 214 |
| 8:9–14 | 214 |
| 8:27 | 102 |
| 9 | 214 |
| 9:24 | 214 |
| 10 | 56 |
| 12 | 56, 137 |
| 12:4 | 102 |
| 12:7 | 214 |

## JOEL

| | |
|---|---|
| 1–2 | 39 |
| 2:30 | 118 |

# SCRIPTURE INDEX

## JONAH

| | |
|---|---|
| 3:4–9 | 23 |
| 4:10–11 | 181 |

## ZECH

| | |
|---|---|
| 6:1–8 | 33 |
| 13:8–9 | 216 |

## MATT

| | |
|---|---|
| 4:1–11 | 92 |
| 6:26 | 29 |
| 8:29 | 180 |
| 11:25 | 201 |
| 11:27 | 201 |
| 12:1–14 | 188 |
| 12:41–42 | 88 |
| 16:13–27 | 187 |
| 16:21 | 178 |
| 16:22–23 | 92 |
| 17:1–6 | 196 |
| 17:1–8 | 50 |
| 17:22 | 187 |
| 18:16 | 112 |
| 21:33–44 | 73, 103 |
| 22:37 | 33 |
| 22:42–46 | 143 |
| 23:34–35 | 50 |
| 24 | 137, 176 |
| 24:29 | 118 |
| 26:52 | 63 |
| 26:60 | 112 |
| 28:18–20 | 91 |

## MARK

| | |
|---|---|
| 2:23—3:6 | 188 |
| 2:27b–28 | 187 |
| 8:31 | 178 |
| 8:31–38 | 187 |
| 9:2–8 | 50 |
| 12:1–11 | 103 |
| 12:30 | 33 |
| 13:24 | 118 |
| 13:26 | 187 |

## LUKE

| | |
|---|---|
| 2:41–52 | 178 |
| 4:1–13 | 92 |
| 4:16–18 | 189 |
| 6:1–11 | 188 |
| 8:26–37 | 207 |
| 9:22 | 178 |
| 9:22–26 | 187 |
| 9:28–36 | 50 |
| 10:27 | 33 |
| 11:29b–30 | 195 |
| 11:31–32 | 88 |
| 13:10–16 | 188 |
| 14:1–6 | 188 |
| 20:9–17 | 103 |
| 20:18 | 205 |
| 20:20–26 | 207 |
| 23:8–9 | 195 |
| 24:13–35 | 151 |

## JOHN

| | |
|---|---|
| 1:1 | 114 |
| 1:1–2 | 203 |
| 1:3 | 98, 124 |
| 3:18 | 210 |
| 4:22b–23 | 72 |
| 4:24 | 117 |
| 5:1–18 | 188 |
| 5:17 | 86, 153 |
| 5:24 | 88 |
| 5:27 | 193 |
| 8:44 | 164 |
| 9:13–16 | 188 |
| 13:25 | 184 |
| 14:6 | 143 |
| 14:16 | 158 |
| 14:26 | 158 |
| 16:11 | 210 |
| 16:33 | 31 |
| 19:30 | 97, 98 |

## ACTS

| | |
|---|---|
| 2:1–12 | 139 |
| 7:55 | 187 |
| 20:7 | 15, 24 |

## ROM

| | |
|---|---|
| 5:19 | 200 |
| 7:3 | 81 |
| 8:18–22 | 154 |
| 8:19 | 30, 200 |
| 8:19–22 | 100, 126 |
| 12:19 | 112 |
| 14:10–12 | 93 |

## 1 COR

| | |
|---|---|
| 15:52 | 209 |

## 2 COR

| | |
|---|---|
| 5:10 | 93 |
| 12:9 | 94 |
| 13:1 | 112 |

## GAL

| | |
|---|---|
| 6:7b–8 | 197 |

## EPH

| | |
|---|---|
| 1:9–10 | 115 |
| 4:7–8 | 85 |

## PHIL

| | |
|---|---|
| 2:12 | 198 |

## 1 THESS

| | |
|---|---|
| 4 | 176 |

## 1 TIM

| | |
|---|---|
| 5:19 | 112 |
| 6:15 | 192 |

## 2 TIM

| | |
|---|---|
| 3:16 | xiii |

## HEB

| | |
|---|---|
| 1:13 | 55 |
| 2:5–8 | 197 |
| 2:11 | 140 |
| 3:13 | 94 |
| 9:4 | 123 |
| 10:13 | 55 |
| 11 | 154 |
| 11–13 | 97 |
| 11:4 | 87 |
| 11:7 | 123 |
| 11:40—12:1 | 97 |
| 12:1 | 88 |
| 13:8 | 202 |

## JAS

| | |
|---|---|
| 1:17b | 96 |
| 2:8 | 94 |
| 2:19 | 58 |

## 2 PET

| | |
|---|---|
| 3:8 | 21, 216 |
| 3:19 | 101 |

# 1 JOHN

| | |
|---|---|
| 1 | 184 |
| 1:1–3 | 184 |
| 2:8 | 182 |

# JUDE

| | |
|---|---|
| 3 | 194 |

# REV

| | |
|---|---|
| 1 | 105 |
| 1–3 | 157 |
| 1:1 | 24, 87, 155, 160, 201 |
| 1:1–3 | 211 |
| 1:2 | 87 |
| 1:3 | 12, 23, 103, 199 |
| 1:4 | 22, 25, 215 |
| 1:5 | 87, 101 |
| 1:7 | 78 |
| 1:8 | 22, 160 |
| 1:9 | 22, 37, 87, 112 |
| 1:10 | 24 |
| 1:11 | 162 |
| 1:12 | 112 |
| 1:12–17 | 22 |
| 1:13 | 67, 122, 187 |
| 1:13–16 | 160 |
| 1:16 | 61 |
| 1:17 | 4, 22, 160, 184 |
| 1:17–18 | 202 |
| 1:17b–18 | 22, 184 |
| 1:18 | 101, 160, 165, 197 |
| 1:18b–19 | 201 |
| 1:19 | 63 |
| 1:20 | 112 |
| 2–3 | 25, 69, 105, 160, 162, 179 |
| 2:9 | 143 |
| 2:12 | 61 |
| 2:20 | 138 |
| 2:21 | 12 |
| 3:3 | 209 |
| 3:9 | 143 |
| 4 | 26–27, 31, 33–34, 69, 99, 124, 137, 156, 212 |
| 4–5 | 26, 83, 105, 126 |
| 4–22 | 105, 138, 179 |
| 4:1 | 27, 201 |
| 4:1—22:5 | 157 |
| 4:3 | 26, 116, 158, 166 |
| 4:5 | 117 |
| 4:6 | 96 |
| 4:6–7 | 31 |
| 4:6a | 175 |
| 4:6b | 34 |
| 4:6b–7 | 162 |
| 4:7 | 34 |
| 4:8 | 22, 26, 29, 32 |
| 4:8–11 | 159 |
| 4:11 | 166 |
| 5 | 27, 65, 66, 98, 100, 114, 124, 156 |
| 5:1 | 159 |
| 5:3 | 184 |
| 5:4 | 184 |
| 5:5 | 160 |
| 5:6 | 101, 155 |
| 5:6–7 | 160 |
| 5:8 | 116 |
| 5:9 | 101, 128 |
| 5:9–10 | 28 |
| 5:9–13 | 162 |
| 5:10 | 89 |
| 5:11 | 43, 160 |
| 5:12 | 28, 101 |
| 5:13 | 29, 128 |
| 5:13–14 | 167 |
| 6 | 84, 212 |
| 6–8 | 160 |
| 6:1–8 | 163, 167 |
| 6:1—8:1 | 30–38, 105 |
| 6:6 | 72 |
| 6:9 | 43 |
| 6:9–11 | 87, 162 |
| 6:10–11 | 112 |
| 6:11 | 119 |
| 6:12–14 | 118, 163 |
| 6:12–17 | 35, 167 |
| 6:12—8:1 | 117 |

## REV (CONTINUED)

| | |
|---|---|
| 6:15 | 92 |
| 6:15–17 | 163 |
| 6:16 | 168 |
| 7 | 84 |
| 7:1 | 128 |
| 7:1–2 | 128 |
| 7:1–3 | 119, 122 |
| 7:1–8 | 35, 162 |
| 7:3 | 117, 119, 120 |
| 7:3–4 | 61 |
| 7:9 | 128 |
| 7:9–14 | 122 |
| 7:9–17 | 35, 162 |
| 7:13–14 | 36 |
| 7:14 | 67, 83, 112 |
| 7:14b | 199 |
| 8:1 | 74, 89, 129, 167 |
| 8:2—11:19 | 39, 107 |
| 8:3 | 116 |
| 8:3–4 | 112, 116 |
| 8:4 | 116 |
| 8:5 | 117 |
| 8:7—9:20 | 167 |
| 8:12 | 55 |
| 8:13 | 64, 85, 144 |
| 8:13b | 145 |
| 9:1 | 160 |
| 9:1–2 | 160 |
| 9:2 | 68 |
| 9:4 | 163 |
| 9:6 | 163 |
| 9:7–11 | 160 |
| 9:11 | 167 |
| 9:12 | 145 |
| 9:13 | 69 |
| 9:13–21 | 42 |
| 9:14 | 128 |
| 9:15 | 49, 128, 153 |
| 9:16 | 43 |
| 9:16–19 | 163 |
| 9:17 | 43 |
| 9:20–21 | 163 |
| 10 | 42, 44 |
| 10:1 | 123 |
| 10:3 | 60 |
| 10:3–4 | 121 |
| 10:5 | 56, 60 |
| 10:6 | 12, 74, 79 |
| 10:11 | 45, 199 |
| 11 | 21, 55, 65, 78, 107, 111, 112, 149, 152, 155, 156, 165, 167 |
| 11–12 | 57, 100 |
| 11–13 | 96 |
| 11:1–10 | 52 |
| 11:1–13 | 42, 46–53 |
| 11:2 | 51, 147, 163, 196, 214 |
| 11:2–3 | 214 |
| 11:3 | 50, 51, 214 |
| 11:3–6 | 160 |
| 11:5 | 60 |
| 11:6 | 214 |
| 11:7 | 50, 51, 52, 60, 74, 136, 161, 164, 198 |
| 11:7–12 | 160 |
| 11:8 | 69, 82 |
| 11:9 | 50, 128 |
| 11:11 | 50, 52 |
| 11:11–13 | 52, 74 |
| 11:11–13a | 112 |
| 11:13 | 117 |
| 11:13b | 162 |
| 11:14 | 145 |
| 11:15 | 37 |
| 11:15–17 | 53 |
| 11:15–18 | 125 |
| 11:15–19 | 53 |
| 11:17–18 | 209 |
| 11:18 | 12, 53, 82, 96, 163, 167 |
| 11:18–19 | 123 |
| 11:19 | 117, 123 |
| 12 | 49, 55, 56, 64, 73, 89, 104, 108, 138, 142, 151, 166, 174, 203 |
| 12–13 | 215 |
| 12–15 | 121, 122 |
| 12–19 | 52, 95, 156, 209 |
| 12–20 | 53, 54 |
| 12–22 | 155 |
| 12:1 | 149 |

| Reference | Pages |
|---|---|
| 12:1–5 | 162 |
| 12:3 | 125, 164 |
| 12:3–4 | 160 |
| 12:5 | 88, 112, 161 |
| 12:6 | 57, 162, 214 |
| 12:7 | 164 |
| 12:7–9 | 160, 161 |
| 12:9–10 | 203 |
| 12:10 | 88, 125 |
| 12:11 | 203 |
| 12:12 | 12, 56, 74, 92 |
| 12:13 | 162 |
| 12:14 | 12, 13, 57, 208, 214 |
| 12:15–16 | 167 |
| 12:16 | 56, 162 |
| 12:17 | 87, 140, 144, 162 |
| 13 | 55, 59, 61, 66, 73, 75, 77, 85, 86, 89, 108, 109, 133, 135, 138, 146, 147, 152, 165, 166, 174, 204, 214 |
| 13–14 | 108 |
| 13:1 | 133, 161, |
| 13:2 | 75 |
| 13:2–4 | 136 |
| 13:3 | 60, 74, 161 |
| 13:4 | 76, 160, 161, 163 |
| 13:5 | 57, 196, 214 |
| 13:6 | 161 |
| 13:7 | 128, 161, 198 |
| 13:8 | 59, 63, 101 |
| 13:9 | 62, 112 |
| 13:9–10 | 66 |
| 13:11 | 75, 133 |
| 13:11–15 | 161 |
| 13:12 | 74, 163 |
| 13:14 | 59, 60, 61, 74, 163 |
| 13:16–17 | 163 |
| 13:16–18 | 161 |
| 13:19b | 204 |
| 14 | 63, 66, 78, 83, 84, 108, 119, 144, 152, 178, 203, 210 |
| 14–19 | 96 |
| 14:1 | 70, 133, 161 |
| 14:1–3 | 198 |
| 14:1–5 | 162 |
| 14:1–13 | 112 |
| 14:2–3a | 205 |
| 14:4 | 64 |
| 14:6 | 85, 128, 155 |
| 14:6–7 | 202 |
| 14:6–11 | 113, 162, 165 |
| 14:6–12 | 158 |
| 14:7 | 13, 128, 167 |
| 14:8 | 70, 81 |
| 14:11 | 163 |
| 14:12 | 87 |
| 14:12–13 | 66 |
| 14:13 | 65, 93, 158, 162, 181, 191, 198 |
| 14:14 | 161 |
| 14:14–20 | 119, 121, 122 |
| 14:15 | 162 |
| 14:15–20 | 168 |
| 14:18 | 162 |
| 14:20 | 99, 204 |
| 15 | 109, 152 |
| 15–16 | 66, 109 |
| 15:1 | 125 |
| 15:2–4 | 162, 204 |
| 15:8 | 159 |
| 15:18 | 68 |
| 16 | 83, 135, 136, 147, 152 |
| 16:2–9 | 168 |
| 16:4–6 | 68 |
| 16:5 | 127 |
| 16:7 | 127 |
| 16:8 | 163 |
| 16:12 | 75 |
| 16:12–18 | 69 |
| 16:13 | 69 |
| 16:13–14 | 163 |
| 16:14b | 165 |
| 16:15 | 209 |
| 16:16 | 72 |
| 16:17 | 37, 98, 125 |
| 16:18–21 | 117 |
| 16:19 | 109, 135, 164 |
| 17 | 71, 73–78, 109, 135, 136, 146, 147, 152, 153, 155 |

## REV (*CONTINUED*)

| | |
|---|---|
| 17–18 | 37, 70, 83, 136, 138 |
| 17–20 | 146 |
| 17:1 | 81 |
| 17:2 | 81 |
| 17:3 | 161, 165 |
| 17:5 | 81 |
| 17:6 | 87 |
| 17:8 | 76 |
| 17:8–13 | 161 |
| 17:8a & 8b | 74 |
| 17:9–12 | 74 |
| 17:10 | 14, 76 |
| 17:11 | 74, 75, 76 |
| 17:12 | 14, 74, 76 |
| 17:12–13 | 76 |
| 17:13 | 74 |
| 17:14 | 75, 192 |
| 17:15 | 81 |
| 17:16 | 81, 165 |
| 17:16–17 | 164 |
| 17:16–18 | 161 |
| 18 | 14, 80–83, 95, 109, 135, 151, 152, 146 |
| 18–20 | 11 |
| 18:1 | 82, 148, 164 |
| 18:2 | 80, 82, 101 |
| 18:2–3 | 164 |
| 18:3 | 80, 81 |
| 18:4 | 82, 158 |
| 18:7 | 81, 164 |
| 18:8 | 80 |
| 18:9 | 80, 81 |
| 18:10 | 14, 80, 82, 209 |
| 18:11 | 80, 82 |
| 18:12–13 | 80 |
| 18:13 | 80 |
| 18:15 | 80 |
| 18:16 | 82 |
| 18:17 | 80, 82, 209 |
| 18:18 | 82 |
| 18:19 | 80, 82, 209 |
| 18:21 | 82, 204 |
| 18:22 | 81 |
| 18:23 | 80, 81 |
| 19 | 73, 83, 84, 95, 109, 146, 147, 152, 165 |
| 19:1–4 | 204 |
| 19:1–7 | 162 |
| 19:2 | 81, 164 |
| 19:7b–8 | 199 |
| 19:8 | 83 |
| 19:9–10 | 186 |
| 19:10 | 87, 199 |
| 19:11–16 | 84 |
| 19:11–18 | 161 |
| 19:12 | 184 |
| 19:15 | 60, 61, 88, 161, 204 |
| 19:15–18 | 112 |
| 19:15b | 161 |
| 19:16 | 192 |
| 19:17–18 | 148, 162 |
| 19:17–21 | 204 |
| 19:18 | 164 |
| 19:19–21 | 165 |
| 19:20 | 11, 135, 161, 165 |
| 19:21 | 61, 161, 204 |
| 20 | 7–12, 70, 78, 85–97, 110, 130, 146, 151, 153, 156, 162, 163, 166, 197, 200, 216 |
| 20:1 | 95, 98 |
| 20:1–2 | 125 |
| 20:1–3 | 85 |
| 20:2 | 160 |
| 20:2–7 | 14, 86 |
| 20:3 | 12, 14, 95, 160 |
| 20:3b | 94 |
| 20:4 | 87, 88, 161, 163 |
| 20:4–6 | 85 |
| 20:4–9 | 166 |
| 20:5 | 94 |
| 20:5a | 94 |
| 20:6 | 87, 88, 163 |
| 20:7 | 95 |
| 20:7–10 | 86 |
| 20:8 | 128 |
| 20:8–9 | 164 |
| 20:9 | 165 |

| | | | |
|---|---|---|---|
| 20:10 | 11, 74, 95, 160, 165 | 21:23 | 70, 161, 174 |
| | | 21:24 | 122 |
| 20:11 | 159, 168, 174 | 21:24–25 | 163 |
| 20:11–15 | 86, 91 | 21:24–26 | 140 |
| 20:12 | 91, 92, 93, 163 | 21:26 | 122 |
| 20:13 | 91, 93 | 22:1–2 | 160 |
| 20:14 | 163 | 22:1–3 | 168 |
| 20:15 | 164 | 22:5 | 174 |
| 20:16 | 72 | 22:6 | 22, 24, 155, 201 |
| 20:17 | 74 | 22:6–21 | 102 |
| 20:19 | 74 | 22:6—22:21 | 110 |
| 21 | 27, 70, 139, 148, 154, 174 | 22:7 | 22, 199 |
| | | 22:8 | 186 |
| 21–22 | 12, 49, 83, 126, 147, 174 | 22:10 | 12, 23, 44, 199 |
| | | 22:13 | 4, 22, 160 |
| 21:1 | 174 | 22:15 | 101, 147, 164, 210 |
| 21:1—22:5 | 110 | 22:16 | 25, 53, 87, 157, 179 |
| 21:2 | 142 | | |
| 21:6 | 98, 160 | 22:16–20 | 161 |
| 21:8 | 101, 164 | 22:17 | 158 |
| 21:9 | 148 | 22:18–19 | 199 |
| 21:10 | 98 | 22:19 | 168 |
| 21:17 | 21, 158 | 22:20 | 87 |
| 21:22–24 | 160 | 22:21 | 87 |

www.ingramcontent.com/pod-product-compliance
Lightning Source LLC
Chambersburg PA
CBHW051634230426
43669CB00013B/2299